Muhammad Ibn Sa'd's

Kitab at-Tabaqat al-Kabir

Volume VIII:

The Women of Madina

translated by
Aisha Bewley

Ta-Ha Publishers Ltd

First published in January 1995/1415AH

Reprinted: 1997, 2001, 2006, 2015

This edition published by:

Ta-Ha Publishers Ltd.
Unit 4, The Windsor Centre
Windsor Grove, West Norwood
London, SE27 9NT, UK

www.tahapublishers.com

Translated by Aisha Bewley
Typeset by Bookwork, Slough

A catalogue record of this book is available from the British Library

ISBN 978-1-897940-24-2

Printed and bound by IMAK Ofset, Turkey

بِسْمِ اللهِ الرَّحْمَنِ الرَّحِيمِ

Preface

Abu 'Abdullah Muhammad ibn Sa'd is one of the greatest authorities on Muslim biography. His collection, the *Kitab at-Tabaqat al-Kabir*, is one of the most important and earliest surviving biographical collection of narrations. Its scope extends from the time of the Prophet down to his own time.

Ibn Sa'd was born in 168/764-5 in Basra, and died in 230/845 at the age of 62. He moved to Baghdad where he studied under various people, especially Muhammad ibn 'Umar al-Waqidi. He came to be known as "the secretary of al-Waqidi" because of his close connection to him. Where the text refers to the opinion of Muhammad ibn 'Umar, that means al-Waqidi. He also visited Kufa and Madina in the course of his quest for knowledge. Various authorities have testified to his reliability. These include Ibn Hajar, adh-Dhahabi, al-Khatib al-Baghdadi, and Ibn Khallikan.

This translation is abridged and several repetitions have been eliminated as well as the chain of authorities for the various narrations. This translation covers Volume 8, which deals exclusively with women who met the Prophet, may Allah bless him and grant him peace, or transmitted from him. The *Tabaqat* is a great storehouse of information compiled from all the sources available to Ibn Sa'd, including weak ones. Sometimes there are conflicting reports about various matters, and so a degree of caution is called for when deciding if the narration is actually a basis for action. The great joy in reading something like the *Tabaqat* is that, because of its great scope, it gives the reader a vivid taste and feel for what the people in Madina must have been like and how extraordinary they were. It makes them come alive for the reader.

Aisha Bewley

Contents

Chapter One:
The Manner in which the Messenger of Allah Received Women's Allegiance

'Amir ash-Sha'bi said, "When the Prophet ﷺ received allegiance (*bay'a*) from women, his hand was covered with a cloth."

Ash-Sha'bi said that when the Prophet ﷺ received allegiance from women, he first placed a Qatari cloak over his hand. He said, "I do not shake hands with women."

'Urwa said that the Prophet ﷺ did not shake hands with women when he received their allegiance.

Umayma bint Ruqayqa said, "I went to the Messenger of Allah with a group of women to offer him our allegiance. We said, 'We will give you allegiance, Messenger of Allah, on the basis that we will not associate anything with Allah, nor steal, nor commit fornication, nor kill our children, nor bring a lie that we forge between our hands and feet, and that we will not disobey you in anything correct.' The Messenger of Allah ﷺ said, 'Inasmuch as you are capable and able.' We said, 'Allah and His Messenger are more merciful to us than ourselves. Come and receive our allegiance, Messenger of Allah!' The Messenger of Allah said, 'I do not shake hands with women. My word to a hundred women is like my word to one woman.'"

Umayma bint Ruqayqa said, "I went to the Messenger of Allah ﷺ with a group of women to give him allegiance. He imposed on us the preconditions from the Qur'an that we should not steal nor commit fornication nor kill our children nor forge a lie. Then he said, 'Inasmuch as you are capable and able.' I said, 'Allah and His Messenger are more merciful to us than ourselves.' He said, 'I do not shake hands with women. My word to one woman is like my word to a hundred women.'"

'A'isha said that the Prophet ﷺ never shook hands with a woman.

Ibrahim said that the Prophet ﷺ shook hands with women with a cloth covering his hand.

Qays ibn Abi Hazim said that when women came to offer allegiance to the Prophet, he laid his cloak over his hand and received their allegiance through the cloak. He sent some women away without receiving their allegiance since they were apprehensive about the preconditions, and he received the allegiance of other women through his cloak. He said, "Some of you are in the Garden," and he clenched his fingers together as if to indicate it was few of them.

Asma' said, "I went to the Messenger of Allah with a group of women to offer him allegiance. The Messenger of Allah stated the preconditions to us, and a niece of mine stretched out her hand to take that of the Messenger of Allah. She was wearing a gold bracelet and gold rings. The Messenger of Allah ﷺ withdrew his hand, saying, "I do not shake hands with women."

Tariq at-Taymi said, "I went to the Messenger of Allah ﷺ while he was sitting in the sun wearing a yellow garment and he had his head pulled down inside it. Then he stood up and went to a room where there were six women. He greeted them and received allegiance from them with the yellow garment covering his hand."

Umm 'Atiyya said, "When the Messenger of Allah ﷺ came to Madina, he gathered the women of the Ansar together in a house. Then he sent 'Umar ibn al-Khattab to them. 'Umar came to the door of the house and greeted us, saying, 'Peace be upon you,' and we returned the greeting to him. He said, 'I am the messenger of the Messenger of Allah to you.' We said, 'Welcome to the Messenger of Allah and the messenger of the Messenger of Allah!' He said, 'Give allegiance on the basis that you do not associate anything with Allah, nor steal, nor commit fornication, nor kill your children, nor bring a lie which you forge between your hands and feet.' We said, 'Yes.' He put in his hand from outside the house and we extended our hands from inside the house. Then he said, 'O Allah, bear witness!' He commanded us to go out to the *'ids*, both mature girls and menstruating women. *Jumu'a* was not obliged for us. He forbade us to follow the funeral procession."

Isma'il said, "I asked my grandmother (Umm 'Atiyya) about the words of Allah, *'nor disobey you in respect of anything correct,'* (60:12) and she said, 'He forbade us to wail.'"

Usayd al-Barrad said that one of the women who gave allegiance said, "Part of the basis on which we gave allegiance to the Messenger of Allah ﷺ was that we should not disobey him in anything that was correct. This meant we should not scratch our faces nor tear our garments nor pull out our hair nor cry out shrieking."

'Ubada ibn as-Samit said, "The Messenger of Allah ﷺ said to us, 'Will you give allegiance to me on the same basis that the women do? That you will not associate anything with Allah, steal, commit fornication, kill your children, nor bring a lie which you forge between your hands and feet, and that you do not disobey me in anything correct?' We said, 'Yes, indeed, Messenger of Allah.' So we gave allegiance to him on that basis. The Messenger of Allah ﷺ said, "Whoever commits a wrong action afterwards and is punished for it, that is its expiation. If he is not punished for it, then his affair is left to Allah. If He wishes, He will forgive him, and if He wishes, He will punish him.'"

It is related that Umm Salama al-Ansariyya was one of the women from whom the Messenger of Allah ﷺ received allegiance. Her maternal aunt was with her, and she related more than one *hadith* from the Prophet ﷺ. She said, "One of the women said, 'Messenger of Allah, what is the 'correct' in which we must not disobey you?' He said, 'Do not wail.'"

Umm 'Atiyya said, "The oath of allegiance - or part of it - was that we should not wail. That was only fulfilled by five women among us: Umm Sulaym, Umm al-'Ala', the daughter of Abu Sabra, the wife of Mu'adh, the mother of Mu'adh, and another woman."

Mus'ab ibn Nuh said, "I met one of our old women who was one of those who gave allegiance to the Prophet ﷺ. She went to him to give him allegiance. She said, 'Part of what he enjoined on us was that we should not wail. An old woman said, "Messenger of Allah, some people lamented with me over a loss which I sustained, and they have sustained a loss and so I want to go and lament with them." He said, "Go and lament with them."' She went and then came back to him and gave allegiance.'

"She said, 'This is the "correct" to which Allah refers when He says, *"nor disobey you in respect of anything correct."*(60:12)'"

Abu'l-Mulayh al-Hudhali said, "A woman came to the Messenger of Allah ﷺ to give him allegiance. He recited this *ayat* to her. When he said, *'nor disobey you in respect of anything correct,'* (60:12) he said, 'Do not wail.' She said, 'Messenger of Allah, a woman lamented with me, should I lament with her?' The Messenger of Allah ﷺ did not say anything until she had repeated it two or three times. Then he granted her a respite. Then she agreed and then he received her allegiance."

Bakr ibn 'Abdullah said, "The Messenger of Allah ﷺ received allegiance from the women on the basis that they would not tear their clothes nor wail nor scratch their faces nor speak unseemly language."

Ash-Sha'bi was heard to mention that when the women gave allegiance, the Messenger of Allah ﷺ said, "Give allegiance on the basis that you do not associate anything with Allah." Hind said, "We say that." "Nor should you steal." Hind said, "I took something from Abu Sufyan's property." Abu Sufyan said, "What you took of my property is lawful for you." He said, "You should not commit fornication." Hind said, "Does a free woman fornicate?" He said, "You should not kill your children." Hind said, "You have killed them."

Maymun ibn Mahran reported that some women, including Hind, the daughter of 'Utba ibn Rabi'a and the mother of Mu'awiya, came to the Prophet ﷺ to give him allegiance. When he said, "Do not associate anything with Allah and do not steal," Hind said, "Messenger of Allah, Abu Sufyan is a stingy man. Is there anything held against me if I take some of his food without his permission?" The Messenger of Allah ﷺ sanctioned that in fresh food but did not sanction it in dry food. He said, "Do not fornicate." She said, "Does a free woman fornicate?" He said, "Do not kill your children." She said, "Have you left us a child that you did not kill at Badr?" He said, "Do not disobey me in anything correct."

Maymun said, "Allah did not grant His Prophet obedience from them except in what is correct, and what is correct consists of obedience to Allah Almighty."

Salma bint Qays said, "I went to the Prophet with some of the women of the Ansar to give allegiance to him. Part of what he enjoined on us was that we should not cheat our husbands. When we left him, we said, 'By Allah, we should go back to the Messenger of Allah ﷺ and ask him what "cheating our husbands" means.' We went back and asked him and he said, 'It is that you do not give their property to someone else.'"

'Ata' al-Khurasani said that part of what the Messenger of Allah enjoined on the women is that they should not wail nor go off alone with men.

It is related from al-Hasan that when the Prophet ﷺ received allegiance from women, he enjoined on them that they would only socialise with men who were related to them.

Dabi' ibn 'Amr said, "We went to visit al-Hasan when he was ill and he said, "When the allegiance of the women took place, the Messenger of Allah ﷺ received it from them and imposed a precondition that they should not socialise with men, and it is what is in the Book of Allah."

Abu Salama ibn 'Abdi'r-Rahman said, "When 'Umar and 'A'isha came to Makka, they stayed with the daughter of Thabit. She was one of the seven women who gave allegiance to the Messenger of Allah ﷺ in Makka."

Sa'd said, "When the Messenger of Allah received allegiance from the women, a woman who seemed to be a woman of Mudar went up to him and said, 'Messenger of Allah, all is left up to our fathers, husbands and sons, so what part of their property is lawful to us?' He replied, 'The fresh foods you eat and give.'"

Asma' bint Yazid said, "The Prophet passed by me when I was with some women and he greeted us and we returned the greeting to him."

Umm 'Umara said, "The men clasped the hand of the Messenger of Allah ﷺ on the night when the Pledge of 'Aqaba was taken. Al-'Abbas ibn 'Abdu'l-Muttalib took the hand of the Messenger of Allah. Then I and Umm Mani' remained. My husband, 'Arafa ibn 'Amr, called out, 'Messenger of Allah, these two women are with us to give allegiance to you.' The Messenger of Allah ﷺ said, 'I take allegiance from them on the same basis which I took it from you, but I do not shake hands with women.'"

She said, "We went back to our men, and then two men of our people met us - Salit ibn 'Amr and Abu Dawud al-Mazini. They had wanted to attend the Pledge, but they found that the people had already given allegiance. Later they gave allegiance to As'ad ibn Zurara, the leader of the seventy people who took part on the Night of 'Aqaba."

As-Sawda' said, "I went to give allegiance to the Messenger of Allah ﷺ. He said, 'Put on henna.' I put on henna and then came and gave allegiance to him."

'Amr ibn Shu'ayb's grandfather said, "When the Messenger of Allah ﷺ emigrated to Madina, some women who had become Muslim went to him and said, 'Messenger of Allah, our men have given allegiance to you and we also want to give you our allegiance.' The Messenger of Allah ﷺ called for a vessel of water and put his hand in it and then each woman put her hand in it. This was how their allegiance took place."

Asma' bint Yazid said, "We gave allegiance to the Messenger of Allah ﷺ and he enjoined on us, *'that they will not associate anything with Allah nor steal nor fornicate nor kill their children ...'*

(60:12) He said, 'I will not shake your hands, but I enjoin on you what Allah enjoins on you.'"

Umm 'Amir al-Ashhaliyya said, "I, Layla bint al-Khutaym, and Hawwa' bint Yazid went and visited the Prophet between *Maghrib* and *'Isha'*, wrapped up in our capes. I greeted him and he asked me who I was and I told him. Then he asked who my two companions were and they told him. He welcomed us and then said, 'What do you need?' We said, 'Messenger of Allah, we have come to give you allegiance in Islam. We believe in you and we testify that what you have brought is the truth.' The Messenger of Allah ﷺ said, 'Praise belongs to Allah who guided you to Islam!' Then he said, 'You have given allegiance.'"

Umm 'Amir said, "I went up to him and the Messenger of Allah said, 'I do not shake hands with women. My word to a thousand women is like my word to a single woman."

Umm 'Amir used to say, "I was the first one to give allegiance to the Messenger of Allah ﷺ."

'Asim ibn 'Amr ibn Qatada said, "The first to give allegiance to the Prophet ﷺ were Umm Sa'd bint Rafi' ibn 'Ubayd, Umm 'Amir bint Yazid and Hawwa' bint Yazid, as well as Layla bint al-Khutaym of Banu Zafar. There were also Layla, Maryam and Tamima, the daughters of Abu Sufyan, Abi'l-Banat, who was killed at Uhud, ash-Shamus bint Abi 'Amir ar-Rahib and her daughter, Jamila bint Thabit ibn Abi'l-Aqlah, and Tayyiba bint an-Nu'man ibn Thabit."

Az-Zuhri said, "I went to 'Urwa ibn az-Zubayr who was in the process of writing to Hubayra, the companion of al-Walid ibn 'Abdu'l-Malik. He had written to him to ask about the words of Allah Almighty, *'O you who believe! When believing women come to you in emigration, submit them to a test. Allah has best knowledge of their belief.'* (60:10) He wrote back to him, 'On the Day of al-Huday-biyya, the Messenger of Allah made a treaty with Quraysh which stipulated that he would return to them anyone who came to him without his guardian's permission. He returned the men. Then when women emigrated, Allah refused to allow them to be returned until they had been tested by the test of Islam if a woman claimed that she had come desiring Islam. He commanded that women's dowers be repaid when the women were not sent back, and that they should receive the like of what they had paid them if they were the ones who did that [i.e. if their wives went over to the unbelievers]. He said, 'Ask for what you have paid out.'

"The brothers [of one such a woman] came to him in the morning and asked for her return, but the Messenger of Allah ﷺ refused to return her. They went back to Makka and told Quraysh, but they were content to let the women stay. '*Ask for what you paid out and let them ask for what they paid out. That is the judgement of Allah. Allah will judge between them. Allah is Knowing, Wise. If any of your wives abandon you for the rejecters, you should have restitution, and give to those whose wives have gone the same as they paid out.*' (60:11-12) This means: 'If any of your wives abandon you for the unbelievers, and then one of their women comes to you and you obtain booty or spoils, then compensate them from the dower of the woman who comes to you.' The believers affirmed the judgement of Allah Almighty, but the idolworshippers refused to affirm it. 'In the case of what the idolworshippers lose to the Muslims of the dower of those of the wives of the idolworshippers who emigrate, give their husbands the like of what they had spent from the property of the idolworshippers in your hands.' We do not know of any woman of the Muslims who left her husband to join the idolworshippers after she believed, but Allah Almighty gave a judgement about it if it were to happen, and Allah is the judge over them. '*Do not hold to any marriage ties with women who reject,*' (60:10) i.e. who are other than the People of the Book. Therefore 'Umar ibn al-Khattab divorced Mulayka bint Abi Umayya, the mother of 'Ubaydullah ibn 'Umar, and Abu Jahm ibn Hudhayfa married her. 'Umar also divorced the daughter of Jarwal al-Khuza'iyya, Umm al-Hakam bint Abi Sufyan ibn Harb on that day and she married 'Abdullah ibn 'Uthman ath-Thaqifi and she bore him 'Abdu'r-Rahman ibn Umm al-Hakam.

It is related from 'Ikrima about His words, "*submit them to a test,*" that he said, "Who comes to you only for love of Allah and His Messenger and not for love of one of our men nor to flee from her husband."

Chapter Two:
Khadija bint Khuwaylid ibn Asad

Ibn 'Abbas said, "She is Khadija bint Khuwaylid ibn Asad. Her mother was Fatima bint Za'ida ibn al-Asamm, and her mother was Hala bint 'Abdu Manaf ibn al-Harith, and her mother was al-'Araqa or Qilaba bint Su'ayd ibn Sahm, and her mother was 'Atika bint 'Abdu'l-'Uzza ibn Qusayy, and her mother was al-Khutya or Rayta bint Ka'b, and her mother was Na'ila bint Hudhafa. Before anyone married her, Khadija bint Khuwaylid was offered to Waraqa ibn Nawfal, but no marriage took place between them. Then she married Abu Hala. His name was Hind ibn an-Nabbash ibn Zurara of Tamim. His father was a noble among his people. He settled in Makka and formed an alliance there with the Banu 'Abdu'd-Dar ibn Qusayy. Quraysh used to marry their allies. Khadija bore Abu Hala a son called Hind and a son called Hala.

Then after Abu Hala, she married 'Atiq ibn 'Abid of Makhzum. She bore him a girl called Hind, who married her cousin, Sayfi ibn Umayya ibn 'Abid of Makhzum and she bore him Muhammad. This clan was called the "Banu Muhammad" because of the position of Khadija. It existed in Madina and eventually died out. Khadija was called Umm Hind.

It is related from Mughira ibn 'Abdu'r-Rahman al-Asadi that his people said, "We asked Hakim ibn Hizam which of them was older, the Messenger of Allah ﷺ or Khadija? He said, 'Khadija was fifteen years older than him. The prayer was unlawful for my aunt before the Messenger of Allah was born.'"

Abu 'Abdullah said, "Hakim's statement, 'The prayer was unlawful for her' means she menstruated, but he is speaking as the people of Islam speak."

It is related from Ibn 'Abbas that the women of the people of Makka met for a festival which they held in the month of Rajab. They did not think that anything was more important than attending that festival. While they were in retreat with an idol something in the shape of man appeared to them, came up to them, and then called out in his loudest voice, "Women of Tayma'! A Prophet will appear in your land who will be called Ahmad. He will be sent with the Message of Allah. So any woman who is able to be his wife should do so." The women threw pebbles at him, and denounced him and were harsh to him. Khadija ignored what he said but did not treat him as the women did.

It is related that Nafisa bint Umayya, the sister of Ya'la bint Umayya, said, "Khadija had nobility and great wealth. She used to dispatch goods to Syria. Her caravan was equal to the general caravan of Quraysh. She hired men and paid them on the basis of a partnership. When the Messenger of Allah ﷺ reached the age of twenty-five and was known in Makka as 'the Trusty (*al-Amin*)', Khadija bint Khuwaylid sent for him to ask him to take her goods to Syria with her slave Maysara. She said, 'I will give you double what your people give.' The Messenger of Allah ﷺ did that, and he went to the market of Bosra and sold the goods which he had brought and bought other goods and brought them back with double her normal profit. She gave the Prophet twice the amount she had named for him."

Nafisa said, "She sent me to him secretly to ask him to marry her, and he agreed. She sent for her uncle 'Amr ibn Asad ibn 'Abdu'l-'Uzza and he came. The Messenger of Allah ﷺ came with his uncles and one of them performed the marriage. 'Amr ibn Asad said about this, 'This marriage shall not be rejected.' The Messenger of Allah ﷺ married her on his return from Syria when he was twenty-five. She bore al-Qasim, 'Abdullah, who is at-Tahir, and at-Tayyib, who was called that because he was born in Islam, Zaynab, Ruqayya, Umm Kulthum and Fatima. Salma, 'Uqba's client, was her midwife. There were two years between each two children. She used to find wet-nurses for them and arranged that before they were born."

It is related from Ibn 'Abbas that the uncle of Khadija, 'Amr ibn Asad, gave her in marriage to the Messenger of Allah ﷺ. Her father had died on the Day of Fijar. Muhammad ibn 'Umar said, "Our companions agree about this and there is no disagreement about it."

Muhammad ibn 'Umar said, "Khadija was born fifteen years before the Elephant, and she was forty when she married the Messenger of Allah ﷺ."

Hakim ibn Hizam said, "The Messenger of Allah married Khadija when she was forty and the Messenger of Allah was twenty-five. Khadija was two years older than me. She was born fifteen years before the Elephant and I was born thirteen years before the Elephant."

'A'isha and Nafi' ibn Jubayr said, "Khadija was the first to become Muslim."

Az-Zuhri said, "The Messenger of Allah and Khadija prayed in secret for as long as Allah wished."

'Afif al-Kindi said, "During the *Jahiliyya* I came to Makka wishing to purchase clothes and perfume for my family. I stayed with al-'Abbas ibn 'Abdu'l-Muttalib. While I was with him, looking at the Ka'ba when the sun was high, a young man came up to the Ka'ba. He raised his head towards the heaven and concentrated his attention. Then he faced the Ka'ba standing upright. Then a boy came and stood at his right. A woman soon came and stood behind them. Then the young man bowed and the boy and woman bowed. Then the young man raised his head and the boy and woman raised their heads. Then the young man went into prostration and the boy and woman went into prostration. I said, 'Abbas, I see something immense.' Al-'Abbas said, 'Something immense. Do you know who this young man is?' I said, 'No, I do not know.' He said, 'This is Muhammad ibn 'Abdullah ibn 'Abdu'l-Muttalib, my nephew. Do you know who this boy is?' I said, 'No, I do not know.' He said, "Ali ibn Abi Talib ibn 'Abdu'l-Muttalib, my nephew. Do you know who this woman is?' I said, 'No, I do not know.' He said, 'This is Khadija bint Khuwaylid, the wife of this nephew. This nephew of mine whom you see tells us that his Lord is the Lord of the heavens and earth, who enjoined on him this *deen* which he is following. He is following it and, by Allah, I do not know that there is anyone on the face of the earth following this *deen* except these three.'"

'Afif said, "Later I wished I had been their fourth."

Muhammad ibn Salih and 'Abdu'r-Rahman ibn 'Abdu'l-'Aziz said, " Khadija died on the twentieth of Ramadan, three years before the *hijra*. She was sixty-five."

'A'isha said, "Khadija died before the prayer was made obligatory. That was three years before the *hijra*."

Hakim ibn Hizam said, "Khadija bint Khuwaylid died in the month of Ramadan in the tenth year of prophethood. She was sixty-five then. We took her out of her house and buried her at al-Hajun. The Messenger of Allah ﷺ went down into her grave. At that time we did not have the *sunna* of the funeral prayer." He was asked, "When was that, Abu Khalid?" He said, "Three years before the *hijra* or thereabouts. It was shortly after the Banu Hashim left the ravine."

He said, "She was the first woman the Messenger of Allah ﷺ married and all his children were by her, except for Ibrahim, the child of Mariya. Her *kunya* was Umm Hind from her son by her husband, Abu Hala at-Tamimi."

Chapter Three:
The Daughters of the Messenger of Allah

Fatima, daughter of the Messenger of Allah

Her mother was Khadija bint Khuwaylid. She was born while Quraysh were rebuilding the Ka'ba. That was five years before prophethood.

It is related that Abu Bakr asked the Prophet ﷺ for Fatima's hand in marriage. He said, "Abu Bakr, wait for a decision about her." Abu Bakr mentioned that to 'Umar and 'Umar said to him, "He has rejected you, Abu Bakr!" Then Abu Bakr said to 'Umar, "Ask the Prophet for Fatima's hand." So he asked to marry her and he said to him the like of what he had said to Abu Bakr: "Wait for a decision about her." 'Umar went to Abu Bakr and told him, and he said to him, "He has rejected you, 'Umar." Then 'Ali's family said to 'Ali, "Ask the Messenger of Allah for Fatima's hand in marriage." So he proposed and the Prophet ﷺ gave her in marriage to him. 'Ali sold a camel he had and some of his goods and that fetched 480 dirhams. The Prophet said to him, "Invest two-thirds of it in scent and a third in goods."

Musa ibn Qays al-Hadrami reported that Hujr ibn 'Anbas said, "Abu Bakr and 'Umar asked the Messenger of Allah for Fatima's hand. The Prophet ﷺ said, 'She is yours, 'Ali. You are not a fraud,' meaning you are not a liar. That was because he had promised her to 'Ali before Abu Bakr and 'Umar had asked to marry her."

'Ata' was heard to say, "'Ali asked to marry Fatima and the Messenger of Allah ﷺ said to her, '''Ali is mentioning you.' She was silent and so he gave her in marriage to him."

It is related that a man heard 'Ali say, "I want to propose to the Messenger of Allah ﷺ for his daughter. But, by Allah, I have nothing!" The man asked, "How is that?" Then the man mentioned his connections and family and so he asked to marry her. The Prophet said, "Have you got anything?" 'Ali said, "No." He said, "Where is your coat of mail which I gave you on such-and-such a day?" He said, "I have it." He said, "Give it to her." He gave it to her.

It is related from 'Ikrima that 'Ali proposed to Fatima and the Prophet said to him, "What dower will you give her?" He said, "I do not have anything to give her as dower." He said, "Where is your coat of mail which I gave you?" He said, "I have it." He said, "Give it to her." He said, "He gave it to her and married her." 'Ikrima said, "It was worth four dirhams."

It is related that 'Ikrima said, "Fatima married 'Ali for an iron coat of mail."

Burayda said, "A group of the Ansar said to 'Ali, 'You should marry Fatima.' He went to the Messenger of Allah and greeted him. He said, 'What do you need, Ibn Abi Talib?' 'Ali mentioned Fatima. He said, 'Welcome and greetings,' and did not say anything more. 'Ali went out to that group of Ansar who were waiting for him. They said, 'What happened?' He said, 'I only know that he said, "Welcome and greetings," to me.' They said, 'One greeting is enough for you from the Messenger of Allah. He gave you welcome and he gave you greetings.' Later he married her and he said, 'Ali, there must be a wedding feast.' Sa'd said, 'I have a ram.' So a group of the Ansar collected some measures of millet for him. On the wedding night, he said, 'Do not start anything until I join you.'"

He said, "The Messenger of Allah ﷺ called for a vessel and did *wudu'* in it and then poured it over 'Ali. Then he said, 'O Allah, bless them and put blessings on them and bless them in their offspring.'"

It is related that Muhammad said, "'Ali gave Fatima a dower of iron armour and a well-worn garment."

Muhammad ibn 'Ali said, "'Ali married Fatima for a sheepskin and a worn-out garment." Abu Ja'far said something similar.

It is related from 'Ilya' ibn Ahmar al-Yaskari that 'Ali married Fatima and sold a camel of his for 480 dirhams. The Prophet ﷺ said, "Invest two-thirds of it in scent and one third in clothes."

'Ali said, "I married Fatima when I did not have a bed except a ramskin. We slept on it at night and fed the camel on it. I had no servant except her."

Ibrahim said, "The dower of the daughters of the Messenger of Allah ﷺ and of his wives was 500 dirhams, or twelve and a half *uqiyyas*."

It is related that 'Ali ibn Abi Talib married Fatima, the daughter of the Prophet ﷺ in the month of Rajab five months after the Prophet arrived in Madina. He consummated the marriage after he returned from Badr. Fatima was eighteen on the day that the marriage with 'Ali was consummated.

Abu Ja'far said, "When the Messenger of Allah came to Madina, he stayed with Abu Ayyub for a year or thereabouts. When 'Ali married Fatima, he said to 'Ali, 'Look for a house.' 'Ali looked for a house and found something a little distant from the Prophet ﷺ. He consummated the marriage there and the Prophet went to her and said, 'I want to move you near me.' She said to the Messenger of Allah, 'Ask Haritha ibn an-Nu'man to move for me.' The Messenger of Allah said, 'Haritha has moved for us so that I am embarrassed to ask him again.' Haritha heard about that, so he moved and then went to the Prophet ﷺ and said, 'Messenger of Allah, I have heard that you want to move Fatima near you. These are my houses and they are the nearest of the houses of the Banu'n-Najjar to you. Both myself and my wealth are for Allah and His Messenger. By Allah, Messenger of Allah, I prefer the money which you took from me to that which remains.' The Messenger of Allah ﷺ said, 'You have spoken truly. May Allah bless you.' The Messenger of Allah moved her to Haritha's house."

It is related that Asma' bint 'Umays said [to Umm Ja'far], "I prepared your grandmother Fatima for your grandfather 'Ali. There was no stuffing in their bed and pillows except fibre. 'Ali prepared a wedding-feast for Fatima, There was no better wedding feast in that time than his wedding feast. He left his armour in pawn with a Jew for a half measure of barley."

It is related from Muhammad that when 'Ali went to live with Fatima, their bed was a ramskin. When they wanted to sleep, they turned over its wool, and their pillows were made of leather stuffed with fibre."

Muhammad ibn 'Ali said, 'The dower of Fatima was a worn-out garment and a sheepskin."

'Ikrima said, "When the Messenger of Allah gave Fatima in marriage to 'Ali, part of the trousseau prepared for Fatima was a palm-leaf bed, a pillow of leather stuffed with fibre, a small leather vessel and a waterskin."

Umm Ayman said, "The Messenger of Allah ﷺ gave his daughter Fatima in marriage to 'Ali ibn Abi Talib and he told him not to go in to Fatima until he had come to him. The Messenger of Allah came and stood at the door and gave the greeting. He asked for permission to enter and was given it. He said, 'Is my brother there?' Umm Ayman said, 'May my father and mother be your ransom, Messenger of Allah, who is your brother?' He replied, "Ali ibn Abi Talib.' She said, 'How can he be your brother when you have married your daughter to him?' He said, 'That is how it is, Umm Ayman.' He called for water and it was brought in a vessel and he washed his hands in it. Then he called 'Ali who sat before him, and he sprinkled some of that water on his chest and between his shoulders. Then he called Fatima and she came without a head covering, tripping on her garment, and then he sprinkled some of that water on her. Then he said, 'By Allah, I swear that I have married you to the best of my family.'" Umm Ayman said, "I arranged her trousseau. Part of what was prepared for her was a cushion of leather stuffed with fibre and soft sand was spread in her house."

'Ikrima said something similar.

It is related from Darim ibn 'Abdu'r-Rahman ibn Tha'laba al-Hanafi that one of his uncles of the Ansar said that his grandmother had told him that she was one of the women who escorted Fatima to

'Ali. She said, "She was presented in two robes, the first had silver rings coloured with saffron. We entered 'Ali's house and there was a sheepskin on a bench, a cushion stuffed with fibre, a waterskin, a sieve, a napkin and a cup."

'Abdullah ibn 'Amr ibn Hind said, "On the night when Fatima was given to 'Ali, the Messenger of Allah said to him, 'Do not start anything until I come to you.' The Messenger of Allah soon followed them and stood at the door and asked for permission to enter and then entered. 'Ali was apart from her. The Messenger of Allah said, 'I know that you love Allah and His Messenger.' He called for water and rinsed his mouth and then put it back in the vessel and then sprinkled it on her chest and his chest."

It is related from 'Ali that when the Messenger of Allah ﷺ married him to Fatima, he sent with her a woven cloth, a leather cushion stuffed with fibre, two mills, a water vessel, and two waterskins. One day 'Ali said to Fatima, "By Allah, I have drawn water until my chest hurts. Allah has given your father spoils, so go and ask him for a servant." She said, "By Allah, I have ground until my hands are blistered." She went to the Prophet and he said, "What has brought you, girl?" She said, "I have come to greet you," and she was too shy to ask and went back. He said, "What did you do?" She said, "I was too shy to ask him." So they went to him together and 'Ali said, "Messenger of Allah, I have drawn water until my chest hurts." Fatima said, "I have ground until my hands are blistered. Allah has given you some booty and wealth, so give us a servant." He said, "By Allah, I will not give to you and leave the People of the Suffa binding up their bellies [from hunger]. I cannot find anything I can spend on them, but I will sell [the booty] and spend it on them."

So they went back and then the Prophet ﷺ came to them when they were under their blanket. When they covered their heads, their feet showed and when they covered their feet, their heads showed. They jumped up and he said, "Stay where you are. Shall I tell you what is better than what you ask?" They said, "Yes indeed." He said, "Some words which Jibril taught me. After every prayer say 'Glory be to Allah' ten times, 'Praise be to Allah' ten times, and 'Allah is greater' ten times. When you retire to your bed, then say 'Glory be to

Allah' 33 times, 'Praise be to Allah' 33 times, and 'Allah is greater' 34 times."

'Ali said, "By Allah, I have not omitted them since the Messenger of Allah taught them to me." Ibn al-Kiwa' said to him, "Not even on the night of Siffin?" He said, "May Allah fight you, people of Iraq, not even on the night of Siffin!"

'Amr ibn Sa'id said, "'Ali had showed some harshness towards Fatima. She said, 'By Allah, I will complain about you to the Messenger of Allah!' She went and 'Ali went after her. When the Prophet heard them talking, he stood up. She complained to the Messenger of Allah of 'Ali's roughness and harshness to her. He said, 'Daughter, listen, give ear and understand. There is no cleverness in a woman who does not attend to her husband's affection when he is calm.' 'Ali said, 'I will refrain from what I used to do.' He said, 'By Allah, I will never do anything you dislike.'"

Habib ibn Abi Thabit said, "Some words passed between 'Ali and Fatima. The Messenger of Allah entered and 'Ali made him a bed and he lay down on it. Fatima came and lay down beside him. 'Ali came and lay down on the other side. The Messenger of Allah took 'Ali's hand and placed it on his navel and took Fatima's hand and placed it on his navel and continued until he made peace between them. Then he went out."

Habib said, "It was said to him, 'You entered in one state and you have come out and we see joy in your face.' He said, 'What would prevent me when I have made peace between the two I love the most?'"

Abu Ja'far said, "Al-'Abbas came in to visit 'Ali ibn Abi Talib and Fatima. She was saying, 'I am older than you.' Al-'Abbas said, 'Fatima, you were born when Quraysh were building the Ka'ba when the Prophet ﷺ was thirty-five. You, 'Ali, were born a few years before that.'"

Muhammad ibn 'Umar said, "Fatima bore 'Ali al-Hasan, al-Husayn, Umm Kulthum, and Zaynab."

'A'isha said, "I was sitting with the Messenger of Allah ﷺ when Fatima came walking with the same gait as the Messenger of Allah.

He said, 'Welcome, my daughter.' He had her sit at his right or his left and whispered something to her and she wept. Then he whispered something to her and she laughed. I said, 'Why did I see you laugh so soon after weeping? The Messenger of Allah singled you out for something and then you wept. What did the Messenger of Allah whisper to you?' She said, 'I will not divulge his secret.' When the Messenger of Allah ﷺ died, I asked her again and she said, 'He said, "Jibril used to meet me every year and repeat the Qur'an to me once. This year he has come to me twice and repeated it to me. I only think that my end is near. I am the best precursor for you." He added, "You will be the swiftest of my family to join me."' She said, 'I wept at that.' Then he said, "Are you not content to be the mistress of the women of this community, or the women of the worlds?"' She said, 'I laughed at that.'"

It is related that 'Abdu'r-Rahman al-A'raj was heard to say in his gathering in Madina, "The Messenger of Allah assigned 300 *wasqs* of barley and dates to Fatima and 'Ali at Khaybar. 85 *wasqs* were barley. Fatima had 200 *wasqs* of that."

'Amir said, "Abu Bakr went to Fatima when she was ill and asked permission to enter. 'Ali said, 'This is Abu Bakr at the door. Do you wish to give him permission?' She said, 'Do you agree to that?' He said, 'Yes.' So he went in to visit her and comforted her and spoke to her, and she was pleased with him."

Salma said, "Fatima, the daughter of the Messenger of Allah, was ill while we were with her. On the day she died, 'Ali had gone out. She said to me, 'Pour a bath for me.' So I poured a bath for her and she washed in the best manner in which she used to wash. Then she said, 'Bring me my new clothes.' So I brought them to her and she put them on. Then she said, 'Put my bed in the middle of the house.' I did that and she lay down on it and faced the *qibla*. Then she said to me, 'Mother, I will die now. I have washed, so do not let anyone uncover my shoulder.'" She said, "She died. Then 'Ali came and I told him. He said, 'By Allah, no one will uncover her shoulder.' He took her and buried her with that *ghusl*."

It is related from Muhammad ibn Musa that 'Ali ibn Abi Talib washed Fatima.

It is related that 'A'isha, the wife of the Prophet, reported that Fatima, the daughter of the Messenger of Allah, asked Abu Bakr after the death of the Messenger of Allah to allot her inheritance to her from what the Messenger of Allah left of his booty. Abu Bakr said to her, "The Messenger of Allah ﷺ said, 'We do not leave inheritance. What we leave is *sadaqa*.'" Fatima became angry. She only lived six months after the death of the Messenger of Allah.

Az-Zuhri and Abu Ja'far said, "Fatima lived three months after the Prophet ﷺ." It is related that Abu Ja'far and 'Urwa said it was six months.

Muhammad ibn 'Umar, whom I consider to be reliable, said, "She died on the 7th of Ramadan in the year 11 when she was about 29."

Ibn 'Abbas said, "Fatima was the first to be given a bier. Asma' bint 'Umays made it for her. She had seen how it is constructed when she was in Abyssinia."

'Amra bint 'Abdu'r-Rahman said, "Al-'Abbas ibn 'Abdu'l-Muttalib prayed over Fatima, the daughter of the Messenger of Allah, and he, 'Ali and al-Fadl ibn 'Abbas went down into her grave."

It is related from 'Urwa that 'Ali prayed over Fatima.

It is related that ash-Sha'bi said, "Abu Bakr prayed over her, may Allah be pleased with him and her."

It is related that Ibrahim said, "Abu Bakr as-Siddiq prayed over Fatima, the daughter of the Messenger of Allah, and said four *takbirs* over her."

It is related that az-Zuhri said, "Fatima, the daughter of the Messenger of Allah, was buried at night. 'Ali buried her."

'Ali ibn Husayn said, "I asked Ibn 'Abbas, 'When did you bury Fatima?' He said, 'We buried her at night beyond Hada'.' I said, 'Who prayed over her?' He replied, "Ali.'"

It is related that Muhammad ibn 'Umar questioned 'Abdu'r-Rahman ibn Abi'l-Mawali. He said, "I said, 'People say that the grave of Fatima is at the mosque where they say their funeral prayers at al-Baqi'.' He said, 'By Allah, that is the mosque of Ruqayya,' i.e.

the woman who lived there. 'Fatima is buried in the corner of the house of 'Aqil which is next to the house of the Jahshis, directly facing the exit of the Banu Nabih from the Banu 'Abdu'd-Dar at al-Baqi'. There are seven cubits between her grave and the road."

'Abdullah ibn Hasan said, "I found al-Mughira ibn 'Abdu'r-Rahman ibn al-Harith ibn Hisham waiting for me at al-Baqi' at midday in intense heat. I said, 'What has made you stop here, Abu Hashim?' He said, 'I was waiting for you. I have heard that Fatima was buried in this room in the house of 'Aqil next to the house of the Jahshi family. I want you to buy it for me whatever the cost. I will be buried in it.' 'Abdullah said, 'By Allah, I will do it.' He made great efforts to purchase it from the 'Aqili family but they refused to sell."

'Abdullah ibn Ja'far said, "I have not seen anyone who doubts that her grave is located there."

✳✳✳✳✳

Zaynab, daughter of the Messenger of Allah

Her mother was Khadija bint Khuwaylid. She was the oldest of the daughters of the Messenger of Allah ﷺ. He married her to his cousin, Abu'l-'As ibn ar-Rabi' before prophethood. She was the first of the daughters of the Messenger of Allah to marry. Abu'l-'As' mother was Hala bint Khuwaylid, Zaynab's maternal aunt. Zaynab and Abu'l-'As had two children: 'Ali and Umama. 'Ali died when he was still a child and Umama grew up and later married 'Ali ibn Abi Talib after Fatima's death.

It is related from 'Amr ash-Sha'bi that Zaynab, the daughter of the Messenger of Allah, was married to Abu'l-'As ibn ar-Rabi'. She became Muslim and emigrated with her father while Abu'l-'As refused to become Muslim.

It is related from 'A'isha that Abu'l-'As ibn ar-Rabi' was one of those who was with the idolworshippers at Badr. He was captured by 'Abdullah ibn Jubayr al-Ansari. When the people of Makka ransomed their captives, his brother, 'Amr ibn ar-Rabi', came to ransom his brother. Zaynab, the daughter of the Messenger of Allah, was still

in Makka at that time and she sent a necklace made of Zafar onyx she
had which had belonged to Khadija bint Khuwaylid. Zafar is a mountain in Yemen. Khadija bint Khuwaylid had given her the necklace
when she consummated her marriage to Abu'l-'As ibn ar-Rabi'. She
sent it as part of her husband's ransom. When the Messenger of Allah
ﷺ saw the necklace, he recognised it and it moved him and he
remembered Khadija and he felt pity. He said, 'If you could see the
way to releasing her captive to her and returning her goods to her,
then do it.' They said, 'Yes, Messenger of Allah.' They released
Abu'l-'As and returned Zaynab's necklace to her and the Prophet
ﷺ made Abu'l-'As promise that he would let Zaynab join him. He
made that promise and he did it."

Muhammad ibn 'Umar, whom I consider reliable, stated that
Zaynab made *hijra* with her father.

Ma'ruf ibn al-Khurbad al-Makki said, "Abu'l-'As ibn ar-Rabi'
went out on one of his journeys to Syria and thought about his wife,
Zaynab, daughter of the Messenger of Allah, and composed these
verses:

> I remember Zaynab when she leaned on the waymark.
> I said to a person who lived in the Haram, 'Water!'
>
> For the daughter of the Trustworthy.' May Allah reward her!
> Virtuous she is, and every husband praises what he knows."

Muhammad ibn 'Umar said, "The Messenger of Allah ﷺ used to
say, "We find no fault in Abu'l-'As as an in-law."

Yazid ibn Ruman said, "The Messenger of Allah led the people in
the *Subh* prayer. When he stood up for the prayer, Zaynab, daughter
of the Messenger of Allah, said, 'I have given safe-conduct to Abu'l-
'As ibn ar-Rabi'.' When the Messenger of Allah finished, he said,
'Did you hear what I heard?' They said, 'Yes.' He said, 'By the One
who has the soul of Muhammad in His hand, I did not know anything
about what was going to happen until I heard what you heard. Safe-
conduct can be given by the least of people.'"

Isma'il ibn 'Amir said, "Abu'l-'As ibn ar-Rabi' came from Syria. His wife, Zaynab, had become Muslim with her father and emigrated. Then he became Muslim later on and the Prophet did not separate them."

It is related from Qatada that Zaynab, daughter of the Messenger of Allah, was married to Abu'l-'As ibn ar-Rabi'. She emigrated with the Messenger of Allah and then her husband became Muslim and emigrated to the Messenger of Allah and he returned her to him.

Qatada said, "Then *Surat Bara'a* (10) was sent down after that. So when a woman became Muslim before her husband, he had no means to her except by proposing again. Her accepting Islam amounts to a definitive divorce."

It is related from Shu'ayb that the Prophet ﷺ returned his daughter to Abu'l-'As ibn ar-Rabi' by a new marriage. Yazid said, "A new dower."

It is related from Ibn 'Abbas that the Messenger of Allah ﷺ returned his daughter to Abu'l-'As after two years had passed by virtue of the first marriage without any new dower.

Muhammad ibn Ibrahim at-Taymi said, "Abu'l-'As ibn ar-Rabi' went to Syria in the caravan of Quraysh. The Messenger of Allah ﷺ heard that that caravan was returning from Syria, and he sent Zayd ibn Haritha with 170 horsemen. They intercepted the caravan in the vicinity of al-'Is in Jumada al-Ula, 6 AH. They seized it and the goods it contained and captured some of the people who were in the caravan, including Abu'l-'As ibn ar-Rabi'. He went to Madina and went to his wife, Zaynab, daughter of the Messenger of Allah, before daybreak. He asked for her protection and she granted it to him. When the Messenger of Allah prayed *Fajr*, she stood at the door and called out in her loudest voice, 'I have given safe-conduct to Abu'l-'As ibn ar-Rabi'.' The Messenger of Allah ﷺ said, 'O people, did you hear what I heard?' They said, 'Yes.' He said, 'By the One who has the soul of Muhammad in His hand, I did not know anything about what was going to happen until I heard what you heard. The believers are one hand against others. The least of them grants their protection. We protect the one she protects.' When the Prophet ﷺ went to his house, Zaynab came to him and asked him to return to

Abu'l-'As what had been taken from him. He did that. He also commanded her not to go near him for she was not lawful to him as long as he remained an idolworshipper. Abu'l-'As returned to Makka and settled all his obligations. Then he became Muslim and returned to the Prophet as a Muslim, emigrating in the month of Muharram, 7 AH. So the Messenger of Allah ﷺ returned Zaynab to him by virtue of that first marriage."

Anas ibn Malik said, "I saw Zaynab, the daughter of the Messenger of Allah, wearing a striped silk cloak."

'Abdullah ibn Abi Bakr ibn Muhammad ibn 'Amr ibn Hazim said, "The daughter of the Messenger of Allah died at the beginning of 8 AH."

Abu Rafi' said, "Those who washed Zaynab, the daughter of the Messenger of Allah, included Umm Ayman, Sawda bint Zam'a and Umm Salama, the wife of the Messenger of Allah."

Umm 'Atiyya said, "One of the daughters of the Prophet died and the Messenger of Allah commanded us, 'Wash her an odd number of times - three or five or more than that if you think it better. Wash her with water and lotus. Put some camphor in the last washing. When you finish, inform me.'" She said, "We informed him and he gave us his wrapper and said, 'Shroud her with it.'"

Umm 'Atiyya said, "When we washed the daughter of the Messenger of Allah, we plaited her hair into three plaits, on the sides and in front, and put them behind her."

Umm 'Atiyya said, "When we washed the daughter of the Prophet, the Messenger of Allah said to us when we were washing her, 'Begin with the right side and the places of *wudu'*.'"

✳✳✳✳✳

Ruqayya, daughter of the Messenger of Allah

Her mother was Khadija bint Khuwaylid. She was married to 'Utba ibn Abi Lahab ibn 'Abdu'l-Muttalib before prophethood. When the Messenger of Allah was sent and Allah sent down,

"Perish the hands of Abu Lahab," (111) his father, Abu Lahab, said to him, "My head is unlawful to your head if you do not divorce his daughter." So he parted from her without having consummated the marriage. She became Muslim when her mother, Khadija bint Khuwaylid, became Muslim. She and her sisters gave allegiance to the Messenger of Allah when the women gave it.

She married 'Uthman ibn 'Affan and made *hijra* with him to Abyssinia both times. The Messenger of Allah ﷺ said, "They are the first to emigrate for Allah Almighty since Lut." She suffered a miscarriage in the first emigration and then bore 'Uthman a son after that whom they named 'Abdullah. 'Uthman had that *kunya* in Islam. The child lived to the age of two and then a cock pecked his face and his face became swollen and he died. She did not bear any more children. She emigrated to Madina after her husband 'Uthman when the Messenger of Allah had emigrated. She fell ill when the Messenger of Allah was preparing for Badr and so the Messenger of Allah ﷺ left 'Uthman ibn 'Affan behind to care for her. She died while the Messenger of Allah was at Badr in the month of Ramadan, seventeen months after the *hijra* of the Messenger of Allah. Zayd ibn Haritha brought the news of Badr and entered Madina when the earth was being levelled over Ruqayya's grave.

It is related that Ibn 'Abbas said, "When Ruqayya, the daughter of the Messenger of Allah, died, the Prophet ﷺ said, 'Join our forerunner, 'Uthman ibn Maz'un.' The women wept over Ruqayya and 'Umar ibn al-Khattab came and began to hit them with his whip. The Prophet took hold of his hand and then said, 'Let them weep, 'Umar.' Then he said, 'Weep, but beware of the braying of Shaytan. Whatever comes from the heart and eye is from Allah and mercy. Whatever comes from the hand and tongue is from Shaytan.' Fatima sat on the edge of the grave beside the Prophet and began to weep. The Prophet ﷺ wiped the tears from her eyes with the end of his garment."

Muhammad ibn Sa'd said, "I mentioned this *hadith* to Muhammad ibn 'Umar and he said, 'What I consider to be reliable from all transmissions is that Ruqayya died while the Messenger of Allah was at Badr, and he was not present at her burial. Perhaps this *hadith* is about another of the daughters of the Prophet whose burial he attended. If it is about Ruqayya and it is confirmed, then perhaps he came to her grave after he arrived in Madina, and the women wept over it after that."

*****

Umm Kulthum, the daughter of the Messenger of Allah

Her mother was Khadija bint Khuwaylid. She was married to 'Utayba ibn Abi Lahab ibn 'Abdu'l-Muttalib before prophethood. When the Messenger of Allah was sent and Allah sent down, *"Perish the hands of Abu Lahab,"* (111) his father, Abu Lahab, said to him, "My head is unlawful to your head if you do not divorce his daughter." So he parted from her without having consummated the marriage. She remained with the Messenger of Allah in Makka and became Muslim when her mother became Muslim. She and her sisters gave allegiance to the Messenger of Allah with the women. She emigrated to Madina when the Messenger of Allah ﷺ emigrated. She left for Madina with the family of the Messenger of Allah and remained there.

When Ruqayya, the daughter of the Messenger of Allah, died, 'Uthman ibn 'Affan then married Umm Kulthum, who was a virgin. That was in Rabi' al-Awwal 3 AH. He consummated the marriage with her in this year in Jumada al-Akhira. She remained with him until she died without bearing any children. She died in Sha'ban, 9 AH. The Messenger of Allah said,"If I had had ten [i.e. daughters], I would have married them to 'Uthman."

It is related from Anas ibn Malik that he saw Umm Kulthum, daughter of the Messenger of Allah, wearing a striped silk cloak.

Asma' ibn 'Umays said, "I and Safiyya bint 'Abdu'l-Muttalib washed Umm Kulthum, daughter of the Messenger of Allah. I put her on a bier which I ordered be made from freshly cut palm boughs, and I buried her."

'Amra bint 'Abdu'r-Rahman said, "Women of the Ansar washed her, including Umm 'Atiyya. Abu Talha went down into her grave."

Anas ibn Malik said, "I saw the Prophet ﷺ sitting on her grave with his eyes flowing with tears. He said, 'Who among you did not have intercourse last night?' Abu Talha said, 'I, Messenger of Allah.' He said, 'Go down.'"

Muhammad ibn 'Abdu'r-Rahman ibn Sa'd ibn Zurara said, "The Messenger of Allah ﷺ prayed over her and sat on her grave. 'Ali ibn Abi Talib, al-Fadl ibn 'Abbas, and Usama ibn Zayd went down into her grave."

✴✶✴✶✴

Umama bint Abi'l-'As ibn ar-Rabi'

Her mother was Zaynab, daughter of the Messenger of Allah.

Abu Qatada was heard to say, "While we were sitting at the door of the Messenger of Allah, the Messenger of Allah came out to us carrying Umama bint Abi'l-'As ibn ar-Rabi'. Her mother was Zaynab, daughter of the Messenger of Allah. She was a little girl."
He said, "The Messenger of Allah ﷺ prayed with her on his shoulder. He put her down when he bowed and picked her up when he stood up until he finished the prayer, doing that with her."

Abu Qatada ibn Rib'i said, "I saw the Messenger of Allah ﷺ pray while he was carrying Umama bint Abi'l-'As, his granddaughter, on his shoulder. He put her down when he bowed and picked her up when he stood up."
'Abdullah ibn al-Harith ibn Nawfal said, "The Messenger of Allah ﷺ used to pray with Umama bint Abi'l-'As on his shoulder. He put her down when he bowed and picked her up when he stood up."

It is related from 'Ali ibn Zayd ibn Jid'an that the Messenger of Allah ﷺ went to his family with an onyx necklace. He said, "I will give it to the one I love the most." The women said, "He will give it to the daughter of Abu Bakr." He called the daughter of Abu'l-'As by Zaynab and put it in her hand. There was a secretion from her eye and he wiped it away with his hand.

It is related from 'A'isha that the Negus gave the Messenger of Allah ﷺ jewellery which included a gold ring. He accepted it and was about to turn away from it. He sent it to the daughter of his daughter Zaynab. He said. "Adorn yourself with this, little daughter."

It is related that Umama bint Abi'l-'As said to al-Mughira ibn Nawfal ibn al-Harith, "Mu'awiya has proposed to me." He said to her, "Will you marry the son of the liver-eater! Will you leave that to me?" She said. "Yes." He said, "I will marry you."

Ibn Abi Dhi'b said, "His marriage was permitted."

Chapter Four:
The Paternal Aunts of the Prophet

Safiyya bint 'Abdu'l-Muttalib ibn Hisham

Her mother was Hala bint Wuhayb ibn 'Abdu Manaf. She was the half-sister of Hamza ibn 'Abdu'l-Muttalib by his mother. In the Jahiliyya she was married to al-Harith ibn Harb ibn Umayya, and she bore him a son, Safi. Then she was married to al-'Awwam ibn Khuwaylid and bore him az-Zubayr, as-Sa'ib and 'Abdu'l-Ka'ba. Safiyya became Muslim and gave allegiance to the Messenger of Allah. She emigrated to Madina and the Messenger of Allah ﷺ assigned her forty *wasqs* from Khaybar.

It is related from 'Urwa that when the Messenger of Allah ﷺ went out from Madina to fight his enemy, he left his wives and womenfolk in the fortress of Hassan ibn Thabit because it was the most secure fortress of Madina. Hassan remained behind on the Day of Uhud. A Jew came up close to the fortress, listening and spying. Safiyya bint 'Abdu'l-Muttalib said to Hassan, "Go down to this Jew and kill him." He seemed to dread that and so she took a pole and went down and stealthily opened the door little by little and then attacked him and struck him with the pole and killed him.

It is related from Hisham ibn 'Urwa that Safiyya bint 'Abdu'l-Muttalib went out with a spear in her hand on the Day of Uhud when the people were fleeing. She shook it at the faces of the people, saying, "You are fleeing from the Messenger of Allah!" When the Messenger of Allah ﷺ saw her, he said, "Zubayr, the woman!" Hamza's belly had been slit open and the Messenger of Allah did not want her to see him. She was his sister. Az-Zubayr said, "Mother! Get back! Get back!" She said, "Get away! You have no mother!" She came and looked at Hamza.

Safiyya bint 'Abdu'l-Muttalib was buried in al-Baqi' in the court-yard of the house of al-Mughira ibn Shu'ba at the *wudu'* place. Safiyya died in the khalifate of 'Umar ibn al-Khattab and she related things from the Messenger of Allah.

✳✳✳✳✳

Arwa bint 'Abdu'l-Muttalib ibn Hisham

Her mother was Fatima bint 'Amr ibn 'A'idh of Makhzum. In the Jahiliyya she married 'Umayr ibn Wahb ibn 'Abdu Manaf. She bore him Tulayb. Then after him she married Arta ibn Sharahbil ibn Hashim and bore him Fatima. Then Arwa became Muslim in Makka and emigrated to Madina.

Muhammad ibn Ibrahim ibn al-Harith at-Taymi said, "Tulayb ibn 'Umayr became Muslim in the house of al-Arqam ibn Abi'l-Arqam al-Makhzumi. Then he left and went to his mother, Arwa bint 'Abdu'l-Muttalib. He said, 'I have given allegiance to Muhammad and submitted to Allah.' His mother said to him, 'It is most fitting that you help and support your uncle. By Allah, if we were able to do what the men do, we would follow him and defend him.' Tulayb said, 'And what prevents you, mother, from becoming Muslim and following him? Your brother Hamza has become Muslim.' Then she said, 'I will see what my sisters are doing and then I will be one of them.' Tulayb said, 'I ask you by Allah, won't you come and submit to him and believe him and testify that there is no god but Allah and that Muhammad is the Messenger of Allah?' Then she supported the Prophet ﷺ with her tongue and encouraged her son to help him and support him."

Barra bint Abi Tajra said, "Abu Jahl and a number of unbelievers of Quraysh accosted the Prophet ﷺ and injured him, and Tulayb ibn 'Umayr went to Abu Jahl and dealt him a blow which exposed his skull. They seized him and put him in chains. Abu Lahab had him released. Arwa was asked, 'Do you see that your son Tulayb has made himself a target rather than Muhammad?' She said, 'The best of his days are the days when he defends the son of his uncle. He has brought the truth from Allah.' They said, 'And do you follow Muhammad?' She said, 'Yes.' Some of them went to Abu Lahab and told him and he went to visit her. He said, 'I am astonished at you that you follow Muhammad and abandon the religion of 'Abdu'l-Muttalib.' She said, 'That is the case. Take the side of your cousin and support him and defend him. If he is victorious, then you will have the choice of either joining him or keeping your religion. If he fails, you will have an excuse as he is your cousin.' Abu Lahab said, 'Do you think that we have power over all the Arabs! He has brought a new religion.' Then Abu Lahab left."

Other people besides Muhammad ibn 'Umar mentioned that Arwa said on that day, "Tulayb has helped his cousin. I exhort him to be steadfast in life and property."

❋✦❋✦❋

'Atika bint 'Abdu'l-Muttalib ibn Hashim

Her mother was Fatima bint 'Amr ibn 'A'idh of Makhzum. In the Jahiliyya she married Abu Umayya ibn al-Mughira of Makhzum and bore him 'Abdullah, Zuhayr, and Qurayba. Then 'Atika bint 'Abdu'l-Muttalib became Muslim in Makka and emigrated to Madina.

She had had a dream which alarmed her and distressed her. She told her brother al-'Abbas ibn 'Abdu'l-Muttalib about it. She said, "I want you to keep secret what I am going to tell you. I am afraid that it might bring some evil and hardship to your people. I dreamt that before Quraysh went out to Badr, a rider on a camel came and stopped at al-Abtah. Then he shouted in his loudest voice, 'O people of the houses! Go to your slain.' He shouted that three times." She said, "I saw people gather to him and then he entered the mosque and the people were following him. Then his camel appeared on the top of the Ka'ba and he shouted the same thing three times. Then his camel appeared on the top of Abu Qubays and he shouted the same thing three times. Then he took a stone from Abu Qubays and let it go and it came crashing down until it stopped at the bottom of the mountain. There was not a room or a house in Makka but that a piece of it entered it. None of that stone entered a room or house of the Banu Hashim nor the houses of Zuhra."

Her brother al-'Abbas said, "This is a vision." Worried, he went out and met al-Walid ibn 'Utba ibn Rabi'a who was his friend. He mentioned it to him and asked him to keep it secret. The story spread among the people and they talked about 'Atika's dream. Abu Jahl said, "Banu 'Abdu'l-Muttalib! Are you not content with making your men Prophets so that you make your women Prophets! 'Atika claims that she saw such-and-such in a dream. We will wait three days to see if what she says is true. If not, we shall write you down as the most lying people of a house amongst the Arabs." Al-'Abbas said to him, "O yellow-belly, you are more likely to lie and be censured than us!" The third day after 'Atika's dream, Damdam ibn 'Amr arrived. Abu Sufyan ibn Harb had sent him to alert Quraysh about the danger to their caravan. He entered Makka, having slit the ears of his camel and slit open his shirt front and back, with his saddle turned round. He was shouting, "O company of Quraysh! The caravan! The caravan! Muhammad and his companions have attacked it! Help! Help! By Allah, I do not think you will reach it!" They prepared to go to their caravan and went to Abu Lahab to ask him to go out with them. He said, "By al-Lat and al-'Uzza, I will not go out and I will not send anyone out." He only was stopped from that by fear of the dream of 'Atika. He was saying, "Atika's dream has been fulfilled."

❋✳❋✳❋

Umm Hakim

She is al-Bayda' bint 'Abdu'l-Muttalib ibn Hashim. Her mother was Fatima bint 'Amr of Makhzum. In the Jahiliyya she married Kurayz ibn Rabi'a. She bore him 'Amir, Arwa, Talha and Umm Talha. Arwa bint Kurayz married 'Affan ibn Abi'l-'As ibn Umayya ibn 'Abdu Shams, and bore him 'Uthman ibn 'Affan. Then she was married to 'Uqba ibn Abi Mu'ayt and bore him al-Walid, Khalid and Umm Kulthum.

❋✳❋✳❋

Barra bint 'Abdu'l-Muttalib ibn Hashim

Her mother was Fatima bint 'Amr ibn 'A'idh of Makhzum. In the *Jahiliyya* she married 'Abdu'l-Asad ibn Hilal and bore him Abu Salama ibn 'Abdu'l-Asad who was martyred at Badr. He was married to Umm Salama bint Abi Umayya ibn al-Mughira before the Messenger of Allah ﷺ. Then after 'Abdu'l-Asad ibn Hilal, Barra married Abu Ruhm ibn 'Abdu'l-'Uzza and she bore him Abu Sabra who was martyred at Badr.

※✳※✳※

Umayma bint 'Abdu'l-Muttalib ibn Hashim

Her mother was Fatima bint 'Amr ibn 'A'idh of Makhzum. In the Jahiliyya she married Jahsh ibn Riyab, the ally of Harb ibn Umayya ibn 'Abdu Shams. She bore him 'Abdullah who was martyred at Badr, 'Ubaydullah, 'Abd, who is Abu Ahmad, Zaynab bint Jahsh, the wife of the Messenger of Allah, and Hamna bint Jahsh. The Messenger of Allah ﷺ assigned Umayma bint 'Abdu'l-Muttalib forty *wasqs* of the dates of Khaybar.

Chapter Five:
The Daughters of the Uncles of the Messenger of Allah

Duba'a bint az-Zubayr ibn 'Abdu'l-Muttalib

Her mother was 'Atika bint Abi Wahb ibn 'Amr of Makhzum. The Messenger of Allah ﷺ married her to al-Miqdad ibn 'Umar, the ally of al-Aswad ibn 'Abdu Yaghuth az-Zuhri, and the marriage was consummated. He was called al-Miqdad ibn al-Aswad. Duba'a had two children: 'Abdullah and Karima. 'Abdullah was killed in the Battle of the Camel on 'A'isha's side. 'Ali ibn Abi Talib passed by his corpse and said, "An unfortunate nephew! You!" The Messenger of Allah ﷺ assigned Duba'a bint az-Zubayr 40 *wasqs* from Khaybar.

Umm al-Hakam bint az-Zubayr

Her mother was 'Atika bint Abi Wahb ibn 'Amr of Makhzum. She married Rabi'a ibn al-Harith ibn 'Abdu'l-Muttalib, and she bore him Muhammad, 'Abdullah, 'Abbas, al-Harith, 'Abdu Shams, 'Abdu'l-Muttalib, Umayya, a son, and Arwa the elder. The Messenger of Allah ﷺ assigned Umm al-Hakam thirty *wasqs* from Khaybar.

Safiyya bint az-Zubayr

Her mother was 'Atika bint Abi Wahb ibn 'Amr of Makhzum. The Messenger of Allah ﷺ assigned her 40 *wasqs* from Khaybar.

Umm az-Zubayr bint az-Zubayr

Her mother was 'Atika bint Abi Wahb ibn 'Amr of Makhzum. The Messenger of Allah صلى الله عليه وسلم assigned her 40 *wasqs* from Khaybar.

Umm Hani'

Her name was Fatikha bint Abi Talib. Her mother was Fatima bint Asad ibn Hashim. She married Hubayra ibn Abi Wahb al-Makhzumi. She bore him Ja'da ibn Hubayra. The Messenger of Allah صلى الله عليه وسلم assigned her 40 *wasqs* from Khaybar.

Umm Talib bint Abi Talib 'Abdu'l-Muttalib

Hisham ibn al-Kalbi does not mention her in the *Book of Lineages* among the children of Abu Talib. Among Abu Talib's daughters, he mentioned Umm Hani', Jumana, and Rayta. It may be that Rayta is Umm Talib, as Muhammad ibn 'Umar calls her in the *Book of the Feeding of the Prophet*. He says that he assigned Umm Talib bint Abi Talib 40 *wasqs* at Khaybar. The mother of all of the children of Abu Talib except for Tulayq ibn Abi Talib, was Fatima bint Asad.

Jumana bint Abi Talib

Her mother was Fatima bint Asad ibn Hashim. She married Abu Sufyan ibn al-Harith ibn 'Abdu'l-Muttalib, and she bore him Ja'far ibn Abi Sufyan. The Messenger of Allah صلى الله عليه وسلم assigned her 30 *wasqs* from Khaybar.

Umama bint Hamza ibn 'Abdu'l-Muttalib

Her mother was Salma bint 'Umays. Umama is the one about whom 'Ali and Ja'far, the sons of Abu Talib, and Zayd ibn Haritha quarrelled [i.e. over her guardianship].

Umm Habib bint al-'Abbas

Her mother was Umm Fadl Lubana bint al-Harith al-Hilaliyya. Al-Aswad ibn Sufyan ibn 'Abdu'l-Asad married her and she bore him Zurqa' and Lubana. They lived in Makka.

Hind bint al-Muqawwim ibn 'Abdu'l-Muttalib

Her mother was Qilaba bint 'Amr. She married Abu 'Amra, who is Bashir ibn 'Amr, from the Banu'n-Najjar of the Ansar. She bore him 'Abdullah and 'Abdu'r-Rahman.

Arwa bint al-Muqawwim ibn 'Abdu'l-Muttalib

Her mother was Qilaba bint 'Amr. She married Abu Masruh, who is al-Harith ibn Ya'mar of Hawazin. He was an ally of al-'Abbas ibn 'Abdu'l-Muttalib. She bore him 'Abdullah ibn Abi Masruh.

Umm 'Amr bint al-Muqawwim

Her mother was Qilaba bint 'Amr. She married Mas'ud ibn Mu'attib ath-Thaqafi. She bore him 'Abdullah ibn Mas'ud. Then she married Abu Sufyan ibn al-Harith ibn 'Abdu'l-Muttalib and bore him 'Atika bint Abi Sufyan.

Arwa bint al-Harith ibn 'Abdu'l-Muttalib

Her mother was Ghaziyya bint Qays. She married Abu Wida'a ibn Sabara and she bore him al-Muttalib, Abu Sufyan, Umm Hakim, and ar-Rabi'.

Durra bint Abi Lahab ibn 'Abdu'l-Muttalib

Her mother was Umm Jamil bint Harb ibn Umayya. She married al-Harith ibn 'Amr ibn Nawfal and she bore him al-Walid, Abu'l-Hasan and Muslim. Then he was killed as an unbeliever at Badr and after him she married Dihya ibn Khalifa al-Kalbi.

'Uzza bint Abi Lahab ibn 'Abdu'l-Muttalib

Her mother was Umm Jamil bint Harb ibn Umayya. She married Awfa ibn Hakim ibn Umayya and bore him 'Ubayda, Sa'id, and Ibrahim.

Khalida bint Abi Lahab ibn 'Abdu'l-Muttalib

Her mother was Umm Jamil bint Harb ibn Umayya. She married 'Uthman ibn Abi'l-'As ibn Bishr ath-Thaqafi and she bore him children.

Fatima bint Asad ibn Hashim

Her mother was Fatima bint Haram ibn Rawaha. She married Abu Talib ibn 'Abdu'l-Muttalib ibn Hashim and bore him 'Ali, Ja'far, 'Aqil, Talib, the oldest of them, Umm Hani', Jumana, and Rayta.

Ruqayqa bint Sayfi ibn Hashim

Her mother was Hala bint Kalda. She married Nawfal ibn Uhayb ibn 'Abdu Manaf and bore him Makhrama ibn Nawfal.

It is related that Ruqayqa bint Sayfi ibn Hashim said, "I can visualise my uncle Shayba (meaning 'Abdu'l-Muttalib) when I was a girl. Al-Muttalib ibn 'Abd Manaf visited us and I was the first to run to him. I clung to him and told my family he was there."

On that day she was older than 'Abdu'l-Muttalib. She became Muslim and joined the Messenger of Allah ﷺ and she was the harshest of people towards her son, Makhrama [one of the leaders of the unbelievers].

It is related from Miswar that Ruqayqa bint Sayfi ibn Hashim, the mother of Makhrama ibn Nawfal, warned the Messenger of Allah, "Quraysh has gathered together intending to come at you during the night."

Al-Miswar said, "The Messenger of Allah ﷺ left his bed and 'Ali ibn Abi Talib spent the night in it."

Chapter Six:
The Wives of the Prophet

Khadija bint Khuwaylid ibn Asad

She was the first woman whom the Messenger of Allah ﷺ married. We have already discussed her, her lineage, and her marriage with the Messenger of Allah before prophethood and her Islam, children and death in a previous chapter.

After she died, the Messenger of Allah ﷺ married:

Sawda bint Zam'a ibn Qays ibn 'Abdu Shams

Her mother was ash-Shamush bint Qays ibn 'Amr from the an-Najjar of the Ansar. She married as-Sakran ibn 'Amr ibn 'Abdu Shams. She became Muslim in Makka early on and gave allegiance to the Prophet. Her husband, as-Sakran ibn 'Amr, also became Muslim. They both emigrated to Abyssinia in the second emigration.

Bukayr said, "As-Sakran ibn 'Amr came to Makka from Abyssinia with his wife, Sawda bint Zam'a. He died in Makka, leaving her a widow. When she became lawful [i.e. after the waiting-period], the Messenger of Allah ﷺ sent to her and proposed to her. She said, 'My business is up to you, Messenger of Allah.' The Messenger of Allah said, 'Tell a man of your family to give you in marriage.' He told Hatib ibn 'Amr ibn 'Abdu Shams to marry her to him. She was the first woman that the Messenger of Allah ﷺ married after Khadija.

'Abdullah ibn Muslim said, "The Messenger of Allah ﷺ married Sawda in Ramadan, the tenth year of prophethood, after the death of Khadija and before he married 'A'isha. He consummated the marriage with her in Makka and emigrated with her to Madina.

It is related that 'A'isha said, "Sawda bint Zam'a became old and the Messenger of Allah ﷺ did not have much to do with her. She knew my position with the Messenger of Allah and that he spent a lot of time with me. She was afraid that he would divorce her and she would lose her place with him. So she said, 'Messenger of Allah, my day which falls to me is for 'A'isha and you are in the lawful in it.' The Prophet ﷺ kissed her. About that it was sent down, *'If a woman fears evil treatment, or aversion, on the part of her husband.'"* (4:128)

It is related from 'A'isha that Sawda gave her day and night to 'A'isha wanting to please the Messenger of Allah.

It is related that an-Nu'man ibn Thabit at-Taymi said that the Messenger of Allah ﷺ said to Sawda bint Zam'a, "Begin a waiting period." So she waited for him on his way in the night and said, "Messenger of Allah, I do not have any desire for men, but I want to be raised up among your wives, so take me back." The Messenger of Allah ﷺ took her back.

It is related from al-Qasim ibn Bazza that the Prophet ﷺ sent to Sawda about divorcing her. When he came to her, she waited on his way by 'A'isha's room. When she saw him, she said, "I adjure you by the One who sent down His Book on you and chose you over His creation, why do you wish to divorce me? Do you have some ill feelings towards me?" He said, "No." She said, "I adjure you by the like of the first, will you take me back! I am old and have no need of men but I want to be raised up among your wives on the Day of Rising." So the Prophet ﷺ took her back and she said, "I have given my day and night to 'A'isha, the beloved of the Messenger of Allah."

Ma'mar said, "I heard that the Messenger of Allah ﷺ wanted to divorce Sawda, and she spoke to him about that and said, 'Messenger of Allah, I have no urge for husbands, but I want Allah to raise me up as your wife on the Day of Rising.'"

'A'isha said, "There is no woman whose skin I would more prefer to be in than that of Sawda bint Zam'a, except she was a woman with some envy."

It is related from Ibrahim that Sawda said to the Messenger of Allah, "I prayed behind you yesterday and bowed behind you until I held my nose fearing that the blood would drip." He said, "He laughed, and she sometimes used to make him laugh at things."

'A'isha said, "One day the wives of the Messenger of Allah ﷺ gathered and we said, 'Messenger of Allah, which of us will be the quickest to join you?' He said, 'The one with the longest hand.' So we took a cane to measure and Sawda bint Zam'a bint Qays had the longest hand. The Messenger of Allah died and Sawda was the swiftest of them to join him, so later we knew that the length of her hand meant *sadaqa*, and she was a woman who loved to give *sadaqa*."

Muhammad ibn 'Umar said, "This *hadith* is weak about Sawda. It is about Zaynab bint Jahsh. She was the first of the wives of the Messenger of Allah ﷺ to join him. She died in the khalifate of 'Umar ibn al-Khattab while Sawda bint Zam'a was still alive. 'Abdullah ibn Muslim tells us that Sawda died in Shawwal, 54 AH, in Madina during the khalifate of Mu'awiya ibn Abi Sufyan. Muhammad ibn 'Umar considered this to be reliable.

Abu Hurayra said, "The Messenger of Allah went on *hajj* with his wives in the year of the Hajj of Farewell. Then he said, 'It is this *hajj* and then there is confinement.'" Abu Hurayra said, "All the wives of the Messenger of Allah went on *hajj* again except for Sawda bint Zam'a and Zaynab bint Jahsh. They said, 'We will not ride an animal after the Messenger of Allah.'"

Sawda said, "I have done *hajj* and *'umra*, and I will remain in my house as Allah Almighty has commanded me."

'A'isha said, "On the night of Muzdalifa, Sawda asked the Messenger of Allah ﷺ for permission to go on before him and before the crush of people. She was a slow woman." Al-Qasim said, "This means she was heavy." She said, "He gave her permission and she left before the surge of the people. We waited until morning and then we set off when he did. I wanted to ask permission from the Messenger of Allah as Sawda had asked permission, so that I could go ahead of the people with him being happy about it."

'A'isha said, "I wanted to ask permission of the Messenger of Allah ﷺ as Sawda had asked permission so that I could pray *Subh* at Mina before the people came." They said to 'A'isha, "Did Sawda ask his permission?" She said, "Yes. She was a slow heavy woman and so he gave her permission."

'Abdullah ibn Abi Farwa said, "I heard 'Abdu'r-Rahman al-A'raj tell us in his assembly in Madina, 'The Messenger of Allah ﷺ used to assign Sawda bint Zam'a 80 *wasqs* of dates and 20 *wasqs* of barley or wheat from Khaybar.'"

It is related from Muhammad ibn 'Umar that 'Umar ibn al-Khattab sent a sack of dirhams to Sawda bint Zam'a. She said, 'What is this?" They said, "Dirhams." She said, "A sack is a container for dates. Girl, bring me a scarf." He said, "She divided them."

Ibn 'Abbas said, "Sawda bint Zam'a was married to as-Sakran ibn 'Amr, the brother of Suhayl ibn 'Amr. She dreamt that the Prophet came and trod on the back of her neck. She told her husband about that and he said, 'By your father, if your dream is true, I will die and you will marry the Messenger of Allah.' She said, 'Oh, never!' (Hisham said, 'That means she denied it to herself.') Then another night she dreamt that the moon swooped down on her from the sky while she was lying down. She told her husband and he said, 'By Allah, if your dream is true, then I will shortly die and you will remarry after me.' That very day as-Sakran fell ill and he died shortly thereafter and she married the Messenger of Allah ﷺ."

Abu Salama ibn 'Abdu'r-Rahman and Yahya ibn 'Abdu'r-Rahman said, "Khawla bint Hakim ibn al-Awqas as-Salamiyya, the wife of 'Uthman ibn Maz'un, came to the Messenger of Allah ﷺ and said, 'Messenger of Allah, 'I seem to see that you are experiencing a lack by the loss of Khadija.' He said, 'Yes. She was the mother of the family and the lady of the house.' She said, 'Shall I propose to someone on your behalf?' He said, 'Yes, the women are more delicate in that.' So she proposed on his behalf to Sawda bint Zam'a of the Banu 'Amir ibn Lu'ayy, and she proposed to 'A'isha bint Abi Bakr, and he married her. He consummated the marriage with Sawda in Makka. 'A'isha at that time was six years old. He consummated her marriage later when he was in Madina."

'Abdullah ibn Muslim said, "Sawda bint Zam'a died in Madina in Shawwal of 54, during the khalifate of Mu'awiya ibn Abi Sufyan.

✳✳✳✳✳

'A'isha bint Abi Bakr as-Siddiq ibn Abi Quhafa

Her mother was Umm Ruman bint 'Umayr of Kinana.

Ibn 'Abbas said, "The Messenger of Allah ﷺ asked Abu Bakr for 'A'isha's hand and Abu Bakr said, 'Messenger of Allah, she has been promised to Jubayr, Mu'tim ibn 'Adi's son. Let me secure her release from them.' He did that and then she married the Messenger of Allah, and she was a virgin."

'A'isha said, "The Messenger of Allah ﷺ married me in Shawwal of the tenth year of prophethood, three years before the *hijra*. I was six. The Messenger of Allah emigrated and reached Madina on Tuesday the 12th of the month of Rabi' al-Awwal. We had a wedding in Shawwal on the eighth month of *hijra* and I was nine at that time."

'A'isha said, "The Messenger of Allah married me while I was playing with the girls. I did not know that the Messenger of Allah had married me until my mother took me and made me sit in the room rather than being outside. Then it occurred to me that I was married. I did not ask her and my mother was the one who told me."

'A'isha said, "The Messenger of Allah married me when I was six and consummated the marriage when I was nine. He came in while I was playing with dolls with the girls. When he came in, my friends would withdraw from him and slip out. The Messenger of Allah ﷺ would go out and bring them back to me."

'Atiyya said, "The Messenger of Allah ﷺ asked for the hand of 'A'isha bint Abi Bakr when she was a child. Abu Bakr said, 'Messenger of Allah, will you marry your brother's daughter?' He said, 'You are my brother in the *deen*.'"

He said, "So he gave her in marriage to him for some household goods which were worth about fifty dirhams. Her nurse came to her while she was playing with the girls and took her hand and brought her to the house and tidied her and took a veil with her and brought her to the Messenger of Allah."

'A'isha said, "The Messenger of Allah ﷺ married me when I was six and consummated the marriage when I was nine. I was playing on a see-saw and had become dishevelled. I was playing on it and I was taken and prepared and then brought in to him. He was shown my picture in silk."

'Abdullah ibn 'Abdullah ibn 'Ubayd ibn 'Umayr said, "The Messenger of Allah ﷺ was so grieved about Khadija that people feared for him, until he married 'A'isha."

It is related from Abu 'Ubayda that the Prophet married 'A'isha when she was seven years old and consummated the marriage when she was nine and died when she was 18.

'A'isha said, "The Messenger of Allah ﷺ married me in Shawwal and consummated the marriage with me in Shawwal. Which of his wives is more fortunate than me?" She used to like it for women to have their marriage consummated in Shawwal.

Abu 'Asim said, "People disliked to consummate marriage with women in Shawwal. The plague occurred in Shawwal for the first time."

'A'isha said, "The Prophet ﷺ married me when I was seven and consummated the marriage with me when I was nine. I used to play dolls with my friends. When he came and they were with us, the Prophet would say to us, 'Stay where you are.'"

'A'isha said, "The Messenger of Allah ﷺ came in to me one day while I was playing with dolls. He said, 'What is this, 'A'isha?' I said, 'The horses of Sulayman.' He laughed."

'A'isha was asked, "When did the Messenger of Allah ﷺ consummate the marriage with you?" She said, "When the Messenger of Allah emigrated to Madina, we and his daughters stayed behind. When he reached Madina, he sent Zayd ibn Haritha and Abu Rafi', his client, to fetch us. He gave them two camels and 500 dirhams which the Messenger of Allah ﷺ took from Abu Bakr with which to purchase whatever camels they needed. Abu Bakr sent 'Abdullah ibn Urayqit ad-Dili with them along with two or three camels. He wrote to 'Abdullah ibn Abi Bakr to order him to take my mother, Umm Ruman, me and my sister Asma', the wife of az-Zubayr. When they reached Qudayd, Zayd ibn Haritha purchased three camels with those 500 dirhams. Then they left Makka together and chanced upon Talha ibn 'Ubaydullah who wanted to make *hijra* with the family of Abu Bakr. We left together, and Zayd ibn Haritha and Abu Rafi' left with Fatima, Umm Kulthum, and Sawda bint Zam'a. Zayd took Umm Ayman and Usama ibn Zayd. 'Abdullah ibn Abi Bakr took Umm Ruman and his two sisters. Talha ibn 'Ubaydullah set out and we all travelled in company until my camel bolted at al-Bayd. I was in a sedan with my mother, and my mother began to say, 'Daughter! Bride!' until our camel was caught when it descended, and Allah Almighty preserved us. Then we reached Madina and I alighted with the family of Abu Bakr, and the family of the Messenger of Allah alighted. On that day the Messenger of Allah was building the mosque and there were houses around the mosque. His family stayed in one of them.

"We stayed for some days in the house of Abu Bakr. Then Abu Bakr said, 'Messenger of Allah, what prevents you from consummating your marriage with my daughter?' The Messenger of Allah said, 'The dower.' So Abu Bakr as-Siddiq gave him 12½ *uqiyyas* and the Messenger of Allah sent them to us. The Messenger of Allah consummated the marriage with me in this house which I am now in. The Messenger of Allah died in it."

The Messenger of Allah made himself a doorway into the mosque opposite the door of 'A'isha. She said, "The Messenger of Allah ﷺ consummated the marriage with Sawda in one of those houses beside me. The Messenger of Allah was with her."

It is related from 'A'isha that Sawda gave her day to 'A'isha and said, "My day is for 'A'isha." The Messenger of Allah ﷺ allotted 'A'isha her day and Sawda's day.

'A'isha said, "I said, 'Messenger of Allah, the women have *kun-yas*, so give me a *kunya*.' He said, 'Use the *kunya* of your nephew 'Abdullah.'"

'A'isha said, "O Prophet of Allah, will you give me a *kunya*?" The Prophet ﷺ said, "Use the *kunya* of your nephew 'Abdullah," and so she was given the *kunya* of Umm 'Abdullah.

'A'isha said, "I was preferred over the wives of the Prophet ﷺ by ten things." It was asked, "What are they, Umm al-Mu'minin?" She said, "He did not marry any other virgin but me. He did not marry a woman whose parents were both Muhajirun except me. Allah Almighty revealed my innocence from heaven. Jibril brought my picture from the heaven in silk and said, 'Marry her. She is your wife.' He and I used to do *ghusl* from the same vessel, and he did not do that with any of his wives except me. He used to pray while I was stretched out in front of him, and he did not do that with any of his wives except me. The revelation would come to him while he was with me, and it did not come down when he was with any of his wives except me. Allah took his soul while he was against my chest. He died on the night when it was my turn and he was buried in my room."

It is related that 'Ammar mentioned 'A'isha and said, "We know that she is the wife of the Messenger of Allah in this world and the Next."

It is related from 'Urwa that the Messenger of Allah ﷺ said to 'A'isha, "I saw you twice in a dream. I saw a man carrying you on a piece of silk and he was saying this is your wife. Then it was uncovered and it was you. So I said, 'If this is from Allah, He will bring it about.'"

It is related from ash-Sha'bi about Masruq that when he reported from 'A'isha, Umm al-Mu'minin, he would say, "The truthful daughter of the true, whose innocence was proclaimed, told me such-and-such." Another said in this *hadith*, "The beloved of the beloved of Allah."

It is related from Masruq that a woman said to 'A'isha, "O Mother!" She said, "I am not your mother. I am the mother of your men."

It is related from 'A'isha that she had dolls, i.e. toys. When the Prophet ﷺ entered, she concealed them from him with her garment. Abu 'Awana said, "But she did not stop."

'A'isha said, "I was given characteristics which no other woman was given. The Messenger of Allah ﷺ married me when I was seven. The angel brought him my picture in his hand and he looked at it. He consummated that marriage when I was nine. I saw Jibril and no woman except me saw him. I was the most beloved of his wives, and my father was the most beloved of his Companions. The Messenger of Allah ﷺ became ill in my house, and I nursed him, and he died when no one but me and the angels saw him."

Humayd ibn 'Urayb said, "A man attacked 'A'isha in the Battle of the Camel and the people gathered against him. 'Ammar said, 'What is this?' They said, 'A man is attacking 'A'isha!' 'Ammar said to him, 'Stop, you ugly yelper! Do you attack the beloved of the Messenger of Allah? She is his wife in the Garden.'"

'A'isha said to the Messenger of Allah, "Who are your wives in the Garden?" He said, "You are among them."

Mus'ab ibn Ishaq ibn Talha said, "I was informed that the Messenger of Allah ﷺ said, 'I saw her in the Garden so that my death would be easy for me on that account, as if I was seeing her hands,'" i.e. 'A'isha.

Muslim al-Batin said that the Messenger of Allah ﷺ said, "'A'isha is my wife in the Garden."

It is related that Masruq was asked, "Was 'A'isha good in the *fara'id* [shares of inheritance]?" He said, "Yes, by the One who has my soul in His hand. I saw the old great Companions of Muhammad ask her about the *fara'id*."

'Urwa said, "I saw 'A'isha giving 70,000 dirhams away as *sadaqa*."

Umm Dharra said, "Ibn az-Zubayr sent 'A'isha some money in two sacks which amounted to 100,000 dirhams, and she called for a bowl. She was fasting that day and she began to divide it between people. In the evening, she said, 'Girl, bring me my fast-breaking.' Umm Dharra said, "O Umm al-Mu'minin, out of what you spent you could have used some dirhams to buy some meat with which to break your fast.' She said, 'Do not scold me. If you had reminded me, I would have done it.'"

Mus'ab ibn Sa'd said, "'Umar allotted the wives of the Prophet 10,000 dirhams and added 2000 more to 'A'isha's lot. He said, 'She was the beloved of the Messenger of Allah.'"

'Amr ibn al-'As said, "Messenger of Allah, who is the most beloved of people to you?" He said, "'A'isha." He said, "I was speaking about men." He said, "Her father."

Masruq said, "'A'isha said to me, 'I saw Jibril standing in this room of mine on a horse while the Messenger of Allah was talking to him. When he came in, I said, 'Messenger of Allah, who is it I saw you talking to?' He said, 'Did you see him?' I said, 'Yes.' He said, 'In what form?' I said, 'Like Dihya al-Kalbi.' He said, 'You have seen a great blessing. That was Jibril.' A short time later he said, "A'isha, this is Jibril who conveys the greeting to you.' I said, 'And peace upon him. May Allah repay him with good as a guest.'"

'A'isha said, "The Messenger of Allah ﷺ said to me, 'Jibril conveys the greeting to you.' I said, 'And peace upon him and the mercy of Allah.'"

It is related from al-Qasim that 'A'isha used to fast all the time.

It is related from Ibn Jurayh that 'Ata' said, "I used to go to 'A'isha with 'Ubayd ibn 'Umayr. She was near the water-course of Thabir." I said, "What was her screen that day?" He said, "At that time she was in a tent which had a covering over it which was a screen between us and her, but I saw her wearing a red garment when I was a child."

'A'isha said, "The Prophet of Allah ﷺ came and said, 'I will present something to you. You should not be hasty until you have consulted your parents.' I said, 'What is this business?' He recited to me, *'O Prophet, say to your wives, "If it is the life of this world and its finery you desire..."'* to *'Allah has prepared, for those among you who do good, an enormous wage.'* (33:28-29)'"

'A'isha said, "Why do you tell me to consult my parents! Rather, I desire Allah and His Messenger and the Next Abode." The Prophet was delighted by that and liked it. He said, "I will present to your companions what I have presented to you." She said, "Do not tell them what I chose." He did not. He said to them what he had said to 'A'isha. Then he said, "'A'isha chose Allah and His Messenger and the Next Abode." 'A'isha said, "Allah gave us a choice and we did not see that as a divorce."

'Urwa said, "'A'isha said to me, 'Nephew, the Messenger of Allah said to me, "It is not hidden from me when you are angry and when you are pleased." I said, "How do you recognise that, may my father and mother be your ransom?" He said, "When you are pleased, you say when you swear, 'No, by the Lord of Muhammad.' When you are angry, you say, 'No, by the Lord of Ibrahim.'" She said, "You have spoken truly, Messenger of Allah!"'"

Ishaq al-A'ma [the blind] said, "I visited 'A'isha and she veiled herself from me. I said, 'Why do you veil yourself from me when I cannot see you?' She said, 'Even if you do not see me, I see you.'"

'Abdu'r-Rahman al-A'raj said in his assembly in Madina, "The Messenger of Allah ﷺ used to assign 'A'isha 80 *wasqs* of dates from Khaybar and 20 *wasqs* of barley or wheat."

'Urwa said, "'A'isha had a dress of rough silk which she wore which had been given to her by 'Abdullah ibn az-Zubayr."

It is related from Shumaysa that she visited 'A'isha who was wearing clothes from wolfskin, a chemise, a head covering and a skirt. They were coloured with safflower red.

It is related that a woman said that 'A'isha used to wear safflower red clothes.

'Abdu'r-Rahman ibn al-Qasim said, "'A'isha used to wear safflower clothes when she was in *ihram*."

It is related from al-Qasim ibn Muhammad that 'A'isha used to wear the two red ones: gold and safflower red when she was in *ihram*.

Al-Qasim ibn Muhammad was asked, "People claim that the Messenger of Allah ﷺ forbade two red ones, safflower and gold." He said, "They have lied. I saw 'A'isha wearing safflower dye and wearing gold rings."

Ibn Abi Mulayka said, "I saw 'A'isha wearing a red chemise." Umm Shayba said, "I saw 'A'isha wearing a safflower red garment."

'A'isha said, "A woman must have three clothes in which to pray: a chemise, a dress and a head covering." 'A'isha used to undo her wrapper and put it round her."

The mother of 'Alqama ibn Abi 'Alqama said, "I brought Hafsa bint 'Abdu'r-Rahman to 'A'isha, Umm al-Mu'minin. Hafsa was wearing a thin head covering, and 'A'isha tore it in half and put a thick head covering on her."

The mother of 'Alqama ibn Abi 'Alqama said, "I saw Hafsa bint 'Abdu'r-Rahman ibn Abi Bakr visit 'A'isha wearing a thin head covering which showed her breast. 'A'isha tore it in half and said, 'Do you not know what Allah sent down in *Surat an-Nur*?' Then she called for a head covering and put it on her."

Mu'adha said, "I saw 'A'isha wearing a safflower red wrap."

Safiyya said, "I saw 'A'isha doing *tawaf* of the House with loose trousers."

'Abdullah ibn Abi Mulayka said, "I saw 'A'isha wearing a red (*muddarij*) garment. I said, 'What is *muddarij*?" He said, "That which they call red."

Habiba bint 'Abbad al-Bariqiyya said that her mother said, "I saw 'A'isha wearing a red chemise and a black head covering."

Umm al-Mughira, the client of the Ansar, said, "I asked 'A'isha about silk. She said, 'We used to wear a garment in the time of the Messenger of Allah ﷺ which was called "*sayra*" which contained some silk.'"

Al-Qasim ibn Muhammad reported that he wore a garment of rough silk on a cold day which he gave to 'A'isha to wear. She did not remove it."

It is related from 'Urwa that 'A'isha gave 'Abdullah ibn az-Zubayr a shawl of rough silk which she used to wear.

Muhammad ibn al-Ash'ath said to 'A'isha, "Shall we give you a skin? It is warmer to wear.' She said, "I dislike the skins of carrion." He said, "I will see to it and only give you one which has been slaughtered." He arranged it for her and sent it to her and she used to wear it."

'Ikrima said that 'A'isha and the wives of the Prophet ﷺ used to use henna when they were in *ihram*. That was after the death of the Prophet and then they went on *hajj* wearing safflower red garments.

'A'isha, the wife of the Prophet, said, "We set out with the Prophet ﷺ until we were at al-Qaha and yellow ran on my face from the scent I had put in my head when I set out. The Prophet said, 'Your colour now, O fair-skinned one, is better!'"

'A'isha, the wife of the Prophet, said, "I asked the Prophet ﷺ about *jihad* and he said, 'Your *jihad* is the *hajj*.'"

'Urwa said, "Sometimes 'A'isha would recite a *qasida* of 60 verses or 100 verses."

'Ikrima said, "'A'isha used to conceal herself from Hasan and Husayn." He said that Ibn 'Abbas said, "It is lawful for them to visit you."

Abu Ja'far said, "Hasan and Husayn used to not visit the wives of the Prophet. Ibn 'Abbas said, 'It is lawful for them to visit the wives of the Prophet.'"

Abu Hanifa and Malik ibn Anas said, "When a man marries a woman, it is not lawful for his son or his grandson to ever marry her, not they nor their sons nor the sons of their daughters. This is agreed upon."

It is related from Abu Sa'id that someone visited 'A'isha while she was mending her trousers and he said, "Umm al-Mu'minin, has not Allah given you a lot of wealth?" She said, "We've had enough of you! Someone who has nothing old and worn has nothing new."

Al-Qasim said, "When the Umm al-Mu'minin became used to something worn, she did not like to get rid of it."

The mother of 'Abdu'r-Rahman ibn al-Qasim said, "I saw 'A'isha wearing a red garment like sparks while she was in *ihram*."

'A'isha said, "I wish that when I die I could be *'something discarded and forgotten.'*" (19:23)

'Abdullah ibn 'Ubayd ibn 'Umayr said, "'A'isha ordered, 'Do not follow my bier with fire and do not place a red blanket under me.'"

It is related that 'A'isha said when she was dying, "Would that I had not been created! Would that I had been a tree glorifying and had done what was obliged for me!"

It is related that 'A'isha said, "Would that I had been a tree! By Allah, I wish that I had been a clod of earth! By Allah, I wish that Allah had not created me as something at all!"

'Isa ibn Dinar said, "I asked Abu Ja'far about 'A'isha and he said, 'I ask Allah's forgiveness for her. Do you know that she used to say, "Would that I had been a tree! Would that I had been a stone! Would that I had been a clod of earth!"?' I said, 'Why did she do that?' He said, 'Repentance.'"

It is related from Qays that 'A'isha said when she was dying, "I have caused mischief after the Messenger of Allah, so bury me with the wives of the Prophet."

It is related from Ibn Abi Mulayka that Ibn 'Abbas visited 'A'isha before she died and praised her, saying, "Good news to the wife of the Messenger of Allah! He did not marry a virgin other than you and your vindication was sent down from heaven.' Ibn az-Zubayr visited her after him and she said, "'Abdullah ibn 'Abbas praised me and I did not want anyone to praise me today. I wish I had been something discarded and forgotten."

It is related from Ibrahim that 'A'isha said, "Would that I had been a leaf on this tree!"

It is related that Khaythama said, "When 'A'isha was asked, 'How are you?' she would say, 'Sound, praise be to Allah.'"

It is related that Dhakwan, the doorman of 'A'isha, said, "I went in and 'A'isha's nephew, 'Abdullah ibn 'Abdu'r-Rahman, was by her head. I said, 'Abdullah ibn 'Abbas asks permission to visit you.' His nephew leant down to her and said, ''Abdullah ibn 'Abbas asks permission to visit you.' She was dying. She said, 'Spare me Ibn 'Abbas. I have no need of him or his commendation.' He said, 'Mother! Ibn 'Abbas is one of the virtuous men of your people who would greet you and bid you farewell!' She said, 'Give him permission if you like.' So he entered and when he had given the greeting and sat down, he said, 'Good news!' She said, 'Of what?' He said, 'Nothing remains between you and meeting Muhammad ﷺ and the beloveds except for the spirit to leave your body. You were the most beloved of the wives of the Messenger of Allah to the Messenger of Allah, and the Messenger of Allah only loved the good. You dropped your necklace on the night of al-Abwa' and the Messenger of Allah began to look for it until morning found him still in the campsite. The people had no water and so Allah revealed that they should do *tayammum* with good soil. What Allah allowed this community of lenience was through you. Allah sent down your innocence from above the seven heavens. The Trusty Spirit brought it and so there is none of the mosques of Allah in which He is remembered but that it is recited in it at the ends of the night and day.' She said, 'Leave me be, Ibn 'Abbas. By the One who has my soul in His hand, I wish that I had been something discarded and forgotten.'"

It is related that Ibn 'Abbas went to 'A'isha about something which had made her cross with him. He said, "Umm al-Mu'minin, you are only called Umm al-Mu'minin because you will be fortunate, and it was your name before you were born."

'A'isha said, "The Messenger of Allah ﷺ said to me, "A'isha, if you want to join me, then enough for you of the provision of this world is the provision of a rider. Beware of sitting with the wealthy, and do not replace a garment until you have already mended it.'"

'A'isha said, "When I have been shrouded and scented, then Dhakwan should lower me into my grave and level the earth over me. Then he is to be set free."

Abu'z-Zinad said, "Ibn Abi 'Atiq visited 'A'isha when she was gravely ill and said, 'O mother, how do you feel?' She said, 'By Allah, it is death.' He said, 'Nothing, then.' She said, 'This will not remain unchanged,' i.e. this condition."

Salim Sablan said, "'A'isha died on the night of the 17th of Ramadan after the *witr*. She commanded that she be buried on the same night, and the people gathered and attended. We have not seen a night with more people present than that. Even the people of al-'Awali came down. She was buried in al-Baqi'."

Abu 'Atiq said, "On the night that 'A'isha died, a palm branch had rags wrapped around it and then it was drenched in oil and ignited, and it was carried with her."

Abu 'Atiq said, "On the night that 'A'isha died, I saw a palm branch with ignited rags carried with her at night, and I saw women at al-Baqi' as if it were an *'id*."

Nafi' said, "I saw Abu Hurayra pray over 'A'isha at al-Baqi' and Ibn 'Amr who was among the people did not object. When Marwan did *'umra* that year, he appointed Abu Hurayra as his deputy."

'Abdullah ibn Abi Bakr said, "Abu Hurayra prayed over 'A'isha in Ramadan in 58 and she was buried after the *witr*."

'Urwa said, "I was one of five in the grave of 'A'isha: 'Abdullah ibn az-Zubayr, al-Qasim ibn Muhammad, 'Abdullah ibn Muhammad ibn 'Abdu'r-Rahman ibn Abi Bakr, and 'Abdullah ibn 'Abdu'r-Rahman. Abu Hurayra prayed over her after the *witr* in the month of Ramadan."

Muhammad ibn 'Umar said, "'A'isha was buried on the night of Tuesday, the 17th of Ramadan, 58, and she was buried that night after the *witr*. On that day she was 66."

Habib, the *mawla* of 'Urwa said, "When Khadija died, the Prophet ﷺ was terribly grieved over her, and Allah sent Jibril who brought him the picture of 'A'isha. He said, 'Messenger of Allah, this one will remove some of your sorrow. This one has some of the qualities of Khadija.' Then he took it back. The Messenger of Allah used to frequent the house of Abu Bakr. He said, 'Umm Ruman, take good care of 'A'isha and watch over her for me.' On that account 'A'isha had a special position among her family, but they were not aware that Allah had commanded that. The Messenger of Allah came to them one day as he used to come to them, and he did not miss a single day without coming to the house of Abu Bakr since he became Muslim until he emigrated. He found 'A'isha hiding behind the door of the house of Abu Bakr, weeping with great distress. He questioned her and she complained about her mother and said that she was after her. The eyes of the Messenger of Allah overflowed with tears and he went in to Umm Ruman and said, 'Umm Ruman, did I not tell you to watch over 'A'isha for me?' She said, 'Messenger of Allah, she spoke to the Siddiq about me and made him angry with us.' The Prophet said, 'And if she did?' Umm Ruman said, 'I will never trouble her.' 'A'isha was born at the beginning of the fourth year of prophethood, and she married the Messenger of Allah in the tenth year, in Shawwal, when she was six. He married her a month after Sawda."

'A'isha said, "The Messenger of Allah ﷺ said, 'The excellence of 'A'isha over women is like the excellence of *tharid* over other foods.'"

It is related from 'A'isha that the Messenger of Allah ﷺ said one day, "O 'A'isha, this is Jibril who gives you the greeting." She said, "Peace be upon him and the mercy of Allah and His blessings." She said, "I did not see him. He used to see what I did not see."

Rabi'a ibn 'Uthman said, "The Messenger of Allah ﷺ travelled by night and then said to 'A'isha, 'You are dearer to me than butter with dates.'"

Fatima al-Khuza'iyya said, "I heard 'A'isha say one day, 'The Messenger of Allah ﷺ visited me and I said, "Where were you today?" He said, "Humayra! I was with Umm Salama." I said, "Did you have your fill from Umm Salama?" He smiled and I said,

"Messenger of Allah, tell me. If you were to alight at two slopes, one of which had been grazed and the other not grazed, which one would you graze in?" He said, "The one which was not grazed." I said, 'I am not like any of your other wives. Each of your wives has had another husband except me." The Messenger of Allah ﷺ smiled.'"

'A'isha said, "Safiyya and I exchanged insults, and I insulted her father and she insulted my father. The Messenger of Allah ﷺ heard it and said, 'Safiyya, do you insult Abu Bakr! Safiyya! Do you insult Abu Bakr!'"

Ibn al-Musayyab said, "The Messenger of Allah ﷺ said to Abu Bakr, 'Abu Bakr, will you obtain my right from 'A'isha?' So Abu Bakr raised his hand and struck her hard on the chest. The Messenger of Allah ﷺ said, 'May Allah forgive you, Abu Bakr, I did not mean this!'"

It is related when 'A'isha, peace be upon her, recited this verse, *'Remain in your houses,'* (33:33), she was heard to weep until her head covering was wet.

✳✳✳✳✳

Hafsa bint 'Umar ibn al-Khattab

Her mother was Zaynab bint Maz'un, the sister of 'Uthman ibn Maz'un.

'Umar said, "Hafsa was born when Quraysh were building the House five years before the Prophet ﷺ was sent."

Abu'l-Huwayrith said, "Khunays ibn Hudhafa ibn Qays married Hafsa bint 'Umar ibn al-Khattab. She was married to him and emigrated with him to Madina and he died, leaving her a widow after the *hijra* when the Prophet ﷺ arrived from Badr."

Ibn 'Umar said, "When Hafsa was widowed, 'Umar met 'Uthman and offered her to him and 'Uthman said, 'I have no need of women.'

He met Abu Bakr and offered her to him and he was silent. He became angry with Abu Bakr. When the Messenger of Allah proposed to her, he gave her in marriage to him. 'Umar met Abu Bakr and said, 'I offered my daughter to 'Uthman and he rejected me. I offered her to you and you were silent. I was more angry with you because of your silence to me than with 'Uthman when he rejected me.' Abu Bakr said, 'The Prophet ﷺ had mentioned something about her, and it was a secret. I disliked to disclose his secret.'"

It is related that 'Abdullah ibn 'Umar said in reference to when Hafsa bint 'Umar was widowed by the death of Khunays ibn Hudhafa as-Sahmi, one of the Companions of the Messenger of Allah who died in Madina, that 'Umar ibn al-Khattab said, "I went to 'Uthman ibn 'Affan and offered Hafsa to him. I said, 'If you like, I will marry you to Hafsa.' He said, 'I will look into it.' Then I met him some days later, and he said, 'It seems to me that I should not marry at this time.' I met Abu Bakr as-Siddiq and I said, 'If you like, I will marry you to Hafsa.' Abu Bakr was silent and did not reply to me at all and I was more vexed with him than I had been with 'Uthman. Some days later, the Messenger of Allah ﷺ proposed to her and I gave her in marriage to him. Abu Bakr met me and said, 'Perhaps you are vexed with me about when you offered Hafsa to me and I did not reply to you at all?' I said, 'Yes.' Abu Bakr said, 'Nothing prevented me from replying to your offer but that I knew that the Messenger of Allah ﷺ had mentioned her and I will not divulge the secret of the Messenger of Allah. If the Messenger of Allah had left her, I would have accepted her.'"

It is related from al-Hasan that one of the Prophet's daughters was married to 'Uthman and then she died. 'Umar met him and saw that he was desolate and noticed his grief. He spoke to him and offered him Hafsa. Then he went to the Prophet ﷺ and said, "I met 'Uthman and I saw his grief so I offered him Hafsa." The Prophet said to him, "Shall I show you an in-law better than 'Uthman and show 'Uthman an in-law better for him than you?" He said, "Indeed, Messenger of Allah!" So the Messenger of Allah ﷺ married Hafsa and gave his daughter in marriage to 'Uthman.

'Umar said, "When Khunays ibn Hudhafa died, I offered Hafsa to 'Uthman and he turned away from me. I mentioned that to the Prophet ﷺ and said, 'Messenger of Allah, are you not surprised at 'Uthman! I offered him Hafsa and he turned away from me.' The Messenger of Allah said, 'Allah will marry 'Uthman to better than your daughter and will marry your daughter to better than 'Uthman.'" They say that 'Umar offered Hafsa to 'Uthman after the death of Ruqayya, daughter of the Prophet, but at that time 'Uthman wanted to marry Umm Kulthum, the daughter of the Prophet, and so 'Uthman turned away from 'Umar on that account. The Messenger of Allah married Hafsa and gave Umm Kulthum in marriage to 'Uthman ibn 'Affan.

Husayn ibn Abi Husayn said, "The Messenger of Allah ﷺ married Hafsa in Sha'ban thirty months before Uhud."

Sa'id ibn al-Musayyab said, "Hafsa was widowed by the death of her husband and 'Uthman was widowed by the death of Ruqayya. 'Umar passed by 'Uthman who was depressed and sad. He said, 'Will you have Hafsa? She has finished her waiting-period.' He did not give him any reply, so 'Umar went to the Prophet ﷺ and mentioned that to him. He said, 'There is something better than that. Marry Hafsa to me and I will give Umm Kulthum, her sister, in marriage to him.' So the Messenger of Allah married Hafsa and 'Uthman married Umm Kulthum."

Sa'id said, "Allah was good to both of them. The Messenger of Allah ﷺ was better for Hafsa than 'Uthman, and the daughter of the Messenger of Allah was better for 'Uthman than Hafsa bint Umar."

It is related from Qays ibn Zayd that the Messenger of Allah divorced Hafsa bint 'Umar. Her uncles, 'Uthman and Quddama, sons of Maz'un, went to her and found her weeping. She said, "By Allah, the Prophet has not divorced on account of being fed up with me." The Messenger of Allah came and visited her and she put on her outer garment. The Messenger of Allah said, "Jibril came to me and told me, 'Take Hafsa back. She fasts and prays at night. She is your wife in the Garden.'"

Qatada said, "The Messenger of Allah ﷺ divorced Hafsa. Jibril came and said, 'O Muhammad, take Hafsa back,' or he said, 'Do not divorce Hafsa. She fasts and prays at night and she is one of your wives in the Garden.'"

It is related from Ibn 'Abbas from 'Umar ibn al-Khattab that the Prophet ﷺ divorced Hafsa and then took her back. That is also related from Anas ibn Malik.

Abu Bakr ibn Sulayman ibn Abi Hathma said "The Messenger of Allah visited Hafsa when a woman called ash-Shifa' was with her making a charm against skin disease. He said, 'Teach it to Hafsa.'"

Bukayr said, "The Messenger of Allah ﷺ intended to divorce Hafsa so that he mentioned something of that, and Jibril came down on him and said, 'Hafsa fasts and prays. She is a righteous woman.'" Ibn Sirin said something similar.

'A'isha said, "The Messenger of Allah ﷺ liked sweet things and honey. When he had prayed '*Asr*, he would go around to his wives and visit them. He visited Hafsa and lingered with her more than his custom. I asked about that and was told, 'A woman of her people gave her a jar of honey and she gave the Messenger of Allah a drink of it.' I said, 'By Allah, I have a stratagem for that!' So I mentioned that to Sawda and said, 'When he visits you and comes near you, say to him, "Messenger of Allah, have you eaten manna-gum [which has an unpleasant smell]?" If he says no to you, then say to him, "What is this smell?" The Messenger of Allah would be vexed to have a smell issue from him. He will say to you, "Hafsa gave me a drink of honey." Then say, "Its bees must have visited mimosa." I will also say that. You say it as well, Safiyya!' Sawda said, "By Allah - There is no god but Him! I almost gave away what you said to me. He is at the door." When the Messenger of Allah drew near, she said, "Messenger of Allah, have you eaten manna-gum?" He said, "No." She said "What is this smell?" He said, "Hafsa gave me a drink of honey." I said, "Its bees must have visited mimosa." When he visited me, I said the like of that, and then he visited Safiyya and she said the like of that. When he visited Hafsa, she said to him, 'Messenger of Allah, shall I give you some of it to drink?' He said, 'I have no need of it.'" She said, "Sawda said 'Glory be to Allah! By Allah, we have deprived him.' I said to her, 'Be quiet.'"

Nafi' said, "Hafsa died not having broken the fast."

Muhammad ibn 'Umar said, "The Messenger of Allah assigned Hafsa 80 *wasqs* of barley or wheat."

It is related that Salim said from his father, "Hafsa died and Marwan ibn al-Hakam prayed over her. He was the governor of Madina at that time."

A woman client of the family of 'Umar said, "I saw a bier on the bed of Hafsa, and Marwan prayed over her at the place of the funeral prayers. Marwan followed her to al-Baqi' and stayed until her burial was over."

It is related that the father of al-Maqburi said, "I saw Marwan between Abu Hurayra and Abu Sa'id in front of the funeral prayer of Hafsa. I saw Marwan carry the leg of her bed from the house of the Banu Hazm to the house of al-Mughira ibn Shu'ba and Abu Hurayra carried it from the house of al-Mughira to her grave."

Nafi' said, "'Abdullah and 'Asim, the sons of 'Umar, went down into Hafsa's grave, as well as Salim, 'Abdullah, and Hamza, the sons of 'Abdullah ibn 'Umar."

Muhammad ibn 'Umar said, "Hafsa died in Sha'ban, in 45 during the khalifate of Mu'awiya ibn Abi Sufyan at the age of 60."

※✴※✴※

Umm Salama

Her name was Hind bint Abi Umayya. Her father was Suhayl, who is called Zad ar-Rakib. Her mother was 'Atika bint 'Amir ibn Rabi'a, of Kinana. Abu Salama married her. His name was 'Abdullah ibn 'Abdu'l-Asad, of Makhzum. He emigrated with her to Abyssinia on both the emigrations. There she bore him Zaynab. After that she bore him Salama, 'Umar, and Durra.

'Umar ibn Abi Salama said, "My father went to Uhud and Abu Salama al-Jashami shot him in the arm with an arrow. His wound was treated for a month and then the wound healed. The Messenger of Allah ﷺ sent my father to Qatan in Muharram at the beginning of the thirty-fifth month [after the *hijra*]. He was away for 29 days and then returned and entered Madina on the 8th of Safar 4 AH and the wound had become septic. He died from it on the 8th of Jumada al-Akhira in 4 AH. My mother observed her waiting-period and became lawful on the 10 Shawwal in 4 AH. Then the Messenger of Allah married her at the end of the month of Shawwal, 4 AH. She died in Dhu'l-Qi'da, 59."

It is related from Umm Salama that the Messenger of Allah ﷺ said to her, "When you are afflicted by a calamity, you should say, 'O Allah, reward me for my affliction and give me something better than it in return.'" She said, "I said it on the day that Abu Salama died. Then I said, 'Who will I have to replace Abu Salama?' Allah soon gave me someone better than Abu Salama in return."

It is related from Umm Salama, the wife of the Prophet, that Abu Salama said that he had heard the Messenger of Allah ﷺ say, "If anyone is afflicted by a calamity and he says what Allah has commanded him to say: *'Inna lillahi wa inna ilayhi raji'un!'* (2:156) - 'Surely we come from Allah and surely to Him we return!' and then: 'O Lord, reward me for my affliction and give me something better than it in return,' Allah will reward him for his affliction and he is worthy of Allah giving him something better than it in return." She said, "When Abu Salama died, I remember what he had reported to me from the Messenger of Allah ﷺ and I said, 'Surely we come from Allah and surely to Him we return! O Lord, reward me for my affliction and give me something better than it in return.' Then I said, 'What replacement can I be given who is better than Abu Salama?' I was given someone better than Abu Salama in return, and I hope that Allah will reward me for my affliction."

Ziyad ibn Abi Maryam said, "Umm Salama said to Abu Salama, 'I have heard that there is no woman whose husband dies when he is one of the people of the Garden and she is one of the people of the Garden, and then she does not marry anyone after him, but that Allah will re-unite them in the Garden, and that this is also the case when a woman dies and the man remains after her. Let us make a pact that neither one of us will marry after the death of the other.' He said, 'Will you obey me?' She said, 'I have never consulted you but that I wanted to obey you.' He said, 'When I die, re-marry.' Then he said, 'O Allah, provide Umm Salama after me with a man better than me who will not grieve her nor injure her!'"

She said, "When Abu Salama died, I said, 'Who is this man who will be better for me than Abu Salama?' After some time the Messenger of Allah ﷺ came and stopped at the door. He mentioned the proposal to her nephew or her son and to her guardian. Umm Salama said, 'I either reject the Messenger of Allah or bring him my family.' The following day he repeated the proposal and I said the like of that." Then she said to her guardian, "If the Messenger of Allah ﷺ returns, then marry me to him." The Messenger of Allah returned, and married her.

Umm Salama said, "The Messenger of Allah ﷺ said, 'When you are near death, speak well. The angels say *"Amin"* to what you say.' When Abu Salama died, I went to the Prophet ﷺ and said, 'Messenger of Allah, Abu Salama has died. What should I say?' He said, 'O Allah, forgive me and him and give me better than him after him.' I said, 'So Allah gave me better than him, the Messenger of Allah.'"

It is related from Damra ibn Habib that the Messenger of Allah visited Umm Salama to console her for the loss of Abu Salama. "He said, 'O Allah, assuage her sorrow and comfort her for her loss and replace him with someone better!'" He said, "Allah assuaged her sorrow and comforted her for her loss and replaced him with someone better and she married the Messenger of Allah ﷺ."

Umm Salama said, "Abu Salama said, 'The Messenger of Allah said, "Whenever any of you is afflicted by a calamity, he should say, 'Surely we come from Allah and surely to Him we return! O Allah, I expect the repayment for my calamity from You, so reward me for it.' I wanted to say it and for Him to give me better in exchange, and then I said, 'But who is better than Abu Salama?' But nevertheless I said it."

The narrator said, "When her waiting period was over, Abu Bakr proposed to her and she rejected him. Then 'Umar proposed to her and she rejected him. The Messenger of Allah ﷺ sent to her and she said, 'Welcome to the Messenger of Allah and to his messenger. Tell the Messenger of Allah that I am a jealous woman and I have young children, and none of my relatives who can act as guardian is present.' So the Messenger of Allah ﷺ sent to her, 'As for what you say about having young children, Allah will provide you with enough for your children. As for what you say about your being jealous, I will pray to Allah to remove your jealousy. As for relatives, none of them, present or absent, will not be pleased with me.' She said, "Umar, get up and marry me to the Messenger of Allah.' The Messenger of Allah said, 'I will not give you less than what I gave your sister, so-and-so: two mills, two jars, and a leather cushion stuffed with fibre.'"

He said, "The Messenger of Allah used to come to her, and when he arrived, she had taken Zaynab to her room to nurse her. The Messenger of Allah was shy and noble and diffident and he went back. He did that several times. Then 'Ammar ibn Yasir realised what she had done and said, 'I will go that day.' 'Ammar came. He was her brother by the same mother. He went in where she was and took her from her room. He said, 'Stop this ugly foul thing by which you injure the Messenger of Allah!' He ﷺ then entered and began to direct his gaze around the room, saying, 'Where is little Zaynab? What is little Zaynab doing?' She said, "Ammar came and took her.' The Messenger of Allah consummated the marriage with his wife and then said, 'If you like, I will give you the seven days which I give women.'"

Umm Salama said, "When my waiting-period for Abu Salama was over, the Messenger of Allah ﷺ came to me and spoke to me with a screen between me and him. He proposed to me, and I said, 'Messenger of Allah, what do you want with me? I only say this to discourage you in regard to me. I am an older woman. I am the mother of orphans. I am a woman with intense jealousy and you, Messenger of Allah, have several wives.' The Messenger of Allah said, 'That should not stop you. As for what you said about jealousy, Allah will remove it. As for what you said about your age, I am older than you. As for what you said about your orphans, they are the business of Allah and His Messenger.' So I gave permission and he married me. On the night when we had arranged the consummation, I went in the day to my mill and the skin which went under it and set them up, and took some extra barley for my family and ground it, and some excellent fat and made a paste for the Messenger of Allah. When the Messenger of Allah, came to us, the food was offered to him and he took some of it. He spent that night and in the morning, he said, 'You are an honour to your family and you have a position with them. If you like for this to be your night and day, it will be that. If you wish, I will give you seven nights. If I give you seven, then I will give seven to your co-wives.'" She said, "Messenger of Allah, do what you like."

It is related from Abu Bakr ibn 'Abdu'r-Rahman that the Messenger of Allah ﷺ proposed to Umm Salama and part of what he said to her was, "What prevents you, Umm Salama?" She said, "I have three qualities. I am old, I have children, and I am jealous." He said, "As for what you say about jealousy, we will pray to Allah to remove it from you. As for what you say about age, I am older than you. Children are the business of Allah and His Messenger." So he married her and used to spend time with her without touching her because she was breast-feeding, until 'Ammar ibn Yasir came one day and said, "Give me this girl who distracts the wife of the Messenger of Allah." So he took her and found her a nurse at Quba'. The Messenger of Allah ﷺ entered and asked about the little girl. "Where is little Zaynab?" A woman was sitting with Umm Salama and she told him that 'Ammar had taken her to be nursed. He said, "We will allot you tomorrow." So he came the following day and was with his wife. When he was about to leave, he said, "Umm Salama, you have honour with your family. If you want me to allot you seven days, I have not allotted seven to any woman before you. If I allot you seven, I will allot them seven."

Umm Salama said, "When the Messenger of Allah proposed to me, I said, 'I have some qualities which make me not fit to marry the Messenger of Allah: I am an older woman, I am the mother of orphans, and I am intensely jealous.' The Messenger of Allah sent to me, 'As for what you say about being an older woman, I am older than you and it is no fault for a woman to marry someone older than her. As for what you say about being the mother of orphans, all of them are the business of Allah and His Messenger. As for what you say about intense jealousy, I will pray to Allah to remove it from you.'"

She said, "The Messenger of Allah married me and moved me to the room of Zaynab bint Khuzayma, Mother of the Poor, after she had died. There was a jar and I looked in it and there was some barley. There was a mill, an earthenware pot and a cooking pot. I looked and it contained some knobs of melted fat. I took that barley and ground it and then mixed it in the earthenware pot. I took the knobs of melted fat and seasoned it with it. That was the food of the Messenger of Allah and the food of his wife on the night of his wedding."

Al-Muttalib ibn Hantab said, "The widow of the Arabs visited the Master of the Muslims at the beginning of the evening as a bride and she spent the end of the night grinding," i.e. Umm Salama.

It is related from Muhammad ibn 'Umar ibn Abi Salama that the Messenger of Allah ﷺ made his marriage proposal for Umm Salama to her son, 'Umar ibn Abi Salama, and he gave her in marriage to the Messenger of Allah and he was a young boy at that time.

It is related from Abu Bakr ibn 'Abdu'r-Rahman that when the Messenger of Allah ﷺ consummated his marriage with Umm Salama, he said to her in the morning, "You are not in low esteem with your family. If you like, I will spend seven days with you and seven days with them," meaning his other wives. If you like, three with you, and then the turns will resume." She said, "Three."

Salih ibn Ibrahim said, "When Umm Salama began her marriage to the Messenger of Allah, she was nursing the daughter of Abu Salama. 'Ammar ibn Yasir said, 'This little fair one is keeping the Messenger of Allah from his wife,' and he took her and found her a nursemaid."

It is related that 'Abdu'l-Malik ibn Abi Bakr reported that Umm Salama, the wife of the Prophet, told him that when she came to Madina, she told them that she was the daughter of Abu Umayya ibn al-Mughira, and they called her a liar and said, "How the foreigners lie!" This went on until some people went on *hajj* and they said, "Will you write to your family?" So she wrote and sent it with them. When they returned to Madina, they said that she was telling the truth and she had more honour with them. She said, "When I gave birth to Zaynab, the Messenger of Allah came and proposed to me. I said, 'One like me does not marry! I will have no more children and I am a jealous woman with a family.' He said, 'I am older than you. As for the jealousy, Allah will remove it from you. As for the family, they are the business of Allah and His Messenger.'" So she married him and he began to come to her, saying, "Where is little Zaynab?" until 'Ammar came and took her. He said, "This one is obstructing the Messenger of Allah!" She was nursing her. So the Prophet came and said, "Where is little Zaynab?" She replied, "She is with Qurayba bint Abi Umayya. 'Ammar ibn Yasir took her." The Prophet said, "I will come to you tonight." She said, "I set out the skin and brought out some grains of barley which was in my jar and brought out some fat and mixed them together. Then he spent the night and said in the morning, 'You have honour with your family. If you wish, I will spend seven nights with you, and if I spend seven, I will give seven to my wives.'"

It is related that 'A'isha said, "When the Messenger of Allah married Umm Salama, I felt very unhappy when they mentioned her beauty to us. I was civil about her until I saw her. By Allah, she was even more beautiful than how she had been described to me. I mentioned that to Hafsa and we were as a single hand. She said, 'No, by Allah, this is only jealousy. She is not as they say!' Hafsa was civil about her until she saw her and said, 'I have seen her, and by Allah, she is not as they say, not nearly. She is indeed very beautiful.' I saw her later and by my life, she was as Hafsa had said, but I was jealous."

It is related from Abu Bakr ibn al-Harith al-Makhzumi that the Messenger of Allah ﷺ married Umm Salama in Shawwal and consummated the marriage in Shawwal.

Umm Kulthum said, "When the Prophet ﷺ married Umm Salama, he said to her, 'I sent the Negus some *uqiyyas* of musk and jewellery, and I believe that he has died. I think that the gift I sent to him will be returned to me. If it is returned to me, it is yours.'" It was as the Prophet had said. The Negus had died and his gift was returned to him and he gave each of his wives an *uqiyya* of musk, and gave the rest to Umm Salama, and he gave her the jewellery.

'Abdu'r-Rahman ibn al-Harith said, "The Messenger of Allah was on one of his journeys and he was accompanied by both Safiyya bint Huyayy and Umm Salama on that journey. The Messenger of Allah went to the howdah of Safiyya, thinking that it was the howdah of Umm Salama. It was Umm Salama's day. The Messenger of Allah began to chat with Safiyya and Umm Salama became jealous. Then the Prophet realised that it was Safiyya and went to Umm Salama. She said, 'You were chatting with the daughter of the Jew on my day when you are the Messenger of Allah!' She said, 'Then I regretted those words.' She used to ask forgiveness for them. She said, 'Messenger of Allah, ask forgiveness for me. Jealousy provoked me to it.'"

Muhammad ibn 'Umar said, "The Messenger of Allah ﷺ assigned Umm Salama 80 *wasqs* of dates from Khaybar and 20 *wasqs* of barley, or wheat."

Nafi' said, "Umm Salama, the wife of the Prophet, died in 59 and Abu Hurayra prayed over her at al-Baqi'."

It is related that she was 84 when she died.

✳✳✳✳✳

Umm Habiba

Her name was Ramla bint Abi Sufyan ibn Harb ibn Umayya. Her mother was Safiyya bint Abi'l-'As, the aunt of 'Uthman ibn 'Affan. She married 'Ubaydullah ibn Jahsh of Khuzayma, an ally of Harb ibn Umayya. She bore him Habiba from whom she takes her *kunya*. Habiba married Dawud ibn 'Urwa ibn Mas'ud ath-Thaqafi.

'Ubaydullah ibn Jahsh emigrated with Umm Habiba to Abyssinia on the second *hijra*. He apostatised from Islam and died in Abyssinia. Umm Habiba remained firm in her Islam and emigration.

It is related from 'Uthman ibn Muhammad al-Akhnasi that Umm Habiba bint Abi Sufyan bore her daughter Habiba by 'Ubaydullah in Makka before she emigrated to Abyssinia. Muhammad ibn Sa'd said that she gave birth to her in Abyssinia.

It is related that Sa'd said, "She left Makka while she was pregnant with her and gave birth to her in Abyssinia."

It is related from Isma'il ibn 'Amr ibn Sa'd ibn al-'As that Umm Habiba said "In a dream I saw my husband, 'Ubaydullah ibn Jahsh, in the worst and ugliest form, and I became alarmed. I said, 'By Allah, your condition has altered.' In the morning he said, 'Umm Habiba, I thought about religion and I did not think that there was a better religion than Christianity. I took it on. Then I joined the religion of Muhammad, but now I have reverted to Christianity.' I said, 'By Allah, you are without good!' I told him about the dream which I had seen but he paid no attention to it. He gave himself over to drinking wine until he died. Then I saw him in a dream as if he were coming to me saying, 'Umm al-Mu'minin!' I was alarmed and I interpreted it as the Messenger of Allah marrying me."

She said, "When my waiting period came to an end, I was aware of the messenger of the Negus at the door asking permission to come in. It was a slavegirl of his called Abraha who used to attend to his garments and oil him. Then she came in where I was. She said, 'The king says to you that the Messenger of Allah has written to him to marry you to him.' She said, 'May Allah give you good news!' She said, 'The king says to you, "Appoint someone to give you in marriage."'"

So she sent for Khalid ibn Sa'id ibn al-'As and he acted as her guardian. She gave Abraha two silver bracelets and two anklets she was wearing and the silver rings she was wearing out of joy at her good news. In the evening the Negus commanded Ja'far ibn Abi Talib and the Muslims with him to attend, and the Negus spoke and said, "I praise Allah, the King, the Most Pure, the Perfect Peace, the Trustworthy, the Safeguarder, the Almighty, the Compeller. I testify that there is no god but Allah and that Muhammad is His slave and Messenger. He is the one about whom 'Isa ibn Maryam gave the good news. Following on from that, the Messenger of Allah has written to instruct me to marry him to Umm Habiba bint Abi Sufyan, and she has accepted the offer of the Messenger of Allah. I have assigned her a dower of 400 dinars." Then the dinars were poured before the people. Khalid ibn Sa'id spoke and said, "Praise be to Allah! I praise him and seek his help and support. I testify that there is no god but Allah and that Muhammad is His slave and Messenger whom He sent with the Guidance and the *Deen* of Truth to raise it over every other *deen*, even though the idolworshippers are averse. Following on from that, I have replied to the offer of the Messenger of Allah and I have married him to Umm Habiba ibn Abi Sufyan. May Allah bless the Messenger of Allah." He gave the dinars to Khalid ibn Sa'id ibn al-'As and he took them. Then they wanted to get up and he said, "Sit down. The *sunna* of the Prophets when they marry is to provide food for the marriage. So he called for food and they ate and then split up."

Umm Habiba said, "When the money reached me, I sent for Abraha who had given me the good news. I said to her, 'I gave you what I had that day as I had no money in my possession. Here is fifty *mithqals*. Take it and use it.' She refused and then brought out a box which contained what I had given her. She returned it to me and said, 'The King has decided that I should not take anything from you. I am the one who takes care of his clothes and oils him. I have followed the *deen* of Muhammad, the Messenger of Allah, and I have surrendered to Allah. The king has commanded that his women send to you all the scent they have.'"

She said, "On the following day, she brought me aloes, *wars* scent, and amber and much civet. I brought all of that to the Prophet. He saw it on me and with me and did not object. Then Abraha said,

'What I need you to do is to convey my greeting to the Messenger of Allah and inform him that I have followed his *deen*.' She said, "Then she was kind to me and used to attend to me. Whenever she visited me, she used to say, 'Do not forget what I need you to do.'"

She said, "When I came to the Messenger of Allah, I told him how the proposal had taken place and what Abraha had done for me. The Messenger of Allah smiled and I gave him her greeting and he said, 'And peace upon her, and the mercy of Allah and His blessings.'"

Muhammad said, "The Messenger of Allah ﷺ sent 'Amr ibn Umayya ad-Damri to the Negus to propose marriage to Umm Habiba bint Abi Sufyan, who had been married to 'Ubaydullah ibn Jahsh. She married him and the Negus gave her a dower of 400 dinars from him on behalf of the Messenger of Allah."

Abu Ja'far said, "We only think that 'Abdu'l-Malik ibn Marwan stipulated the dower of women at 400 dinars for that reason."

'Abdullah ibn Abi Bakr said, "The one who gave her in marriage and to whom the Negus presented the proposal was Khalid ibn Sa'id ibn al-'As. That was in 7 AH. When she arrived in Madina she was about 30."

Az-Zuhri said, "The Negus made arrangements for her for the Prophet and sent her with Sharahbil ibn Hasana."

'Abdu'l-Wahid ibn Abi 'Awn said, "When Abu Sufyan heard about the marriage of the Prophet ﷺ to his daughter, he said, 'That suitor is rejected!'"

It is related that Ibn 'Abbas said about His words, *"It may well be that Allah will put love between you and those of them who are your enemies,"* (60:7) "The Prophet married Umm Habiba bint Abi Sufyan."

Az-Zuhri said, "When Abu Sufyan ibn Harb came to Madina, he went to the Messenger of Allah when he was intending to invade Makka. He wanted to ask him to extend the Truce of Hudaybiyya. The Messenger of Allah did not agree to that. So he got up and went to his daughter, Umm Habiba. When he went to sit on the bed of the Prophet, she rolled it up from under him. He said, 'Daughter, am I too good for this bed or is it too good for me?' She said, 'It is the bed of the Messenger of Allah and you are an unclean idolworshipper.' He said, 'Daughter, you have gone bad away from me.'"

It is related from Safiyya that when Abu Sufyan, the father of Umm Habiba, the wife of the Prophet ﷺ died, she called for scent and put it on her arms and cheeks, and then said, "I have no need of this were it not that I heard the Messenger of Allah say, 'It is not lawful for a woman who believes in Allah and the Last Day to mourn for a dead person more than three days except for a husband. She mourns for him for four months and ten days.'"

It is related from Ibn Shawwal that Umm Habiba bint Abi Sufyan informed him that the Messenger of Allah ﷺ commanded her to avoid gatherings at night.

Muhammad ibn 'Umar said, "The Messenger of Allah ﷺ assigned Umm Habiba bint Abi Sufyan 80 *wasqs* of dates from Khaybar and 20 *wasqs* of barley."

'A'isha said, "Umm Habiba, the wife of the Messenger of Allah, called me when she was dying. She said, 'There was some bad feeling between us and the co-wives. May Allah forgive me and you for what there was of that.' I said. 'May Allah forgive you all of that and overlook and put you into the lawful in that.' She said, 'You have gladdened me, may Allah gladden you.' She sent for Umm Salama and said the like of that to her."

She died in 46 in the khalifate of Mu'awiya ibn Abi Sufyan.

Zaynab bint Jahsh al-Asadiyya

Her mother was Umayma bint 'Abdu'l-Muttalib ibn Hashim.

'Uthman al-Jahshi said, "The Prophet ﷺ left for Madina, and Zaynab bint Jahsh was one of those who emigrated with the Messenger of Allah to Madina. She was a beautiful woman and the Messenger of Allah ﷺ proposed to her on behalf of Zayd ibn Haritha. She said, 'Messenger of Allah, I am not pleased with him for myself. I am a widow of Quraysh.' He said, 'I am pleased with him for you,' and so Zayd ibn Haritha married her."

Muhammad ibn Yahya ibn Hibban said, "The Messenger of Allah came to the house of Zayd ibn Haritha to look for him. Zayd had been called 'Zayd ibn Muhammad'. The Messenger of Allah ﷺ had missed him for a time and asked, 'Where is Zayd?' He went to his house to look for him but did not find him. Zaynab bint Jahsh, his wife, came out to him wearing a single garment, and the Messenger of Allah turned away from her. She said, 'He is not here, Messenger of Allah. Enter, may my father and mother be your ransom!' The Messenger of Allah refused to enter and Zaynab made haste to put on more clothes on account of what the Messenger of Allah had said to her at the door. She leapt up quickly and the Messenger of Allah admired her, and he turned away muttering something which could hardly be understood, although he said aloud, 'Glory be to Allah the Immense! Glory be to the One who turns the hearts.' Zayd went to his house and his wife told him that the Messenger of Allah had come to his house. Zayd said, 'Didn't you tell him to come in?' She said, 'I offered that to him and he refused.' He said, 'Did you hear anything?' She said, 'When he turned away, I heard him saying some words which I could not understand and I heard him say, "Glory be to Allah the Immense! Glory be to the One who turns the hearts."' Zayd went to the Messenger of Allah and said, 'Messenger of Allah, I heard that you came to my house. Why didn't you come in? May my father and mother be your ransom, Messenger of Allah, perhaps Zaynab pleases you? I will divorce her.' The Messenger of Allah said, 'Keep hold of your wife.' Zayd could not find any way to her after that day. So he went to the Messenger of Allah and informed him. The Messenger of Allah said, 'Keep hold of your wife.' He said, 'Messenger of Allah, I will divorce her.' The Messenger of Allah said, 'Keep your wife.' Zayd separated from her and disassociated himself from her and she became lawful, meaning her waiting-period came to an end.'"

He said, "While the Messenger of Allah ﷺ was sitting and talking with 'A'isha, suddenly the Messenger of Allah was overcome by a swoon and it left him smiling. He said, 'Who will go to Zaynab to give her the good news that Allah has married her to me from the Heaven?' and the Messenger of Allah recited, *'When you said to the one Allah had blessed and you yourself had blessed, "Keep hold of your wife and fear Allah"...'* (33:37) 'A'isha said, 'Far and wide we had heard about her beauty, and another of the greatest and noblest of matters is what was done for her when Allah married him to her from the Heaven. I said, "Will she boast over us on that account?"' 'A'isha said, 'Salma, the servant of the Messenger of Allah, went out in haste and told her that and Zaynab gave her the coins she had on her.'"

Ibn 'Abbas said, "When Zaynab was informed of her marriage with the Messenger of Allah ﷺ to her, she prostrated."

Muhammad ibn 'Abdullah ibn Jahsh said, "Zaynab bint Jahsh said, 'When the messenger brought me my marriage to the Messenger of Allah, I vowed to fast for two months for Allah. When the Messenger of Allah visited me, I could not fast them at home or on a journey for which lots were drawn. When I drew the lot to remain at home, I fasted them.'"

It is related from Ibn Abi 'Awn that Zaynab bint Jahsh said one day, "Messenger of Allah, by Allah, I am not like any of your wives. There are none of your wives but had their father or brother or family give her in marriage to you, except for me. Allah married me to you from the Heaven."

Zaynab bint Umm Salama said, "I heard my mother, Umm Salama, say, 'Zaynab bint Jahsh was mentioned and I asked for mercy on her. I mentioned some of what had gone on between her and 'A'isha. Zaynab said, "By Allah, I am not like any of the wives of the Messenger of Allah ﷺ. They were married with dowers and they were given in marriage by relatives. Allah married me to His Messenger, and there was revelation in the Book about me which the Muslims recite and is not changed or altered: *'When you said to the one Allah had blessed...'* (33:37)"'" Umm Salama said, "The Messenger of Allah liked her and he also used to become vexed with her. She was a righteous woman who fasted and prayed, and worked and gave all of that as *sadaqa* to the poor."

Anas said, "Zayd ibn Haritha came to complain about Zaynab to the Prophet. The Messenger of Allah ﷺ said, 'Keep hold of your wife,' and it was revealed, *'while keeping hidden something in your-self that Allah wished to bring to light.'* (33:37)"
'Arim said in his version of the *hadith*, "The Messenger of Allah married her, and the Messenger of Allah did not have a wedding feast for any of his wives as he had for her. He sacrificed a sheep."

Anas said, "It was revealed about Zaynab bint Jahsh, *'When Zayd no longer had any need of her, We married her to you.'* (33:37)" He said, "She used to boast over the wives of the Prophet, saying, 'Your families gave you in marriage and Allah, from above the seven heavens, gave me in marriage.'"

It is related from 'Asim al-Ahwal that a man of the Banu Asad was boasting against a man and the Asadi said, "Do you have among you a woman whom Allah from above the seven heavens married?" He meant Zaynab bint Jahsh.

Anas ibn Malik said, "When the waiting period of Zaynab bint Jahsh finished, the Messenger of Allah ﷺ said to Zayd ibn Haritha, 'I do not find anyone I consider more trustworthy and reliable than you. Go to Zaynab and propose to her for me.'" He said, "Zayd went to her while she was mixing her dough. Zayd said, "When I saw her, my breast was constricted and I could not look at her since I knew that the Messenger of Allah had mentioned her. I turned my back on her and backed away. I said, 'Zaynab, good news! The Messenger of Allah is mentioning you.' She said, 'I will not do anything until my Lord commands me.' So she went to her prayer place and the Qur'an was revealed, *'When Zayd no longer had any need of her, We married her to you.'* (33:37)" He said, "The Messenger of Allah came and entered without permission."

Thabit al-Bannani said, "I said to Anas ibn Malik, 'How long did you serve the Messenger of Allah?' He said, 'Ten years, and he did not change his manner towards me because of anything I did bad or good.' I said, 'What was the most extraordinary thing that you saw in these ten years?' He said, 'When the Messenger of Allah ﷺ married Zaynab bint Jahsh. She had been married to his client, Zayd ibn Haritha. Umm Sulaym said, "Anas! The Messenger of Allah has married this morning and I do not think he has any food. Give me that jar!" I handed it to her and she made some *hays*-paste from pressed dates in a clay vessel which would be enough for him and his wife. She said, "Take it to him." So I went to him - and that was before the *Ayat* of Screening had been sent down. He said, "Put it down." So I put it down between him and the wall. He told me, "Invite Abu Bakr, 'Umar, 'Uthman and 'Ali," and he went on to mention some of his companions by name. I was astonished at the number of people he told me to invite given the lack of the food. It was a very small amount of food. But I did not like to disobey him and I invited them. He said, "See who is in the mosque and invite them." So I went to every man, whether he was praying or asleep, and said, "Respond to the invitation of the Messenger of Allah on his wedding morning," until the house was full. He said to me, "Is there anyone left in the mosque?" I said, "No." He said, "Go see who is in the street and invite them." I invited people until the room was full. He said, "Is there anyone left?" I said, "No, Messenger of Allah." He said "Bring the vessel." So I placed it before him and he put three of his fingers in it and squeezed it. He said to the people, "Eat in the name of Allah." I began to see the dates growing, or the fat as if it were springs bubbling up, until all who were in the house and in the room had eaten and there still remained in the vessel the amount I had brought. So I placed it before his wife and then went to my mother to astonish her with what I had seen. She said, "Do not be surprised. If Allah had wished all of the people of Madina to eat from it, they could have eaten from it.'" I said to Anas, 'How many do you think there were?' He said, 'Seventy-one men or possibly seventy-two.'"

Anas ibn Malik said, "I am the person with the most knowledge of the *Ayat* of Screening. When Zaynab was given to the Prophet, some food was prepared and he invited the people and they came and entered. Zaynab was with the Messenger of Allah in the house. They began to chat and the Messenger of Allah went out and then came back and they were still sitting there." He said, "Then it was sent down: *'O you who believe! Do not go into the Prophet's rooms except after being given permission to come and eat, not waiting for the food to be prepared. However, when you are called go in and, when you have eaten, then disperse and do not remain wanting to chat together. If you do that it causes injury to the Prophet though he is too reticent to tell you so. But Allah is not reticent with the truth. When you ask his wives for something, ask them from behind a screen.'* (33:53) The people got up and the screen was set up."

Anas said, "The Messenger of Allah ﷺ gave a feast when he consummated the marriage with Zaynab, and gave the Muslims their fill of bread and meat. Then he went to the rooms of the Mothers of the Believers to greet them and supplicate for them. They greeted him and made supplication for him. He used to do that on the morning he consummated a marriage. He returned and I was with him. When he reached Zaynab's room, there were two men in the corner of the room who were chatting. When the Messenger of Allah saw them, he left his room. When the two men saw the Prophet leave his room, they got up quickly." Anas said, "I do not know whether I told him that they had left or he was told, and he went back and entered the room and dropped the curtain between men and him, and Allah sent down the *Ayat* of Screening."

Anas ibn Malik said, "I am the person with the most knowledge of the Screen. Ubayy ibn Ka'b used to ask me about it." Anas said, "The Messenger of Allah became a bridegroom of Zaynab bint Jahsh." He said, "He married her in Madina, and he invited the people to some food after midday. The Messenger of Allah saw that some men remained sitting with him after the people had left. Then the Messenger of Allah went out and I went with him as far as 'A'isha's room. Then he thought that they had gone out and came

back and I came back with him. They were still sitting there. So he
went back and I went with him a second time as far as 'A'isha's
room. Then he went back and I went back with him, and they had
left. He set up a curtain between me and him and the Screen was
revealed."

It is related that 'Ubayd ibn 'Umayr said that he heard 'A'isha
state that the Prophet ﷺ used to linger with Zaynab bint Jahsh and
drink honey with her. She said, "Hafsa and I decided that the Prophet
would not visit her. We would say, 'I detect the smell of manna-gum
from you.' He went to one of them and she said that to him. He said,
'But I have drunk honey with Zaynab bint Jahsh. I will not do it
again.' So it was sent down, *'O Prophet! Why do you make forbidden
what Allah has made lawful for you?'* to *'If the two of you would
turn to Allah.'* (66:1-4)" The two were 'A'isha and Hafsa. *"When the
Prophet confided a certain matter to one of his wives"* (66:3) was his
words, "I have drunk honey."

It is related that 'Abdu'r-Rahman al-A'raj was heard to say in his
assembly in Madina, "The Messenger of Allah assigned Zaynab bint
Jahsh 80 *wasqs* of dates from Khaybar and twenty *wasqs* of barley or
wheat."

'A'isha said, "May Allah have mercy on Zaynab bint Jahsh. She
obtained unsurpassed honour in this world. Allah married her to His
Prophet in this world and the Qur'an described it. The Messenger of
Allah said to us while we were around him, 'The swiftest of you to
join me will be the one with the longest armspan.' So the Messenger
of Allah gave her the good news of the swiftness of her joining him.
She is his wife in the Garden."

'A'isha said, "The Prophet ﷺ said to his wives, 'The one among
you with the longest hand will follow me.'" 'A'isha said, "We used to
meet in one of our rooms after the Prophet's death and stretch out our
hands on the wall to measure their length. We continued to do that
until Zaynab bint Jahsh died. She was a small woman, may Allah
have mercy on her. She did not have the longest hand among us. So
then we knew that by the length of the hand the Prophet had meant
sadaqa." She said, "Zaynab was a woman who did handiwork and
she tanned and pierced leather and gave *sadaqa* in the way of Allah."

Al-Qasim ibn Muhammad said, "When Zaynab bint Jahsh was dying, she said, 'I have prepared my shroud. It may be that 'Umar will send a shroud for me. If he does send a shroud, then give one of them away as *sadaqa*. If you can give away my waist-wrapper as *sadaqa* when you lower me down, do so.'"

Muhammad ibn Ibrahim at-Taymi said, "Zaynab bint Jahsh gave instructions that she be carried on the bed of the Messenger of Allah and the bier be carried on it. Before that, Abu Bakr had been carried on it. When a woman died, she was carried on it until Marwan ibn al-Hakam forbade that any but a noble man be carried on it. In Madina they muttered in groups about the dead being carried on it."

Zaynab's grave was in al-Baqi' at the house of 'Aqil between the house of 'Aqil and the house of Ibn al-Hanafiyya. Milk was brought from Sumayna and placed at the grave. It was a hot summer day.

Baraza bint Rafi' said "When the allowance was paid out, 'Umar sent Zaynab bint Jahsh her share. When it was brought to her, she said, 'May Allah forgive 'Umar! Others among my sisters are more entitled to a share of this than I am!' They said, 'This is all yours.' She said, 'Glory be to Allah!' She shielded herself from it with a garment and said, 'Pile it up and put a cloth over it.' Then she said to me, 'Put your hand in and take a handful of it and take it to the Banu so-and-so, and to the Banu so-and-so,' referring to her relatives and orphans, until only a little remained under the cloth." Baraza bint Rafi' said to her, "May Allah forgive you, Umm al-Mu'minin! By Allah, we have a right in this." She said, "Then you have what is under the cloth." Under it we found 85 dirhams. Then she lifted her hands towards heaven and said, "O Allah, do not let the allowance of 'Umar reach me after this year!" She died. 'Abdu'l-Wahhab said in his *hadith*, "She was the first of the wives of the Prophet ﷺ to join him."

Muhammad ibn Ka'b said, "The allowance of Zaynab bint Jahsh was 12,000 dirhams. She only received it one year. 12,000 dirhams were brought to her and she began to say, 'Do not let the next lot of this money reach me! It is a temptation.' Then she divided it between her relatives and people in need. 'Umar heard about that and said,

'This is a woman who seeks good.' He stopped at her door and gave the greeting and said, 'I have heard that you have distributed the money.' So he sent her 1000 dirhams to spend and it went the same way as the other money."

'Amra bint 'Abdu'r-Rahman said, "When Zaynab bint Jahsh was dying, 'Umar ibn al-Khattab sent her five garments from the treasury which she could choose from. She was shrouded in them and her sister Hamna gave away the shroud which she had prepared for her burial." 'Amra bint 'Abdu'r-Rahman said, "I heard 'A'isha say, 'She departed in a praiseworthy manner and was a great loss for the orphans and widows.'"

'Abdu'r-Rahman ibn Abza said, "Zaynab was the first of the wives of the Messenger of Allah to join him. She died in the time of 'Umar ibn al-Khattab. They said to 'Umar, 'Who will go down into her grave?' He said, 'Whoever was able to visit her when she was alive.' 'Umar prayed over her and did four *takbirs.*"

It is related from al-Qasim ibn 'Abdu'r-Rahman that they said, "When Zaynab bint Jahsh died, she was the first of the wives of the Prophet ﷺ to join him. When she was carried to her grave, 'Umar went to her grave and praised Allah and then said, 'I sent to the women,' meaning the wives of the Prophet, 'when this woman fell ill to ask who should nurse her and attend to her.' They sent back, 'We will.' I saw that they spoke the truth. When she died, I sent to them and said, 'Who should wash her, perfume her and shroud her?' They sent back, 'We will.' I saw that they spoke the truth. Then I sent to them, 'Who should enter her grave?' They sent back, 'Whoever could lawfully visit her when she was alive.' I saw that they spoke the truth. So move back, people!' He moved them back from her grave and then two men of her household entered it."

It is related from Nafi' and others that people used to go out for both men and women. When Zaynab bint Jahsh died, 'Umar commanded that it be announced, "None should go out for Zaynab except her relatives." 'Umays's daughter said, "Amir al-Mu'minin! Shall I show you something which I saw the Abyssinians do for their women?" She made a bier and covered it with a cloth. When he saw it, he said, "How excellent this is! How concealing!" He commanded that it be announced, "Come out for your mother."

It is related that 'Abdu'r-Rahman ibn Abza said that he prayed with 'Umar over Zaynab bint Jahsh. She was the first of the wives of the Messenger of Allah to die after him. He said four *takbirs* over her and then sent to the wives of the Messenger of Allah, "Who do you command me to let enter her grave?" He said, "He wanted to attend to that, but they sent to him, 'Whoever could see her while she was alive should take her into her grave.' 'Umar ibn al-Khattab said, 'They spoke the truth.'"

It is related that Muhammad ibn al-Munkadir said, "'Umar ibn al-Khattab passed by the gravediggers who were digging Zaynab's grave on a hot summer day. He said, 'I should pitch a tent over them.' So it was the first tent pitched over a grave."

Muhammad ibn al-Munkadir said, "'Umar commanded that a tent be pitched at al-Baqi' over her grave due to the intensity of the heat on that day. It was the first tent pitched over a grave at al-Baqi'."

Tha'laba ibn Abi Malik said, "On the day that al-Hakam ibn al-'As died during the khalifate of 'Uthman, I saw a tent pitched over his grave on a summer day. People started talking and criticising the tent. 'Uthman said, 'How quick people move to evil and confuse one another! I adjure by Allah all who are present, are you aware that 'Umar ibn al-Khattab set up a tent over the grave of Zaynab bint Jahsh?' They said, 'Yes.' He said, 'Did you hear any critic?' They said, 'No.'"

'Abdullah ibn Abi Salit said, "I saw Abu Ahmad ibn Jahsh carrying the bed of Zaynab bint Jahsh. He was blind and he was weeping. I heard 'Umar say, 'Abu Ahmad! Leave the bed and people will not fail to help you.' They crowded to the bed. Abu Ahmad said, "Umar! this woman is the one by which we obtained every blessing, and this cools the heat of what I feel.' 'Umar said 'Keep on. Keep on.'"

'Amir ibn Rabi'a said, "I saw 'Umar ibn al-Khattab pray over Zaynab bint Jahsh in 20 AH on a summer day, and I saw a cloth stretched over her grave. 'Umar was at the edge of the grave. Abu

Ahmad, who had gone blind, was with him at the edge of the grave. 'Umar ibn al-Khattab and the great Companions of the Messenger of Allah were present. 'Umar ibn Muhammad ibn 'Abdullah ibn Jahsh and Usama and 'Abdullah, the sons of Abi Ahmad ibn Jahsh, and Muhammad ibn Talha ibn 'Ubaydullah, who was the son of her sister Hamna bint Jahsh, went down into the grave of Zaynab bint Jahsh."

'Uthman ibn 'Abdullah al-Jahshi said, "The Messenger of Allah married Zaynab bint Jahsh at the beginning of the month of Dhu'l-Qi'da in 5 AH. She was 35 at the time."

'Amra bint 'Abdu'r-Rahman said, "I asked 'A'isha about the marriage of the Messenger of Allah to Zaynab bint Jahsh. She said, 'On our return from the expedition of al-Muraysi' or shortly after it.'"

'Uthman ibn 'Abdullah al-Jahshi said, "Zaynab bint Jahsh did not leave a dirham nor dinar. She gave away as *sadaqa* all that she could. She was the refuge of the poor. She left her house and they sold it to al-Walid ibn 'Abdu'l-Malik when the mosque was destroyed for 50,000 dirhams."

It is related from 'Urwa about 'A'isha, the Umm al-Mu'minin, that when Zaynab bint Jahsh died, she began to weep and mention Zaynab and ask for mercy on her. 'A'isha was asked about that and she said, "She was a righteous woman." 'Urwa said, "I said, 'Aunt, which of the wives of the Messenger of Allah ﷺ did he prefer?' She said, 'I was with him a lot, and Zaynab bint Jahsh and Umm Salama had a position with him. I reckon they were the dearest of his wives to him after me."

It is related that 'Abdullah ibn Muhammad said, "Umm 'Ukkasha ibn Mihsan was asked, 'How old was Zaynab bint Jahsh when she died?' She said, 'We arrived in Madina in the hijra when she was about thirty and she died in 20 AH.'"

'Uthman said, "Zaynab bint Jahsh died when she was 35."

❄✶❄✶❄

Zaynab bint Khuzayma

She is the Mother of the Poor. She was called that in the *Jahiliyya*.

Az-Zuhri said, "Zaynab bint Khuzayma al-Hilaliyya was called the Mother of the Poor. She had been married to at-Tufayl ibn al-Harith ibn al-Muttalib, and he divorced her.

'Abdu'l-Wahid ibn Abi 'Awn said, "''Ubayda ibn al-Harith married her and he was killed as a martyr in the Battle of Badr.''

Al-Muttalib ibn 'Abdullah ibn Hantab said, "Zaynab, Mother of the Poor, was married to 'Ubayda ibn al-Harith who was killed at Badr.''

Quddama said, "The Messenger of Allah ﷺ proposed to Zaynab bint Khuzayma al-Hilaliyya, the Mother of the Poor. She entrusted her business to him and the Messenger of Allah married her. He called witnesses and gave her 12 $\frac{1}{2}$ *uqiyyas* as a dower. He married her in Ramadan at the beginning of the thirty-first month of the *hijra*. She remained with him for eight months, and then died at the end of Rabi' al-Akhir at the beginning of the thirty-ninth month. The Messenger of Allah prayed over her and buried her at al-Baqi'.''

Muhammad ibn 'Umar said, "I asked 'Abdullah ibn Ja'far, 'Who went down into her grave?' He replied, 'Three of her brothers.' I said, 'How old was she when she died?' He said, 'Thirty or thereabouts.'''

It is related from 'Ata' ibn Yasir that the Hilaliyya woman who was married to the Messenger of Allah ﷺ had a black slavegirl. She said, "Messenger of Allah, I want to free this girl." The Messenger of Allah said to her, "Will you not offer her to your nephews to tend sheep?"

✳✱✳✱✳

Juwayriyya bint al-Harith ibn Dirar

She was married to Musafi' ibn Safwan who was killed in the Battle of al-Muraysi'.

'A'isha said, "The Messenger of Allah captured some of the women of the Banu'l-Mustalaq and took the *khums* (fifth) from them and then divided them among the people. He gave a horseman two shares and a man on foot two shares. Juwayriyya bint al-Harith ibn Dirar fell to the share of Thabit ibn Qays al-Ansari. She was married to a cousin of hers called Safwan ibn Malik ibn Judhayma who had been killed. Thabit ibn Qays gave her a *kitaba* contract for herself for nine *uqiyyas*. She was a charming woman and almost no one who saw her was not taken with her. While the Prophet ﷺ was with me, Juwayriyya came to him to ask him for her *kitaba*. By Allah, as soon as I saw her, I disliked the fact that she had come in where the Prophet was. I knew that he would see in her what I saw. She said, 'Messenger of Allah, I am Juwayriyya bint al-Harith, the master of his people, and you know what has befallen me. I have fallen to the portion of Thabit ibn Qays and he has given me a *kitaba* for the sum of nine *uqiyyas*. Help me with my ransom.' He said, 'Or better than that?' She said, 'What is that?' He said, 'I will pay your *kitaba* for you and marry you.' She said, 'Yes, Messenger of Allah.' The Messenger of Allah said, 'I have done it.' The news went out to the people and they said, 'In-laws of the Messenger of Allah enslaved!' So they freed their prisoners from Mustaliq. The number they set free reached a hundred people of a single house because of the fact that he had married her. I do not know of any woman who had greater blessing for her people than she did. That was when he finished the Expedition of al-Mursayi'."

Ash-Sha'bi said, "Juwayriyya was property. Then the Messenger of Allah ﷺ set her free and married her."

Al-Hasan said, "The Messenger of Allah ﷺ was gracious to Juwayriyya and married her."

Mujahid said, "Juwayriyya said, 'Messenger of Allah, your wives will boast over me. They will say, 'The Messenger of Allah did not marry you.' The Messenger of Allah said, 'Did I not make your dower great? Did I not free forty of your people?'"

Abu'l-Abyad, the client of Juwayriyya said, "The Messenger of Allah ﷺ captured the Banu'l-Mustaliq and Juwayriyya was among the captives. Her father came and ransomed her and then the Messenger of Allah ﷺ married her."

It is related from Abu Qilaba that the Prophet ﷺ captured Juwayriyya bint al-Harith and her father went to the Prophet and said, "Someone like my daughter is not kept as a captive. I am too noble for that. Release her." He said, "Do you think that if we gave her a choice, we would do well?" He said, "Indeed, and I will pay what you are due." Her father went to her and said, "This man has given you a choice, so do not disgrace me." She said, "I have chosen the Messenger of Allah." He said, "By Allah, you have disgraced us."

'Amir said, "The Messenger of Allah ﷺ freed Juwayriyya bint al-Harith and married her. He made her dower consist of the setting free of every captive of the Banu'l-Mustaliq."

Az-Zuhri said, "Juwayriyya was one of the wives of the Messenger of Allah. He set up the screen for her, and allotted her what he allotted his other wives."

Ibn 'Abbas said, "The name of Juwayriyya bint al-Harith had been Barra. The Messenger of Allah ﷺ changed her name and called her Juwayriyya. He disliked for it to be said, 'He has left *barra* (good).'"

It is related from Zaynab bint Salama from Juwayriyya bint al-Harith that her name had been Barra and the Messenger of Allah changed it and named her Juwayriyya. He disliked for it to be said, 'He has left *barra* (good).'"

Ibn 'Abbas said, "The name of Juwayriyya had been Barra and the Messenger of Allah ﷺ re-named her Juwayriyya." He said, "He prayed *Fajr* and then left her after he had prayed *Fajr* and stayed away until morning. Then he came and she was still in her prayer place. She said, 'I have continued since you left, Messenger of Allah.' The Prophet ﷺ said, 'After I left you I said some words which, if they had been weighed, would have outweighed what you said. I said, "Glory be to Allah as much as the number of his creations. Glory be to Allah according to His pleasure. Glory be to Allah according to the weight of His Throne. Glory be to Allah according to the ink of His words.""

It is related from 'Abdullah ibn 'Amr that the Messenger of Allah visited Juwayriyya bint al-Harith on a Friday and found that she was fasting, He said to her, "Did you fast yesterday?" She said, "No." He said, "Do you intend to fast tomorrow?" She said, "No." He said, "Then break your fast."

'Abdu'r-Rahman al-A'raj said in his assembly in Madina, "The Messenger of Allah ﷺ assigned Juwayriyya bint al-Harith 80 *wasqs* of dates from Khaybar and 20 *wasqs* of barley or wheat."

Abu'l-Abyad said, "Juwayriyya bint al-Harith, the wife of the Prophet, died in the month of Rabi' al-Awwal in 56 during the khalifate of Mu'awiya ibn Abi Sufyan and Marwan ibn al-Hakam, the governor of Madina then, prayed over her."

It is related from Muhammad ibn Yazid's grandmother, who was the client of Juwayriyya bint al-Harith, that Juwayriyya said, "The Messenger of Allah married me when I was 20." She said, "Juwayriyya died in 50 when she was 65 and Marwan ibn al-Hakam prayed over her."

✳✳✳✳✳

Safiyya bint Huyayy ibn Akhtab

She was from the Banu Israel of the tribe of Harun ibn 'Imran. Her mother was Barra bint Samwa'il, the sister of Rifa'a ibn Samwa'il of the Banu Qurayza, the brothers of an-Nadir. Safiyya had been married to Sallam ibn Mishkam al-Qurazi. Then he divorced her and she married Kinana ibn ar-Rabi' an-Nadiri who was killed at Khaybar.

When the Messenger of Allah ﷺ attacked Khaybar and Allah gave him their property, Safiyya bint Huyayy and a cousin of hers were taken captive. He commanded Bilal to take them to his camel. The Messenger of Allah had the best of all booty, and Safiyya was part of what he chose on the Day of Khaybar. The Prophet ﷺ offered to free her if she chose Allah and His Messenger. She said, "I have chosen Allah and His Messenger." She became Muslim and he set her free and married her and made her emancipation consist of her dower.

He saw a greenish mark near her eye. He said, "What is this?" She said, "Messenger of Allah, I had a dream in which I saw the moon come from Yathrib and fall into my room. I mentioned that to my husband Kinana. He said, 'You want to be married to this king who comes from Madina?' And he hit me in the face." She observed a waiting-period of one menstrual period. The Messenger of Allah did not leave Khaybar until she was pure of her menstruation. Then the Messenger of Allah left Khaybar without wedding her. When the camel was brought up to the Messenger of Allah so that he could leave, the Messenger of Allah placed his foot for Safiyya so that she could put her foot on his thigh. She refused and placed her knee on his thigh. The Messenger of Allah shielded and carried her behind him. He put his cloak over her back and face and then he tied it under his foot. He carried her and put her in the position of his wives. Then he went to a site called Tabbar six miles from Khaybar, meaning to wed her. She refused him and the Messenger of Allah ﷺ felt annoyed on that account. When he was at as-Sahba', which was about twelve miles from Khaybar, the Messenger of Allah said to Umm Sulaym, "Attend to your companion and comb her." The Messenger of Allah wanted to wed her there.

Umm Sulaym said, "We had no tent with us. So I took two robes or cloaks and tied them to a tree to make a shelter. Then I combed her and perfumed her."

Umm Sulaym al-Aslamiyya also said, "I was among those who were present when the Messenger of Allah married Safiyya. We combed and perfumed her. A girl collected some jewellery from what the women had and there is no scent more fragrant than what was used that night. The Messenger of Allah came to her and she stood up for him. We had told her to do that. We left her and the Messenger of Allah wedded her there and spent the night with her. In the morning she wanted to wash and we took her to the waters of the army and she took care of what she needed and washed. I asked her about what she had experienced from the Messenger of Allah ﷺ and she said that he was happy with her and did not sleep that night, and kept on chatting with her. He said to her, 'What moved you to do what you did when I wanted to set up the first camp and consummate the marriage with you?' She said, 'I was afraid for you on account of the proximity of the Jews.' That increased her position with the Messenger of Allah. The Messenger of Allah gave a wedding feast for her there and the feast consisted only of *hays*, and their bowls were only leather-mats. The people ate on that day and then the Messenger of Allah travelled to al-Qusabiyya which was a distance of sixteen miles.

It is related from Anas ibn Malik that Safiyya bint Huyayy had fallen to the share of Dihya al-Kalbi. The Messenger of Allah ﷺ was told, "A beautiful girl has fallen to the share of Dihya al-Kalbi." So the Messenger of Allah bought her for seven camels and handed her over to Umm Sulaym to prepare her and do her up and for her to do her waiting period with her.

Abu'l-Walid says in his *hadith*, "The wedding feast of the Messenger of Allah ﷺ consisted of ghee and cheese and dates." He said "Leather mats were placed on the earth and then the fat, cheese and dates were put on them."

Yazid ibn Harun says in his *hadith*, "The people said, 'By Allah, we do not know whether the Messenger of Allah has married her or she is his captive.' When he carried her, he shielded her and put her behind him, so the people knew that he had married her. When they were near Madina, the people hurried and the Messenger of Allah hurried. They used to do that. Then the camel stumbled and the Messenger of Allah fell and she fell with him. The wives of the Messenger of Allah looked and said, 'May Allah put this Jewess far away and do this and that to her!' The Messenger of Allah got up and shielded her and put her behind him."

Ja'far said, "When Safiyya was brought to the Prophet ﷺ, he said to her, 'Your father was one of the Jews with the strongest enmity to me until Allah killed him.' She said, 'Messenger of Allah, Allah says in His book, *"No burden-bearer can bear another's burden."*

(53:38)' The Messenger of Allah said to her, 'Choose. If you chose Islam, I will keep you for myself. If you choose Judaism, then I will free you so that you can join your people.' She said, 'Messenger of Allah, I desired Islam and I believed in you before you called me when I went to your mount. I have no desire for Judaism, and I have neither father nor brother in it. You give me a choice between disbelief and Islam. I prefer Allah and His Messenger to freedom and returning to my people.' The Messenger of Allah kept her for himself. Her mother was one of the women of the Banu Qaynuqa', one of the Banu 'Amr. The Prophet was never heard to mention her father with even a syllable which she might dislike. She had been married to Sallam ibn Mishkam and he divorced her and then she had married Kinana ibn Abi'l-Huqayq."

Anas ibn Malik said, "Safiyya went to Dihya in his share." He said, "They began to praise her to the Messenger of Allah, saying, 'We have seen an unparalleled woman among the captives.'" He said, "The Messenger of Allah sent for her and paid Dihya a satisfactory amount for her, and then handed her over to my mother and said, 'Put her in order.' The Messenger of Allah left Khaybar and put her behind him. He stopped and then put a tent over her and then said, 'Whoever has some extra provision should bring it.'" He said, "They brought mash, dates and ghee until they had a pile of food. They made *hays* and began to eat and drink with him. That was the wedding feast of the Messenger of Allah for her. When we saw the walls of Madina, we were elated and speeded up our mounts. So we saw the walls and we speeded up our mounts again. The Messenger of Allah speeded his mount with her riding behind him, but his mount stumbled, and the Messenger of Allah fell and she fell." He said, "No one was looking at him or her. The Messenger of Allah shielded her and they went to him. He said, 'I'm not hurt.' We entered Madina and the slavegirls of his wives came out looking at her and gloating at her fall."

Anas ibn Malik said, "When we arrived with the Messenger of Allah, he had Safiyya behind him on his camel, and Abu Talha and I were behind them. Suddenly the camel of the Messenger of Allah stumbled and both he and the woman fell. Abu Talha rushed from his camel and went to the Prophet, saying, 'O Prophet of Allah, are you hurt at all?' He said, 'No. See to the woman.' So Abu Talha threw his garment over his face and then went to the woman and threw the garment over her. She got up and he put her on his mount. We rode until we were at Madina, or looking down on Madina." He said, 'Coming, repenting, worshipping our Lord, praising.' We kept saying this until we reached Madina."

It is related from Anas ibn Malik that the Messenger of Allah freed Safiyya and married her. Thabit al-Bannani asked him, "What was her dower?" He said, "Her self. He set her free and married her."

It is related from Sahl ibn Sa'd that when the Messenger of Allah consummated his marriage with Safiyya bint Huyayy ibn Akhtab, he had a feast. He was asked, "What was in the feast?" He said, "Dates and mush." He said, "On that day I saw Safiyya giving people *nabidh* to drink." He was asked, "What was this *nabidh* which she was giving them to drink?" He said, "Dates which were soaked in a stone vessel or pot, overnight. In the morning Safiyya gave it to the people to drink."

It is related that 'Abdullah ibn 'Umar said, "When the Prophet arrived with Safiyya, he saw 'A'isha standing veiled in the middle of the people. He recognised her and joined her and took hold of her garment, saying, 'O fair one, what did you see?' She said, 'I saw some Jewess.'"

Abu Hurayra said, "When the Messenger of Allah consummated the marriage with Safiyya, Abu Ayyub spent the night at the door of the Prophet. In the morning, the Messenger of Allah ﷺ said the *takbir* and there was Abu Ayyub with his sword. He said, 'O Messenger of Allah, she is a girl who is new to Islam and marriage, and you killed her father and brother and husband. I did not trust her with you.' The Messenger of Allah laughed and spoke kindly to him."

'Ata' ibn Yasir said, "When the Messenger of Allah ﷺ came from Khaybar with Safiyya, he put her in one of the houses of Haritha ibn an-Nu'man. The women of the Ansar heard about her and her beauty and began to look at her. 'A'isha came in a veil and went in where she was and the Prophet recognised her. When she

89

left, the Messenger of Allah went after her and he said, 'What did you think of her, 'A'isha?' She said, 'I saw a Jewess.' He said 'Do not say this, 'A'isha. She has become Muslim and she is a good Muslim.'"

Umm Sinan al-Aslamiyya said, "When we arrived in Madina, we did not enter our houses until we had taken Safiyya to her house. The women of the Muhajirun and Ansar had heard of her and went to her frequently. I saw four of the wives of the Prophet ﷺ in veils: Zaynab bint Jahsh, Hafsa, 'A'isha and Juwayriyya. I heard Zaynab say to Juwayriyya, 'Daughter of al-Harith, I can only think that this girl will overcome us regarding the time of the Messenger of Allah.' Juwayriyya said, 'No, she is one those women who have little luck with husbands.'"

It is related from 'A'isha that the Messenger of Allah ﷺ was on a journey when Safiyya's camel fell ill. Zaynab had some extra camels, so the Messenger of Allah said, "Safiyya's camel has fallen ill. Could you give her one of your camels?" She said, "Me give to that Jewess!" The Messenger of Allah left her alone throughout Dhu'l-Hijja and Muharram. Two or three months passed in which he did not go to her. She said, "Until I despaired of him and moved my bed. Then one day in the middle of the day there was the shadow of the Messenger of Allah ﷺ advancing."

Ibn Abi 'Awn said, "'A'isha and Safiyya insulted each other and the Messenger of Allah said to Safiyya, 'Why didn't you say, "My father is Harun and my uncle is Musa"?' That was when 'A'isha boasted over her."

Sa'id ibn al-Musayyab said, "Safiyya bint Huyayy came with some gold earrings and gave some of them to Fatima and the women with her."

'Ata' said, "The Messenger of Allah did not assign a share to Safiyya bint Huyayy."

Az-Zuhri said, "Safiyya was one of his wives, and he used to assign her a share as he did to his wives."

It is related from 'Umar and Abu Hurayra that the Messenger of Allah set up the screen for her and used to allot her a share as he did for his other wives.

Muhammad ibn 'Umar said, "The Messenger of Allah assigned her 80 *wasqs* of dates from Khaybar and twenty *wasqs* of barley or wheat."

It is related from Zayd ibn Aslam that when the Prophet of Allah was in his final illness, his wives gathered to him and Safiyya bint Huyayy said, "By Allah, O Messenger of Allah, I wish it was I who was suffering instead of you." The wives of the Prophet winked at that and the Messenger of Allah looked at them and said, "Rinse out your mouths!" They said, "For what, Prophet of Allah? " He said, "Whoever of you winked at her companion. By Allah, she spoke truthfully."

It is related that Kinana said, "I was leading Safiyya to defend 'Uthman. Al-Ashtar met her and he struck the face of her mule until it turned aside. She said, 'Take me back. This one will not disgrace me.'" Al-Hasan said in his *hadith*, "Then she placed a plank between her house and that of 'Uthman to convey food and drink to him."

It is related from Yahya ibn Sa'id that Safiyya left a legacy to one of her Jewish relatives.

Husayn ibn 'Abdu'r-Rahman said, "I saw an old man and they said, 'This is the heir of Safiyya bint Huyayy. He became Muslim after her death and so he did not inherit directly from her.'"

Muhammad ibn 'Umar said, "Safiyya bint Huyayy died in 50 AH in the khalifate of Mu'awiya ibn Abi Sufyan."

Abu Salama ibn 'Abdu'r-Rahman said, "Safiyya bint Huyayy left 100,000 dirhams after the sale of her land and goods and she left a third of that as a legacy to her nephew who was a Jew." Abu Salama said, "They refused to give it to him until 'A'isha, the wife of the Prophet, spoke to them, and told them, 'Fear Allah and give him his bequest.' So he took a third of it, which amounted to thirty-three and a half thousand dirhams. She had a house which she gave as *sadaqa* during her lifetime."

It is related that Amina bint Abi Qays al-Ghifariyya said, "I was one of the women who conducted Safiyya to the Messenger of Allah. I heard her say, 'It is not quite seventeen years since I was married to the Messenger of Allah.'"

Safiyya died in 52 in the khalifate of Mu'awiya ibn Abi Sufyan and was buried at al-Baqi'.

※※※※※

Rayhana bint Zayd ibn 'Amr

She was married to a man of the Qurayza called al-Hakam. That is why some transmitters ascribe her lineage to the Banu Qurayza.

Tha'laba ibn Abi Malik said, "Rayhana bint Zayd ibn 'Amr was from the Banu'n-Nadir. She married one of their men called al-Hakam. When the Banu Qurayza were captured, the Messenger of Allah ﷺ took her as a captive and he freed her and married her and she died with him."

'Umar ibn al-Hakam said, "The Messenger of Allah freed Rayhana bint Zayd ibn 'Amr. She had had a husband whom she loved and honoured. She said, 'No one will replace him.' She was very beautiful. She said, 'When the Banu Qurayza were captured, the captives were presented to the Messenger of Allah and I was among those who were presented to him. He commanded me and I drew back. He had the best of every booty. When I withdrew, Allah chose for me. He sent me to the house of Umm al-Mundhir bint Qays for some days until the prisoners had been killed and the captives divided. Then the Messenger of Allah came to me. I was shy before him. He called me and had me sit before him. He said, "If you choose Allah and His Messenger, the Messenger of Allah will choose you for himself." I said, "I choose Allah and His Messenger." When I became Muslim, the Messenger of Allah set me free and married me and gave me a dower of 12 ½ *uqiyyas* as he gave as a dower to his wives. He wedded me in the house of Umm al-Mundhir. He allotted a share to me as he did for his wives and set up the Screen for me.' The Messenger of Allah liked her and she did not ask him for anything but that he gave it to her. She was asked, 'If you had asked the Messenger of Allah for the Banu Quryaza, he would have freed them.' She used to say, 'He was not alone with me until after the captives had been divided.' She remained with him until she died on his return from the Hajj of Farewell and he buried her at al-Baqi'. He married her in Muharram, 6 AH."

Muhammad ibn Ka'b said, "Rayhana was part of the booty Allah gave him. She was a beautiful graceful woman. When her husband was killed, she fell among the captives, and the Messenger of Allah had the pick on the Day of the Banu Qurayza. The Messenger of Allah ﷺ gave her a choice between Islam and her religion, and she chose Islam. So the Messenger of Allah freed her and married her and set up the Screen for her. She was very jealous about him and so he divorced her with a single divorce. She remained in her place and did not go out. It was hard on her and she wept a lot. The Messenger of Allah ﷺ visited her while she was in that state and took her back. She remained with him. She died before he died."

Wahb said, "Rayhana was from the Banu'n-Nadir and she was married to a man in the Banu Qurayza called al-Hakam. The Messenger of Allah freed her and married her. She was among his wives and he allotted her a share as he did for his wives and the Messenger of Allah set up the Screen for her."

Az-Zuhri said, "Rayhana bint Zayd bint 'Amr was from Qurayza. She was part of the property of the Messenger of Allah. He set her free and married her and then divorced her. She was part of his family. She said, 'No one saw me after the Messenger of Allah.'"

Muhammad ibn 'Umar said, "There is weakness in this *hadith* on two points. She was from an-Nadir and she died during the lifetime of the Messenger of Allah. What is related about her being set free and her marriage is the firmest of the statements I have and it is the position of the people of knowledge. I have heard some relate that she was owned by the Messenger of Allah and he did not free her before her death."

Ayyub ibn Bashir al-Ma'awi said, "When the Banu Qurayza were captured, the Messenger of Allah ﷺ sent Rayhana to the house of Salma bint Qays, Ummi al-Mundhir. She stayed with her until she had menstruated once and then become pure after her period. Umm al-Mundhir came and informed the Messenger of Allah. So the Messenger of Allah came to her in the house of Umm al-Mundhir. The Messenger of Allah said to her, 'If you like, I will free you and marry you. If you like, you can remain my property.' She said, 'Messenger of Allah, it will be easier for me and you if I remain your property.' So she was the property of the Messenger of Allah ﷺ and he had intercourse with her until her death."

Abu Bakr ibn 'Abdullah ibn Abi Jahm said, "When the Messenger of Allah ﷺ took Rayhana captive, he offered her Islam and she refused. She said, 'I will remain with the religion of my people.' The Messenger of Allah said, 'If you become Muslim, the Messenger of Allah will choose you for himself.' She refused. That was hard on the Messenger of Allah. While the Messenger of Allah was sitting among his companions, he heard the sound of sandals and said, 'This is Ibn Sa'iyya to give me the good news of the Islam of Rayhana.' He came and informed him that she had become Muslim. The Messenger of Allah ﷺ had intercourse with her by the right of ownership until she died."

❋✦❋✦❋

Maymuna bint al-Harith

Her mother was Hind bint 'Awf ibn Zuhayr. Mas'ud ibn 'Amr ath-Thaqafi married Maymuna in the Jahiliyya and then he divorced her. After him she was married to Abu Ruhm ibn 'Abdu'l-'Uzza. He died and then the Messenger of Allah ﷺ married her. Al-'Abbas ibn al-Muttalib married her to him. He took care of her affairs. She was the full sister of Umm al-Fadl bint al-Harith al-Hilaliyya. The Messenger of Allah married her at Sarif ten miles from Makka. She was the last wife the Messenger of Allah ﷺ married. That was in 7 AH, during the Fulfilled *'Umra.*

Muhammad ibn Ibrahim said, "The Messenger of Allah ﷺ married Maymuna bint al-Harith in Shawwal in 7 AH.

It is related that when the Messenger of Allah ﷺ wanted to leave for Makka in the Year of the Fulfilled *'Umra*, he sent Aws ibn Khawli and Abu Rafi' to al-'Abbas to marry him to Maymuna. Their camel got lost and they remained some days at the flat of Rabigh until the Messenger of Allah caught up with them at Qudayd. They went with him to Makka. Then he sent to al-'Abbas and mentioned that to him. Maymuna entrusted her affair to the Messenger of Allah. The Messenger of Allah came to the house of al-'Abbas and asked al-Abbas for her hand in marriage and he married her to him.

It is related from Sulayman ibn Yasir that the Prophet sent Abu Rabi' and a man of the Ansar and they married him to Maymuna before he left Madina.

Muhammad ibn Ibrahim said, "The Messenger of Allah married her in Shawwal when he was out of *ihram* in the Year of the Fulfilled *'Umra* and married her at Sarif. She also died at Sarif.

Maymun ibn Mahran said, "I visited Safiyya bint Shayba when she was a very old woman. I asked her, 'Did the Messenger of Allah carry Maymuna when he was in *ihram*?' She said, 'No, by Allah, he married her when they were both out of *ihram*.'"

'Amr ibn Maymun ibn Mahran said, "'Umar ibn 'Abdu'l-'Aziz wrote to my father to ask Yazid ibn al-Asamm about whether the Messenger of Allah ﷺ was in *ihram* or out of it when he married Maymuna. My father summoned him and I wrote the letter for him. He said, 'He proposed to her when he was not in *ihram*, and consummated the marriage when he was not in *ihram*.' I heard Yazid say that."

Maymun ibn Mahran said, "'Umar ibn 'Abdu'l-'Aziz wrote to me to ask Yazid ibn al-Asamm about the marriage of the Messenger of Allah ﷺ to Maymuna and whether he married her when he was in *ihram*. I asked him and he said, 'He married her when they were both out of *ihram*, and he consummated the marriage with her when he was out of *ihram*.'"

Maymun ibn Mahran said, "I was sitting with 'Ata' when a man came and said, 'Can someone in *ihram* marry?' 'Ata' said, 'Allah has not made marriage unlawful since He made it lawful.' I said, "Umar ibn 'Abdu'l-'Aziz wrote to me, (and Maymun was at that time in Mesopotamia) to ask Yazid ibn al-Asamm whether the Messenger of Allah married Maymuna when he was in *ihram* or out of it.' Yazid ibn al-Asamm said, 'He married her when he was out of *ihram*.' Maymuna was the aunt of Yazid ibn al-Asamm. 'Ata' said, 'We only take this from Maymuna and we heard that the Messenger of Allah married her when he was in *ihram*.'"

Abu Rafi' said, "The Messenger of Allah ﷺ married Maymuna when he was out of *ihram*, and I was the messenger between them."

It is related from Sulayman ibn Yasir that the Messenger of Allah sent Abu Rafi' and a man of the Ansar and they married him to Maymuna while he was still in Madina before he had set out.

'Ata' al-Khurasani said, "I said to Ibn al-Musayyab that 'Ikrima claims that the Messenger of Allah married Maymuna while he was in *ihram*. He said, 'A wicked liar! Go to him and abuse him! I will tell you: the Messenger of Allah came in *ihram*, and when he came out of *ihram* he married her.'"

Ibn 'Abbas said, "The Messenger of Allah married Maymuna when he was in *ihram*, and he was cupped at al-Qaha while he was in *ihram*."

It is related from Ibn 'Abbas that the Messenger of Allah ﷺ married Maymuna bint al-Harith at Sarif while he was in *ihram* and then consummated it with her at Sarif on his return." Yazid ibn Qarun said, "She died at Sarif and her grave is there."

It is related from Ibn 'Abbas that the Messenger of Allah ﷺ married Maymuna, his aunt, at Sarif while he was in *ihram*. Ibn 'Abbas did not see anything wrong in it.

It is related from 'Ata', ash-Sha'bi and Mujahid that the Messenger of Allah ﷺ married Maymuna while he was in *ihram*."

Al-Fadl ibn Dukayn said that he was cupped while he was in *ihram*.

Ibn 'Amir said, "The Prophet married Maymuna while he was in *ihram* and was cupped while he was in *ihram*."

It is related from 'Ikrima that Maymuna bint al-Harith was the woman who gave herself to the Messenger of Allah ﷺ.

It is related that 'Amra was asked whether Maymuna was the one who gave herself to the Messenger of Allah. She said, "The Messenger of Allah ﷺ married her for 500 dirhams and the guardian for her marriage was al-'Abbas ibn al-Muttalib."

Mujahid said, "The name of Maymuna was Barra and the Messenger of Allah ﷺ named her Maymuna."

It is related from Ibn 'Abbas that Maymuna and the Prophet used to do *ghusl* from the same vessel.

Umm Hani' said, "The Messenger of Allah ﷺ and Maymuna did *ghusl* from the same vessel, a bowl which had traces of dough in it."

It is related that Maymuna said, "The Messenger of Allah ﷺ used to pray in the mosque on a mat while I was sleeping beside him. His garment touched me and I was menstruating."

Maymuna said, "I and the Messenger of Allah were both in *janaba* and I did *ghusl* from a bowl and there was some water left over and the Prophet ﷺ came and washed with it. I said, 'I have washed with it.' He said, 'There is no *janaba* in the water.'"

It is related from Ibn 'Abbas that the Messenger of Allah said, "These sisters are believers: Maymuna, Umm al-Fadl and Asma'."

Maymuna said, "The Messenger of Allah ﷺ left me one night and I locked the door after him. He came back and tried to open the door but I refused to open it for him. He said, 'I swear you will open it for me!' I said to him, 'You go to your wives on my night!' He said, 'I did not. But I left bursting from urine.'"

'Ubaydullah al-Khawlani said, "I saw Maymuna, the wife of the Prophet, praying in a loose outer garment with no waist-wrapper on."

Muhammad said, "The Messenger of Allah ﷺ asked Maymuna about a slavegirl of hers and she said, 'I have freed her.' He said,

'You have short-changed yourself. If you had given her to your relatives, it would have been better.'"

Yazid ibn al-Asamm said, "I and Ibn Talha ibn 'Ubaydullah met 'A'isha while she was coming from Makka. He was her nephew. We stopped in one of the gardens of Madina and we ate from it. She heard about that and came to her nephew to rebuke him. Then she turned to me and admonished me severely. Then she said, 'Do you not know that Allah Almighty has brought you to the house of His Prophet? By Allah, Maymuna has given you a free rein! She is a woman with great fear of Allah and someone who is constant in maintaining ties of kinship.'"

Yazid ibn al-Asamm said, "The tooth-stick of Maymuna bint al-Harith, the wife of the Prophet, was soaking in water if she was busy with work or prayer. Otherwise, she took it and cleaned her teeth with it."

It is related from Yazid ibn al-Asamm that a relative of Maymuna visited her, and she sensed the smell of drink from him. She said, "If you do not go out to the Muslims so they can flog you, you will not enter my house ever again."

It is related from Maymuna that she saw a white snake in the earth and she took it and said, "Allah does not love corruption."

Kurayb, the client of Ibn 'Abbas said, "Ibn 'Abbas sent me to lead Maymuna's camel, and I can still hear her saying 'There is no god but Allah,' until she stoned the *Jamra al-'Aqaba*."

It is related from 'Ubaydullah al-Khawlani, who had been in the care of Maymuna, that he used to see Maymuna praying in an outer garment and head covering with no waist-wrapper.

Yazid ibn al-Asamm said, "We buried Maymuna at Sarif in the tent in which the Messenger of Allah ﷺ had consummated her marriage. The day she died she was shaven. She had shaved in the *hajj*. Ibn 'Abbas and I went down into her grave. When we laid her down, her head was sloping down at an angle, so I took my cloak and put it under her head. Ibn 'Abbas removed it and threw it aside and put a stone under her head."

It is related that 'Ata' said, "Maymuna died at Sarif and we went out with Ibn 'Abbas to her. When we lifted her bier, we did not shake it nor rock it. The Prophet ﷺ had nine wives. He allotted a share to eight and not to one." Someone else said, "She died in Makka and 'Abdullah ibn 'Abbas carried her. He kept saying to those who were carrying her, 'Be gentle with her. She is your mother,' until she was buried at Sarif."

Yazid ibn al-Asamm said, "I was present at the grave of Maymuna, and those who went down into it were Ibn 'Abbas, 'Abdu'r-Rahman ibn Khalid ibn al-Walid, 'Ubaydullah al-Khawlani and myself. Ibn 'Abbas prayed over her." Muhammad ibn 'Umar said, "She died in 61 AH during the khalifate of Yazid ibn Mu'awiya. She was the last of the wives of the Prophet ﷺ to die. When she died, she was 80 or 81. She was childless.

It is related that 'Abdu'r-Rahman al-A'raj said in his assembly at Madina, "The Messenger of Allah ﷺ assigned Maymuna bint al-Harith 80 *wasqs* of dates from Khaybar and 20 *wasqs* of barley or wheat."

Chapter Seven:
The Women the Prophet married without consummating the marriage, and those he divorced and why he divorced them

The Kilabi Woman

There is disagreement about her name. Some say she is Fatima bint ad-Dahhak and some say she is 'Amra bint Yazid. Others say she is al-'Aliyya bint Zabyan and still others say that she is Saba bint Sufyan. We have written down all that we have heard about that. Some say, "There was only one woman of Kilab and they disagree about her name." Others say, "They are all involved and each of them has a different story than her companion." We will clarify that and record what we have heard.

Az-Zuhri said, "She is Fatima bint ad-Dahhak ibn Sufyan. She sought refuge from him and he divorced her. She used to collect the camels and said, 'I am the wretch.' The Messenger of Allah ﷺ married her in Dhu'l-Qi'da 8 AH and she died in 60 AH."

'A'isha said, "The Messenger of Allah married the Kilabiyya woman. When she came in to him, he went up to her and she said, 'I seek refuge with Allah from you.' The Messenger of Allah said, 'You have sought refuge with One Immense. Rejoin your family.'"

Ibn Mannah said, "She sought refuge from the Messenger of Allah. She was out of her mind and her wits had left her. She would say when she asked permission to visit the wives of the Prophet, 'I am the wretch,' and she used to say, 'I was deceived.'"

It is related from 'Amr who said, "The Messenger of Allah ﷺ went into her, but when he gave his wives a choice, she chose her people. He divorced her and she used to collect the camels and say, 'I am the wretch.'"

It is related from Musa ibn Sa'id and Ibn Abi 'Awn, "The Messenger of Allah ﷺ divorced her because of some white leprosy she had."

Husayn ibn 'Ali said, "The Messenger of Allah ﷺ married a woman of the Banu 'Amir. When he went out, she stared at the people of the mosque and his wives told the Messenger of Allah about that. He said, 'You are against her.' We said, 'We will show you her staring.' The Messenger of Allah said, 'All right.' So they showed her to him when she was staring at the people. So the Messenger of Allah divorced her." Muhammad ibn 'Umar said, "She sought refuge from him and he gave her refuge. The Messenger of Allah did not marry anyone from the Banu 'Amir except her. He did not marry other than the Jawniyya woman of Kinda."

Abu Wajza said, "The Messenger of Allah ﷺ married her in Dhu'l-Qi'da in 8 AH when he left al-Ji'frana."

It is related from several people that she died in 60 AH.

Ibn 'Umar said, "One of the wives of the Messenger of Allah was Saba bint Sufyan. The Prophet sent Abu Usayd as-Sa'idi to propose on his behalf to a woman to the Banu 'Amir called 'Amra bint Yazid. He carried out the marriage to her and then the Prophet heard that she had some white leprosy and he divorced her."

It is related from a man of the Banu Abi Bakr ibn Kilab that the Messenger of Allah ﷺ married al-'Aliyya bint Zabyan and she was with him for a time and then he divorced her.

✻✷✻✷✻

Asma' bint an-Nu'man ibn Abi'l-Jawn

Abu 'Awn ad-Dawsi said, "An-Nu'man ibn Abi'l-Jawn al-Kindi used to come and camp. His father's relatives were Najd near ash-Sharba. He came to the Messenger of Allah ﷺ as a Muslim and said, 'Messenger of Allah, shall I marry you to the most beautiful widow among the Arabs? She was married to her cousin who has died. She is a widow. She desires you and inclines to you.' So the Messenger of Allah married her for 12 ¹/₂ *uqiyyas*. He said, 'Messenger of Allah, do not give her a small dower.' The Messenger of Allah said, 'I have not given any of my wives more than this, nor have any of my daughters had a higher dower than this.' Nu'man said, 'You are the best model.' He said, 'Messenger of Allah, I will send word to her family who will bring her to you. I will go with your messenger to ensure your wife is sent with him.' So the Messenger of Allah sent Abu Usayd as-Sa'idi. When they reached her, she was sitting in her house and she told him to enter. Abu Usayd said, 'None of the men see the wives of the Messenger of Allah.' Abu Usayd said, 'That was after the Screen had been revealed.' So she sent to him, 'Make things easy for me.' He said, 'There should be a screen between you and the men who speak to you except for your close relatives.' She did that. Abu Usayd said, 'I stayed three days and then I brought her with with me in a camel-sedan. When we arrived in Madina, I lodged her with the Banu Sa'ida. The women of the quarter visited her and welcomed her and then left her, talking about her beauty. The news of her arrival spread in Madina.' Abu Usayd said, 'I went to the Prophet ملعﷺ who was with the Banu 'Amr ibn 'Awf and informed him of her arrival. One the wives visited her and they tricked her on account of what they had heard about her beauty. She was an extremely beautiful woman. She was told, 'You are descended from kings. If you want to have luck with the Messenger of Allah, when he comes to you, seek refuge from him. You will have luck with him and he will desire you.'"

Abu Usayd as-Sa'idi said, "The Messenger of Allah ملعﷺ sent me to the woman of Jawn and I brought her. They were in part of Najd. I lodged her in the fortresses of the Banu Sa'ida. Then I went to the Messenger of Allah and informed him about her. The Messenger of Allah went out to her on foot. He squatted on his knees and then bent over to kiss her. That was what he used to do when he first married his wives. She said, 'I seek refuge with Allah from you.' The Messenger of Allah pulled back from her and said to her,'You have sought refuge with the Refuge.' He left her and commanded that she be returned to her family."

Sa'id ibn 'Abdu'r-Rahman ibn Abza said, "The Jawniyya woman sought refuge from the Messenger of Allah ﷺ as she had been told that that would give her more luck with him. No woman except her had sought refuge from him. She was tricked when her beauty and appearance were noted. The Messenger of Allah was told about what had moved her to say what she had said to him. He said, 'They are the companions of Yusuf. Their deviousness is immense.'" He said that she was Asma' bint an-Nu'man ibn Abi 'Awn.

'Abdullah ibn Ja'far said, "She was Umayya bint an-Nu'man ibn Abi'l-Jawn."

Ibn Abi 'Awn said, "The Messenger of Allah ﷺ married the Kindite woman in the month of Rabi' al-Awwal in 9 AH."

It is related that 'Urwa said that al-Walid ibn 'Abdu'l-Malik wrote to him to ask him whether the Messenger of Allah ﷺ married Qutayla, the sister of al-Ash'ath ibn Qays. He replied, "The Messenger of Allah did not marry her at all. He did not marry any Kindite woman except the woman of the Banu'l-'Awn. He married her and then when she was brought and reached Madina, he looked at her and divorced her without consummating the marriage."

Az-Zuhri said, "The Messenger of Allah ﷺ did not marry any Kindite woman except the woman of the Banu'l-'Awn, and he did not consummate the marriage before he divorced her."

Ibn 'Abbas said, "The Messenger of Allah ﷺ married Asma' bint an-Nu'man who was the most beautiful and youthful of the people of her time. When the Messenger of Allah began to marry foreign Arab women, 'A'isha said, 'He has taken foreign women who are going to divert his attention from us!' He asked her father for her hand when the Kinda came to him. When the wives of the Prophet saw her, they envied her. They said to her, 'If you want to have luck with him, then seek refuge with Allah from him when he comes in to you.' When he came in and drew back the curtain, he stretched out his hand to her and she said, 'I seek refuge with Allah from you.' He said, 'Who seeks refuge with Allah! Join your family!'"

It is related that Abu Usyad as-Sa'idi, who had been at Badr, said, "The Messenger of Allah ﷺ married Asma' bint an-Nu'man al-

Jawniyya and sent me to fetch her. Hafsa said to 'A'isha, or 'A'isha to Hafsa, 'You henna her and I will comb her.' They did that and then one of them said to her, 'The Prophet ﷺ likes it when a woman comes to him and says, "I seek refuge with Allah from you."' When she went in to him and he closed the door and lowered the curtain and stretched his hand to her, she said, 'I seek refuge with Allah from you.' He brought his sleeve over his face and shielded himself from her. He said, 'You have sought refuge with the Refuge.' three times."' Abu Usayd said, "Then he came out to me and said, 'Abu Usayd, take her to her family and provision her with two white dresses.' She used to say, 'Call me "the wretch."'"

Abu Usayd said, "The Messenger of Allah ﷺ married a woman from Jawn. He told me to fetch her. So I brought her and lodged her in a fortress at the garden of ash-Shawt beyond Dhubab. Then I went to the Prophet and said, 'Messenger of Allah, I have brought your wife.' He left on foot and I went with him. When he came to her, he bent down to kiss her. When the Messenger of Allah ﷺ first married his wives, he used to kiss them. She said, 'I seek refuge with Allah from you.' He said, 'You have sought refuge with the Refuge.' He commanded me to take her back to her family, and I did that."

Abu Usayd said, "When I brought her to as-Sarim, they shouted and said, 'You are not blessed! What came over you?' She said, 'I was tricked. I was told such-and-such.' Her family said, 'You have made us notorious among the Arabs.' So she came to me and said, 'What happened happened. What should I do now?' I said, 'Stay in your house and screen yourself from any relative and do not let anyone seek to marry you after the Messenger of Allah. You are one of the Mothers of the Believers.' So no one sought to marry her and she was not seen by anyone except a relative until her death with her family at Najd during the khalifate of 'Uthman ibn 'Affan."

It is related from Zuhayr that she died disconsolate.

Ibn 'Abbas said, "Asma' bint an-Nu'man married al-Muhajir ibn Abi Umayya and 'Umar wanted to punish them. She said, 'The Screen was not set up for me and I was not called Umm al-Mu'minin.' So he left her alone."

Muhammad ibn 'Umar said, "'Ikrima ibn Abi Jahl married her during the Ridda, and the Screen of the Messenger of Allah had not been set up for her. That is not confirmed."

✳✳✳✳✳

Qutayla bint Qays,
the sister of al-Ash'ath ibn Qays of Kinda

Ibn 'Abbas said, "When Asma' bint an-Nu'man sought refuge from the Prophet ﷺ, he left with the anger showing in his face. Al-Ash'ath ibn Qays said to him 'Do not let it vex you, Messenger of Allah. Shall I marry you to someone who is not less than her in beauty and lineage?' He asked, 'Who?' He said 'My sister Qutayla.' He said, 'I will marry her.' Al-Ash'ath went to Hadramawt and then brought her. When they had travelled some distance from the Yemen, he heard of the death of the Prophet and took her back to her country. He apostatised and so did she. That is why she could re-marry, as her marriage was annulled due to apostasy. Qays ibn Makshuh al-Muradi married her."

It is related from Dawud ibn Abi Hind that the Prophet ﷺ died after marrying a woman of Kinda called Qutayla. She apostatised with her people, and after that she married 'Ikrima ibn Abi Jahl. Abu Bakr was very upset about that. 'Umar said to him, "O khalif of the Messenger of Allah, by Allah, she is not one of his wives. He did not give her a choice nor did he veil her. Allah freed her from him by her apostasy with her people. "

It is related that 'Urwa used to deny that and said, "The Messenger of Allah did not marry Qutayla bint Qays. He did not marry any Kindite woman except for the sister of the Banu'l-Jawn. He married her and she was brought to him and when he looked at her, he divorced her without consummating the marriage."

✳✳✳✳✳

Mulayka bint Ka'b al-Laythi

It is related that Abu Ma'shar said, "The Prophet ﷺ married Mulayka bint Ka'b. She was known for her remarkable beauty. 'A'isha visited her and said her, 'Aren't you ashamed to marry the one who killed your father?' So she sought refuge from the Messenger of Allah and he divorced her. Her people came to the Prophet and said, 'O Messenger of Allah, this is a young girl and she has no judgement. She was deceived, so take her back.' The Messenger of Allah refused and they asked his permission to marry her to a relative of hers from the Banu 'Udhra. He gave permission and she married the man. Her father had been killed on the day that Makka was conquered. Khalid ibn al-Walid killed him at al-Khandama."

Muhammad ibn 'Umar said, "Part of what is fabricated in this *hadith* is mentioning that 'A'isha said to her, 'Aren't you ashamed?' 'A'isha was not with the Messenger of Allah on that journey."

Yazid al-Jundi said, "The Messenger of Allah married Mulayka bint Ka'b al-Laythi in Ramadan, 8 AH, and consummated it and she died with him."

Muhammad ibn 'Umar said, "Our companions deny that and say that he did not marry a woman of Kinana at all."

✷✦✷✦✷

The daughter of Jundub ibn Samra al-Jundi

It is related from Yazid ibn Bakr that the Messenger of Allah married the daughter of Jundub ibn Samra al-Jundi.

Muhammad ibn 'Umar said, "Our companions deny that and say that he did not marry a woman of Kinana at all."

✷✦✷✦✷

Saba, or Sana bint as-Salt ibn Habib

It is related that a man of the group of 'Abdullah ibn Khazim as-Sulami said that the Messenger of Allah ﷺ married Sana bint as-Salt as-Sulamiyya, but she died before he reached her.

'Abdullah ibn 'Ubayd ibn 'Umayr al-Laythi said, "A man came from the Banu Sulaym to the Prophet ﷺ and said, 'Messenger of Allah, I have a daughter whose beauty and intelligence make me begrudge her to any but you.' So the Prophet wanted to marry her, and then he said, 'Another point, Messenger of Allah, she has not been afflicted by any illness in my presence.' The Prophet said to him, 'We have no need of your daughter who comes to us bearing her errors. There is no good in property from which *zakat* is not taken and in a body which does not suffer harm.'"

Chapter Eight:
The Women to whom the Prophet proposed but did not marry and those women who offered themselves to the Prophet

Layla bint al-Khutaym,
the sister of Qays ibn al-Khutaym

Ibn'Abbas said, "Layla bint al-Khutaym came to the Prophet while he had his back facing the sun. She tapped his shoulder and he said, 'Who is this whom the lion will eat?' He used to often say that. She said, 'I am the daughter of the one who feeds the birds and outstrips the wind, I am Layla bint al-Khutaym. I have come to offer myself to you in marriage.' He said, 'I have done it.' So she went back to her people and said, 'The Prophet ﷺ has married me!' They said, 'Evil is what you have done! You are a jealous woman and the Prophet has several wives who are jealous about him and will invoke Allah against you. Ask to be released!' She went back and said, 'Messenger of Allah, release me.' He said, 'You are released.' Mas'ud ibn Aws married her and she bore him children. While she was washing in one of the gardens of Madina, a wolf leapt at her by the words of the Prophet and ate part of her. She was found and then died."

It is related from Ibn Abi 'Awn that Layla bint al-Khutaym gave herself to the Prophet, and that women had offered themselves before, but the Prophet had not heeded any of them.

'Asim ibn 'Umar ibn Qatada said, "It was Layla bint al-Khutaym who gave herself to the Prophet ﷺ and he accepted her. She used to ride her mules in an objectionable way and she had bad character. She said, 'No, by Allah, I will make Muhammad not marry any other of the Ansar in this area. By Allah, I will give myself to him,' So she went to the Prophet while he was standing with one of his Companions. He did not notice her until she put her hand on him. He said, 'Who is this whom the lion will eat?' She said, 'I am Layla, daughter of the master of his people. I have given myself to you.' He said, 'I have accepted you. Go back and my command will reach you.' She went to her people and they said, 'You are a woman who will not be patient with co-wives. Allah has allowed His Messenger to marry whomever he wishes.' So she went back and said, 'Allah has allowed you women and I am a woman with a long tongue and no patience for co-wives.' She asked him to release her and the Messenger of Allah said, 'I have released you.'"

❋❋❋❋❋

Umm Hani' bint Abi Talib ibn al-Muttalib

Her name was Fakhita. Hisham ibn al-Kalbi used to say, "Her name was Hind." But Fakhita is more common. Her mother was Fatima bint Asad.

Ibn 'Abbas said, "The Prophet ﷺ made a marriage proposal to Abu Talib for his daughter, Umm Hani' in the Jahiliyya. Hubayra ibn Abi Wahb proposed to her and he married her to Hubayra. The Prophet said, 'Uncle, do you marry her to Hubayra and ignore me?' He said, 'Nephew, we have in-lawship with them and the noble is an equal for the noble.' Then she became Muslim and Islam split her from Hubayra. Then the Messenger of Allah ﷺ proposed to her and she said, 'By Allah, I used to love you in the Jahiliyya, so how much more it is in Islam! But I am an older woman and I dislike to burden you.' The Messenger of Allah said, 'The best of women who ride camels are the women of Quraysh. How kind to children in their youth and how careful of their husband's property!'"

Abu 'Aqrab said, "The Messenger of Allah ﷺ proposed to Umm Hani' and she said, 'Messenger of Allah, you are more beloved to me than my sight and hearing. The right of the husband is immense, and I fear that if I devote myself to my husband, I will fall short in my duty to my children, and if I devote myself to my children, I will fall short in the right of my husband.' The Messenger of Allah said, 'The best of women who ride camels are the women of Quraysh. How kind to children in their youth and how careful of their husband's property!'"

Abu 'Aqrab said, "The Messenger of Allah ﷺ visited Umm Hani' and proposed to her. She said, 'How can I lie with this one and nurse that one?' referring to the two children in front of her. He asked for something to drink and he was brought some milk and drank some and then handed it to her and she drank the rest. She said, 'I have drunk it and I am fasting.' He said, 'What moved you to do that?' She said, 'For the sake of your left-overs. I would not leave that for anything if I was able. Since I was able, I drank it.' The Messenger of Allah said, 'The best of women who ride camels are the women of Quraysh. How kind to children in their youth and how careful of their husband's property! If Maryam ibn 'Imran had ridden the camel, no one would have been preferred to her.'"

Umm Hani' bint Abi Talib said, "The Messenger of Allah proposed to me, and I made an excuse to him and he excused me. Then Allah sent down, *'O Prophet! We have made lawful for you your wives you have given dowries to...'* to *'and the daughters of your maternal aunts, who have emigrated along with you.'* (33:50) So I was not not lawful to him. I had not emigrated with him. I was one of those brought into Islam."

Abu Salih, the client of Umm Hani', said, "The Messenger of Allah ﷺ proposed to Umm Hani' bint Abi Talib. She said, 'Messenger of Allah, I am older, and have young children.' When her sons came of age, she offered herself to him and he said, 'Now, no,' because Allah had sent down on him, *'O Prophet! We have made lawful for you your wives you have given dowries to...'* to *'and the daughters of your maternal aunts, who have emigrated along with you.'* (33:50) She was not one of the women who emigrated." Another said, "Her children by Hubayra were Ja'da, 'Umar, Yusuf and Hani'."

※✳※✳※

Duba'a bint 'Amir ibn Qurat

Ibn 'Abbas said, "Duba'a bint 'Amir was married to Hawdha ibn 'Ali al-Hanafi, and he died and she inherited a great deal of wealth. Then she married 'Abdullah ibn Jid'an at-Taymi and he had no children. She asked him to divorce her and he divorced her. Then she married Hisham ibn al-Mughira and she bore him Salama. He was one of the best Muslims. Then Hisham died. She was one of the most beautiful of Arab women and the largest in physique. When she sat, she took up a lot of room. She used to cover her body with her hair. Her beauty was mentioned to the Prophet ﷺ and he made a proposal for her to her son Salama ibn Hisham ibn al-Mughira. He said, 'Let me consult her.' The Prophet was told, 'She is old.' Her son went to her and said to her, 'The Prophet has proposed for you.' She said, 'What did you say to him?' He said, 'I said that I would consult you.' She said, 'And what are you consulting me about? Return and marry.' He returned to the Prophet but he was silent about it."

✳✳✳✳✳

Safiyya bint Bashshama ibn Nadla

Ibn 'Abbas said, "The Messenger of Allah ﷺ proposed to Safiyya bint Bashshama ibn Nadla al-'Anbari. He took her as a captive. The Messenger of Allah gave her a choice, saying, 'If you wish, it is me, and if you wish, it is your husband.' She said, 'Rather my husband.' So he released her and the Banu Tamim cursed her."

✳✳✳✳✳

Umm Sharik, who is Ghaziya bint Jabir

It is related by various people that she was from Daws from al-Azd.

Ibrahim at-Taymi said, "Umm Sharik was a woman of the Banu 'Amir ibn Lu'ayy. She offered herself to the Messenger of Allah, and he did not accept her. She did not marry until her death.

It is related from 'Amir about His words, *"You may defer any of them you will,"* (33:51) that it was all of the women who offered themselves to the Prophet ﷺ. He accepted some of them, and deferred some of them and they did not marry after him. One of them was Umm Sharik.

Ash-Sha'bi said, "The woman whom the Messenger of Allah dismissed was Umm Sharik al-Ansariyya."

It is related from 'Ali ibn al-Husayn that the woman who gave herself to the Prophet was Umm Sharik, a woman from al-Azd.

Mujahid said, "She did not give herself to the Prophet."

It is related from 'Ikrima about this *ayat, "and any believing woman who gives herself to the Prophet if the Prophet desires to marry her—exclusively for you, not the believers as a whole,"* (33:50) that he said, "She was Umm Sharik ad-Dawsiyya."

Munir ibn 'Abdullah ad-Dawsi said, "The husband of Umm Sharik became Muslim. Her name was Ghaziya bint Jabir al-Dawsiyya, and he was Abu'l-'Akar. He emigrated to the Messenger of Allah with Abu Hurayra when Daws emigrated. Umm Sharik said, 'The family of Abu'l-'Akar came to me and said, "Perhaps you have embraced his religion?" I said, "Yes, by Allah, I have embraced his religion." They said, "Then, by Allah, we must torture you severely." So they took us from our house at Dhu'-Khalasa. They made for a place and brought me on a slow camel with the worst and roughest of their saddles. They fed me bread with honey and would not let me drink a drop of water until midday when the sun was boiling. It was midsummer. They set up their tents and left me in the sun until my wits, sight and hearing left me. They did that to me for three days. On the third day, they said to me, "Abandon your position." I did not know what they were saying except word by word. So I pointed with my finger heavenwards to indicate *tawhid.*' She said, 'By Allah, I was in that state and exhausted. Then I felt the coolness of a bucket on my chest. I took it and drank from it with one breath. Then it was snatched from me. I looked up and it was hanging between the heaven and the earth and I was unable to reach it. Then it came down to me a second time and I drank from it for another breath. Then it went up. I looked at it between the heaven and the earth and then it came down to me a third time and I drank from it until I was quenched and poured it on my head, face and clothes.' She said, 'They came out and looked and said, "Enemy of Allah, from where did you get this?" I said to them, "The enemies of Allah are other than me. It is those who oppose His religion. As for where it came from, it came from Allah as provision, and Allah has provided for me." They rushed to their waterskins and containers and found them secure and unopened. They said, "We testify that your Lord is our Lord, and that the One who gave you the provision in this place after what we did to you is the One who prescribed Islam." So they became Muslim and all emigrated to the Messenger of Allah. They used to acknowledge my excellence over them and what Allah had done for me.'"

She is the one who offered herself to the Prophet and she was from Azd. She offered herself to the Prophet. She was beautiful and advanced in years. She said, 'I offer myself to you and give you myself to you.' The Prophet ﷺ accepted her. 'A'isha said, 'There is no good in a woman who gives herself to a man.' Umm Sharik said, 'I am that.' Then Allah called her a believer. He says, *'and any believing woman who gives herself to the Prophet.'* (33:50) When this *ayat* was revealed, 'A'isha said, 'Allah is swift in what you desire.'"

Muhammad ibn 'Umar said, "I saw those who said, 'This *ayat* was sent down about Umm Sharik.' It is established with us that it was a woman from Daws from Azd, except in the variant of Musa ibn Muhammad ibn Ibrahim who said, 'Umm Sharik related *hadiths* from the Messenger of Allah.'"

Ibn al-Musayyab heard Umm Sharik say, "The Messenger of Allah ﷺ commanded geckos to be killed."

It is related from Umm Sharik that she heard the Messenger of Allah ﷺ say when he was mentioning the Dajjal, "People will flee from him into the mountains." She said, "I said, 'Messenger of Allah, where will the Arabs be on that day?' He said, 'They will be few.'"

Yahya ibn Sa'id said, "Umm Sharik ad-Dawsiyya emigrated and came across a Jew on the road. She was fasting. The Jew said to his wife, 'If you can let her have something to drink, do so.' She passed the entire night like that until the end of the night and then a bucket was placed on her chest and a pouch [for drawing water]. She drank, and then later woke them up when setting out before dawn. The Jew said, 'I heard the voice of the woman saying, "I have drunk."' She said, 'By Allah, I did not give her anything to drink.'"

He said, "She once had a butter container which someone who came had lent to her and a man haggled with her over it. She said, 'There is not much in it.' She blew in it and hung it in the sun and then it was full of ghee. " He said that it was said that the butter container of Umm Sharik was one of the signs of Allah.

It is related from Jabir that Umm Sharik had a butter container in which she gave ghee to the Messenger of Allah ﷺ. He said, "One day her children asked her for ghee and there was none. She went to the butter vessel to look into it and there it was flowing. She poured out some of it for them and they ate for it for a time. Then she looked at what remained and poured it all out and it finished. Then she went to the Messenger of Allah and he said to her, 'Did you pour it out? If you had not poured it put, it would have remained with you.'"

✳✳✳✳✳

Khawla bint Hakim ibn Umayya

She was from the Banu Sulaym. Her mother was Du'ayfa bint al-'As ibn Umayya. Murra came to Makka and formed an alliance with 'Abdu Manaf ibn Qusayy himself and 'Abdu Manaf married his daughter, 'Atika bint Murra. She was the mother of Hashim, 'Abdu Shams and al-Muttalib.

It is related that Muhammad said, "Khawla bint Hakim was one of those who offered themselves to the Prophet. He put her off. She used to serve the Prophet, and 'Uthman ibn Maz'un married her and later left her a widow."

It is related from Sa'id ibn al-Musayyab that it was Khawla bint Hakim who asked the Messenger of Allah ﷺ about the woman who has the same sort of dream that a man has.

Umama bint Hamza ibn 'Abdu'l-Muttalib

Her mother was Salma bint 'Umays ibn Ma'dd, the sister of Asma' bint 'Umays. That is how she is named by Hisham ibn Muhammad al-Kalbi. Someone else said that she is 'Ammara bint Hamza. Hisham said, "'Ammara was a man, the son of Hamza, and his *kunya* is by him. His mother was Khawla bint Qays."

'Ali said, "I said, 'Messenger of Allah, why are you choosy about Quraysh and do not marry with us?' He said, 'You have someone then?' I said, 'Yes, the daughter of Hamza.' He said, 'That is the daughter of my brother by nursing.'"

It is related from Sa'id ibn al-Musayyab that 'Ali said to the Messenger of Allah, "Why don't you marry the daughter of your uncle Hamza? She is the the most beautiful girl in Quraysh." He said, "'Ali, do you not know that Hamza is my brother by nursing, Allah makes unlawful by suckling what lineage makes unlawful."

Ibn'Abbas said, "'Ammara bint Hamza ibn 'Abdu'l-Muttalib. Her mother was Salma bint 'Umays. She was at Makka. When the Messenger of Allah came, 'Ali spoke to the Prophet and said, 'Why do you leave the daughter of our uncle an orphan among the idolworshippers?' The Prophet did not forbid him to bring her out and so he brought her out. Zayd ibn Haritha spoke up. He was the trustee of Hamza and the Prophet had formed brotherhood between them when he formed brotherhood between the Muhajirun. He said, 'I am more entitled to look after my brother's daughter.' When Ja'far ibn Abi Talib heard that, he said, 'The maternal aunt is a mother and I am more entitled to look after her by the position of her maternal aunt, Asma' bint 'Umays, who is married to me.' 'Ali said, 'I see you quarrelling about a cousin when I am the one who brought her out from among the idolworshippers and you have no tie of kinship with her closer than mine. I am more entitled to look after her.' The Messenger of Allah ﷺ said, 'I will judge between you: You, Zayd, are the client of Allah and the client of His Messenger. You, 'Ali, are my brother and my Companion, and you, Ja'far, are the most like me in physique and character. You, Ja'far, are more entitled to look after-her since her aunt is married to you. A woman does not marry someone who is married to her aunt.' So he judged that Ja'far was to care for her."

Muhammad ibn 'Umar said, "Ja'far came and hopped around the Messenger of Allah. The Prophet ﷺ said, 'What is this, Ja'far?' He said, 'Messenger of Allah, when the Negus wanted to please someone, he stood up and hopped around him.'"

The Messenger of Allah ﷺ gave her in marriage to Salama ibn Abi Salama. The Prophet used to say, "Have you repaid Salama?"

※✳※✳※

Khawla bint al-Hudhayl

Her mother was the daughter of Khalifa ibn Farwa al-Kalbi, the sister of Dihya ibn Khalifa.

It is related from ash-Sharqi al-Qattami that the Messenger of Allah ﷺ married Khawla bint al-Hudhayl and she died before reaching him.

※✳※✳※

Sharaf bint Khalifa, the sister of Dihya ibn Khalifa l-Kalbi

It is related from ash-Sharqi al-Qattami, "When Khawla bint al-Hudhayl died, the Messenger of Allah ﷺ married Sharaf bint Khalifa, the sister of Dihya, but the marriage was not consummated."

'Abdu'r-Rahman ibn Sabit said, "The Messenger of Allah proposed to a woman of Kalb. He sent 'A'isha to look at her. She went and came back. The Messenger of Allah said to her, 'What did you see?' She said, 'I did not see anything beneficial.' The Messenger of Allah said to her, 'You saw something beneficial. You saw a mole on her cheek with every hair trembling on account of you.' She said, 'Messenger of Allah, there is nothing hidden from you.'"

Mujahid said, "When the Messenger of Allah proposed and was rejected, he did not repeat the offer. When he proposed to a woman and she said, 'Let me consult my father,' and she met her father and he gave her permission and then met the Messenger of Allah and told him, the Messenger of Allah said to her, 'We have joined someone else.'"

Chapter Nine:
Various Topics Concerning the Prophet's Wives

The Dowers of the Wives of the Prophet

'A'isha said, "The dower of the Messenger of Allah was 12 ½ *uqiyyas*. That was 500 dirhams." 'A'isha said, "An *uqiyya* is forty dirhams and a *nashsh* is twenty dirhams."

Az-Zuhri said, "The dower of the Messenger of Allah ﷺ was ten *uqiyyas* of gold."

'Umar ibn al-Khattab said, "Do not be excessive in the dowers of women. Whether it is out of fearfulness of Allah or nobility in this world, your Prophet was more entitled to that. He did not make the dower of his wives or daughters more than 12 *uqiyyas*, and that is 480 dirhams."

'Umar said, "I do not know that the Messenger of Allah ﷺ married any of his wives nor gave any of his daughters in marriage for more than than 12 *uqiyyas*."

✳✳✳✳✳

The Bowl of Sa'd ibn 'Ubada

Abu Bakr ibn Muhammad ibn 'Amr ibn Hazm said, "When the Messenger of Allah proposed to a woman, he said, 'Tell them about the bowl of Sa'd ibn 'Ubada.'"

It is related about the bowl of Sa'd ibn 'Ubada, "Sometimes it was meat and sometimes ghee and sometimes milk, which he sent to the Prophet. Whenever he made his rounds, it went around with him."

It is related from az-Zuhri that he denied that the Messenger of Allah had said to the one who proposed on his behalf, "Mention the bowl of Sa'd," but he did not deny that the bowl of Sa'd went with him when he made the rounds.

Umm Salama said, "The Ansar who showed a lot of kindness towards the Messenger of Allah ﷺ were: Sa'd ibn 'Ubada, Sa'd ibn Mu'adh, 'Ammara ibn Hazm and Abu Ayyub. That was because they were close neighbours of the Messenger of Allah. Not a day would pass but that one of them would have a gift which would make the rounds with the Prophet when he went round. The bowl of Sa'd ibn 'Ubada went around in the rounds. He did not drink from it every night."

It is related that Ruthayma heard Umm Salama say, "My fellow wives told me that I should speak to the Messenger of Allah." Umm Salama, Umm Habiba ibn Abi Sufyan, Zaynab bint Khuzayma, Juwayriyya bint al-Harith, Maymuna bint al-Harith and Zaynab bint Jahsh were on the eastern side, and 'A'isha, Safiyya and Sawda were on the other side. Umm Salama said, "My companions spoke to me and said, 'Speak to the Messenger of Allah. The people make their gifts to him in the room of 'A'isha and we like what she likes. They should send their gifts to him wherever he is.'" Umm Salama said, "When the Messenger of Allah visited me, I said, 'Messenger of Allah, my companions have asked me to speak to you to command people to send their gifts to you wherever you are. They say, "We like what 'A'isha likes."'" She said, "He did not answer me. So I asked him, 'Why don't you answer me?' He said, 'Do not harm me concerning 'A'isha. Revelation does not come to me under the same blanket with any of you except 'A'isha.'"

It is related that 'Amra said, "People inquired about the day when the Messenger of Allah went to 'A'isha so that they could give their gifts to him, and guests were delighted if the day was when the Messenger of Allah ﷺ was in the room of 'A'isha."

✳✳✳✳✳

The Houses of the Wives of the Prophet

Muhammad ibn 'Umar said, "I asked Malik ibn Abi'r-Rijal, 'Where were the houses of the wives of the Prophet ﷺ?' He informed me that all of them were on the left side when you stand for the prayer behind the Imam facing the minbar. This is unlikely. All those women whom 'Awf ibn al-Harith mentioned were not all together with the Prophet. Zaynab bint Khuzayma was before Umm Salama. Zaynab died and then Umm Salama took her room. In that same year he married Zaynab bint Jahsh. Sawda was married before 'A'isha and before all of them. She and 'A'isha were brought to Madina after the Messenger of Allah reached Madina. Umm Habiba bint Abi Sufyan came in the two ships in 9 AH. He married Safiyya in that year. Hafsa was before Umm Salama and before Zaynab bint Khuzayma."

It is related that Muhammad ibn 'Amr al-'Amiri said, "Sawda bint Zam'a bequeathed her room to 'A'isha. The relatives of Safiyya bint Huyayy sold her room to Mu'awiya ibn Abi Sufyan for 180,000 dirhams."

Ibn Abi Sabra said, "One of the people of Syria informed me that Mu'awiya sent to 'A'isha, 'You are more entitled to pre-emption.' He sent to her about selling, and he bought 'A'isha's house from her. They say the price was 180,000 dirhams. It is said it was 100,000 dirhams. He gave her the precondition that she could live there for her lifetime. The money was taken to 'A'isha and she did not leave her seat before distributing it. It is said that Ibn az-Zubayr bought it from 'A'isha. It is said that he sent her five camels which carried the money and he gave her the precondition that she could continue to live in it during her lifetime. She immediately distributed it. It was said to her, 'If only you had kept back a dirham of it.' 'A'isha said, 'If you had reminded me, I would have done so.'"

It is related from Salim that Hafsa left her house and Ibn 'Umar inherited it. He did not take any price for it. It was demolished and incorporated into the mosque.

It is related from 'Ikrima that the heirs of Umm Salama sold her house for money. Muhammad ibn 'Umar said that it was not sold.

'Asim ibn 'Umar ibn Qatada said, "When the Messenger of Allah came to Madina, he stayed in Abu Ayyub's house. He sent Abu Rafi' and Zayd ibn Haritha with two camels and 500 dirhams which he received from Abu Bakr. He commanded them to bring his family. Abu Bakr sent 'Abdullah ibn Urayqit ad-Di'li with them with two or three camels. He wrote to 'Abdullah ibn Abi Bakr to tell him to bring his family to him. Zayd ibn Haritha set out with the family of the Messenger of Allah: Fatima and Umm Kulthum, the daughters of the Prophet, and Sawda bint Zam'a, the wife of the Prophet. He wanted to take Zaynab, the Prophet's daughter, but her husband, Abu'l-'As ibn ar-Rabi', kept her back. Ruqayya had already emigrated with her husband, 'Uthman ibn 'Affan, to Madina. Zayd ibn Haritha took his wife, Umm Ayman, and Usama ibn Zayd and they travelled with the family of the Messenger of Allah. 'Abdullah ibn Abi Bakr set out with Umm Ruman and his two sisters, 'A'isha and Asma', the daughters of Abu Bakr. They all arrived in Madina while the Messenger of Allah ﷺ was building the mosque and the rooms around the mosque. He put them in a house belonging to al-Haritha ibn an-Nu'man. The Messenger of Allah ﷺ consummated the marriage with 'A'isha in her room in which the Messenger of Allah was buried. He made a doorway into the mosque opposite the door of 'A'isha from which he went out to the prayer. When he was in retreat, he would put his head out from the mosque through the doorway of 'A'isha. She washed his head while she was menstruating."

Muhammad ibn 'Umar said, "Haritha ibn an-Nu'man had houses near the mosque of the Messenger of Allah ﷺ and around it. When the Messenger of Allah married someone, Haritha ibn an-Nu'man would move for him from his house and eventually all his houses were for the Messenger of Allah and his wives."

'Abdullah ibn Yazid al-Hudhayli said, "I saw the houses of the wives of the Messenger of Allah when they were destroyed by 'Umar ibn 'Abdu'l-'Aziz during the khalifate of al-Walid ibn 'Abdu'l-Malik. They were incorporated into the mosque. They were houses made of dried bricks, and they had rooms made of palm stalks held together with mud. There were nine houses with their apartments. They were located from the house of 'A'isha with the door which is next to the Door of the Prophet, to the dwelling of Asma' bint Hasan ibn 'Abdullah. I saw the house of Umm Salama and its room made with bricks. Her grandson said, 'When the Messenger of Allah raided

Dumat al-Jandal, Umm Salama built her room with bricks. When the Messenger of Allah came and looked at the bricks, he went in to her first and said, 'What is this structure?' She said, 'Messenger of Allah, I wanted to obstruct the vision of people.' He said, 'Umm Salama, the worst of that on which the money of a Muslim is spent is building.'"

It is related that 'Amir said, "The Messenger of Allah only bequeathed the houses of his wives and some land he left as *sadaqa*."

It is related that 'Ata' al-Khurasani said in the assembly of 'Imran ibn Abi Anas, "It was between the grave and the minbar that I found the rooms of the wives of the Messenger of Allah made of palm stalks with their doors covered with black wool. I was present when the letter of al-Walid ibn 'Abdu'l-Malik was read commanding that the rooms of the wives of the Prophet be incorporated into the mosque of the Messenger of Allah. I did not see a day with more weeping than on that day." 'Ata' said that he heard Sa'id ibn al-Musayyab say on that day, "By Allah, I wish that they had left them as they were, so that the people of Madina and visitors from afar could see what was enough for the Messenger of Allah in his lifetime. That would be part of what would encourage people to be abstinent in acquiring and boasting about the stuff of this world."

When 'Ata al-Khurasani finished his *hadith*, 'Imran ibn Abi Anas said, "Among them were four houses of brick which had rooms of palm stalks. There were five houses of palm stalks with mud without any stone with hair covering over the doors. I measured the curtain and found it to be three cubits by one cubit, and the area was that, more or less. As for what you say about the amount of weeping, I can recall myself in an assembly which contained some of the Companions of the Messenger of Allah ﷺ, including Abu Salama ibn 'Abdu'r-Rahman, Abu Umama ibn Sahl ibn Hunayf, and Kharija ibn Zayd. They were weeping until their beards were wet with tears. Abu Umama said on that day, 'Would that they had been left and not destroyed so that people would restrain themselves from building and would have what Allah was pleased with for His Prophet even though the keys to the treasures of this world were in his hands.'"

✳✳✳✳✳

The Division of the Prophet between His Wives

It is related from Abu Qilaba that the Messenger of Allah ﷺ used to divide his time between his wives and was fair. Then he would say, "O Allah, this is my division insofar as I have control. Do not blame me for that over which You and not me have power," meaning the love of the heart.

Bilal ibn Ja'far said, "The Messenger of Allah ﷺ used to go around to his wives in a robe."

Sa'd said, "When the Messenger of Allah was ill with his final illness, Fatima went around to his wives and said, 'It is difficult for the Messenger of Allah to go around to you.' They said, 'He is in the lawful.' He was in 'A'isha's room."

Muhammad said, "When the Messenger of Allah was seriously ill in his final illness, he said, 'Where will I be tomorrow?' They said, 'With so-and-so.' He said, 'And where will I be the next day?' They said, 'With so-and-so.' His wives recognised that he meant 'A'isha and they said, 'Messenger of Allah, we give our days to our sister 'A'isha.'"

It is related that the wives of Messenger of Allah put him in the lawful to choose whomever he wished of them over whomever he wished. He used to prefer 'A'isha and Zaynab.

Abu Razin said, "The Messenger of Allah wanted to divorce some of his wives. When they saw that, they put him in the lawful to prefer whomever he wished of them over whomever he wished."

'A'isha said, "When the Messenger of Allah ﷺ went on a journey, he would draw lots between his wives. Whoever had her lot come out would go with him. He used to allot each of his wives a day and a night except for Sawda who gave her day and night to 'A'isha, seeking to please the Messenger of Allah by that."

'A'isha said, "Sawda became old and the Messenger of Allah did not visit her much, and she knew the position of 'A'isha. She was afraid that he would divorce her and that she would lose her position with the Messenger of Allah. She said, 'Messenger of Allah, my day which is mine from you is for 'A'isha and you are in the lawful in it.' The Prophet kissed her. Then there was revelation about that: *'If a woman fears evil treatment, or aversion, on the part of her husband...'* (4:128)"

'A'isha said, "Whenever the Messenger of Allah travelled, he drew lots between his wives. When a lot other than mine came out, his dislike could be seen. He did not return from any journey and visit any of his wives before me. The division began with me."

'A'isha said, "There were few days when the Messenger of Allah ﷺ did not go around to his wives. He would go up to his wife and embrace and kiss each wife until he reached the last of them. If it was her day, he would stay with her. Otherwise, he would leave. When he entered the house of Umm Salama, he lingered with her. Hafsa and I were like a single hand. I said, 'We only think that he lingers with her in order to be alone with her. They are going to have sex.' That was hard on us, so we got someone to find what kept him with her. When he went to her, she brought out a pot of honey and opened it for him and he would have some of it. He used to like honey. We said, 'What is there that he dislikes so that he will not linger in Umm Salama's room?' We said, 'There is nothing he dislikes more than for it to be said, "We perceive some odour from you." When he comes to you and draws near you, then say, "I sense some smell from you." He will say, "It is from the honey which I had with Umm Salama." Say to him, "I think that its bees must have visited mimosa."'" When he visited 'A'isha, he went up to her and she said, "I smell something from you. What have you had?" He said, "Honey from the room of Umm Salama." She said, "Messenger of Allah, I think that its bees must have visited mimosa." Then he left her and went to Hafsa. He came up to her and she said the like of what 'A'isha had said. When they both said it, it was hard on him. So when he went to Umm Salama later and she brought out the honey for him, he said, "Take it away. I have no need of it." She said, "By Allah, I thought that we had done something terrible. We had made unlawful for the Messenger of Allah ﷺ something he desired."

'Abdullah ibn Rafi' said, "I asked Umm Salama about this *ayat*: *'O Prophet! Why do you make forbidden what Allah has made lawful for you?'* (66:1) She said, 'I used to have a pot of white honey whose bees had visited terebinth flowers. The Prophet ﷺ used to have some of it. He liked it. Then 'A'isha said to him, "Its bees have visited mimosa [which has an unpleasant smell]." So he forbade himself it and then this *ayat* was sent down.'"

'Abdu'l-Karim ibn Abi Umayya said, "I asked 'Abdullah ibn 'Utba ibn Mas'ud what was made forbidden to the Messenger of Allah. He said, 'A pot of honey.'"

'Amra said, "I heard Umm Salama in 'A'isha's room when 'A'isha was dying. She said, 'May Allah have mercy on you and forgive you for every wrong action and let me meet you in the Garden.' I said, 'O mother, what about the story of the honey? 'A'isha told me about it.' Umm Salama said, 'It is as she told you.'"

'A'isha said, "The wives of the Prophet ﷺ sent Fatima, the daughter of the Messenger of Allah, and she asked permission to enter. The Messenger of Allah was with 'A'isha in her room. He gave her permission and she went in. She said, 'Messenger of Allah, your wives have sent me to you to ask you to be fair about the daughter of Abu Quhafa.' The Messenger of Allah said, 'Daughter, do you not love what I love?' She said, 'Yes, indeed, Messenger of Allah.' He said, 'Then love 'A'isha.' Fatima said, 'I left and went to the wives of the Prophet and told them.' They said, 'You have not helped us at all! Go back to the Messenger of Allah!' Fatima said, 'No, by Allah, I will never speak to him about her!' So they sent Zaynab bint Jahsh and she asked permission to enter where the Prophet was. He gave her permission and she entered and said, 'Messenger of Allah, your wives have sent me to you to ask you to be fair about the daughter of Abu Quhafa.' Then Zaynab began to insult me, and I started to look at the Messenger of Allah to see if he would give me permission regarding her. I kept looking at him until I recognised that the Messenger of Allah would not dislike for me to defend myself against her. I attacked Zaynab and I did not hesitate to dumbfound her.' The Messenger of Allah smiled and then said, 'She is indeed the daughter of Abu Bakr!'"

'Ali ibn Husayn said, "The wives of the Messenger of Allah sent to Fatima, the daughter of the Messenger of Allah, and asked her to go to the Messenger of Allah and say, 'Your wives have asked you to be fair about the daughter of Abu Quhafa.' Fatima waited some days without doing anything until Zaynab bint Jahsh went to her. There was no one who would come to grips with 'A'isha except Zaynab bint Jahsh. She spoke to Fatima and Fatima said, 'I will do it.' So she went to the Messenger of Allah and said, 'Your wives have sent me to you to ask you to be fair about the daughter of Abu Quhafa.' The Messenger of Allah said, 'Did Zaynab send you?' Fatima said, 'Zaynab and others.' He said, 'I swear that it is she who undertook that!' She said, 'Yes.' The Messenger of Allah smiled. So Fatima went back to them and informed them. Zaynab exclaimed, 'Daughter of the Messenger of Allah! You have not helped us at all!' The wives said to Zaynab, 'You go.' Zaynab went and asked permission of the Messenger of Allah to enter. The Messenger of Allah said, 'This is Zaynab.' He gave her permission and she said, 'It is enough for you that the daughter of Abu Quhafa adorns her arms for you! Be fair between us and her!' Zaynab attacked 'A'isha and maligned her."

Ibn Ka'b al-Qurazi said, "The Messenger of Allah had leeway in the division between his wives. He could divide between them however he wished. That was by the words of Allah, *'It is more likely, then, they will be comforted.'* (33:51) Then they knew that that was from Allah."

Salma, the client of the Messenger of Allah ﷺ, said, "The Messenger of Allah went around in the night to the nine wives who were alive when he died. Whenever he left a woman, he said to Salma, 'Pour out *ghusl* water for me.' He would wash before he went to another. I said, 'Messenger of Allah, is not one *ghusl* enough?' The Prophet ﷺ said, 'This is better and purer.'"

※✶※✶※

The Screen of the Wives of the Messenger of Allah

It is related that Anas ibn Malik said, "The first time the Screen was revealed was when the Messenger of Allah ﷺ married Zaynab bint Jahsh. On the morning the Messenger of Allah married Zaynab, he invited the people and they had some food and then they left. A group of them remained with the Prophet. They stayed with him for a long time. The Messenger of Allah got up and I went out with him until we came to the door of 'A'isha's apartment. Then he thought that they had left and went back. I went back with him until he entered Zaynab's house. They were still sitting there. He left and I went with him to the door of 'A'isha's apartment. When he thought that they had left, he returned and I returned with him, and they had indeed left. So he put a curtain between me and him and the Screen was revealed."

Anas said, "The Screen was revealed when the Messenger of Allah married Zaynab bint Jahsh. That was in 5 AH. On that day his wives were screened from me and I was fifteen at that time."

Anas ibn Malik said, "The Screen was sent down when the Messenger of Allah married Zaynab bint Jahsh. Umm Sulaym gave him some *hays* in a stone bowl. He said, 'Go and invite any Muslim you meet.' I went out and invited all the Muslims I met. They went in and ate and left. The Messenger of Allah placed his hand on the food and made a supplication. A group of them remained and they began to chat. The Messenger of Allah ﷺ was too polite to say anything to them. He went out and left them in the house. Allah sent down, *'O you who believe! Do not go into the Prophet's rooms except after being given permission.'* (33:53)"

Ibn Ka'b said, "When the Messenger of Allah ﷺ went to his house, they went quickly and took their seats. That was not noticed in the face of the Allah and he did not put his hand to the food out of modesty before them. They were censured for that when Allah revealed, *'O you who believe! Do not go into the Prophet's rooms except after being given permission to come and eat, not waiting for the food to be prepared. However, when you are called go in and, when you have eaten, then disperse and do not remain wanting to chat together. If you do that it causes injury to the Prophet though he is too reticent to tell you so.'* (33:53)"

It is related that 'A'isha said, "The wives of the Messenger of Allah ﷺ used to go out at night to al-Manasi' to relieve themselves. 'Umar used to say to the Messenger of Allah, 'Veil your wives,' but he did not do it. One night Sawda went out in the night. She was a tall woman. 'Umar called to her in a loud voice, 'We have recognised you, Sawda!' wanting for the Screen to be sent down."

'A'isha said, "After the Screen was sent down, Sawda and I went out to relieve ourselves in the evening and 'Umar saw her and recognised her. She was a very distinctive tall woman. 'Umar shouted to her, 'By Allah, you are not hidden from us, Sawda!' So she went back to the Messenger of Allah and mentioned that to him. There was a root in the hand of the Messenger of Allah which he was eating. The Messenger of Allah said, 'Allah has permitted you to go out for your needs.'"

Ibn 'Abbas said, "The Screen of the wives of the Messenger of Allah was sent down when 'Umar was eating with the Prophet. His hand touched one of the hands of the wives of the Prophet, and the Screen was commanded."

Az-Zuhri said, "It was asked, 'Who used to visit them, meaning the wives of the Prophet?'" He said, "Everyone who had a relationship by lineage or suckling which prevented marriage." It was asked, "And the rest of people?" He said, "They used to veil themselves from them so that they would speak to them from behind a screen. It was a single curtain."

It is related from Umm Salama that she and Maymuna were with the Prophet ﷺ. She said, "While we were with him, Ibn Umm Maktum entered. That was after the Screen had been commanded. The Prophet said, 'Veil yourselves from him.' We said, 'Messenger of Allah, isn't he blind so that he cannot see or recognise us?' He said, 'Are you blind as well? Don't you see him?'"

✳✳✳✳✳

Concerning what occurred before the Screen

Abu Malik said, "The wives of the Messenger of Allah ﷺ used to go out at night for their needs and some of the hypocrites used to accost them and annoy them. They complained about that. The hypocrites were spoken to about that and they said, 'We do that to slave-girls.' So the *ayat* was sent down, '*O Prophet! Tell your wives and daughters and the believing women to draw their outer garments closely round themselves. That makes it more likely they will be recognised and not be harmed.'* (33:59) "

It is related from al-Hasan about His words, *"O Prophet! Tell your wives and daughters and the believing women to draw their outer garments closely round themselves. That makes it more likely they will be recognised and not be harmed,'* (33:59)" that he said, "Fools accost your slavegirls in Madina and annoy them, A free woman used to go out and be thought to be a slavegirl and be pestered. So Allah commanded them to draw their outer garments closely round themselves."

Ibn Ka'b al-Qurazi said, "A man from among the hypocrites used to accost the believing women and annoy them. He was spoken to about that, and he said, 'I thought they were slavegirls.' So Allah commanded them to dress differently to the slavegirls and to draw their outer garments closely round themselves. They would cover their faces except for their eyes." He said, "That makes it more likely they will be recognised and not be harmed." He said, "That made it more likely that they would be known."

It is related from Mujahid about His words, *"Those who cause injury to believing men and believing women, without their having justly earned it,"* (33:58) that he said, "for other than what they did."

It is related from 'Ubayd ibn Hunayn about his words, *"If the hypocrites, and those with sickness in their hearts, and the rumour-mongers, in Madina do not desist, We will set you onto them,"* to *"You will not find any changing in the usual practice of Allah,"* (33:60-62) that he said, "The hypocrites themselves were made known in this *ayat: 'those with sickness in their hearts, and the rumour-mongers.'"* He said, "They are all hypocrites."

✳✦✳✦✳

Those who were allowed to visit the wives of the Prophet

Az-Zuhri was asked, "Who used to visit the wives of the Prophet?" He said, "Everyone who had a relationship by lineage or suckling which prevented marriage." It was asked, "And the rest of people?" He said, "They used to veil themselves from them so that they would speak to them from behind a screen. This was one curtain - with the exception of slaves and slaves with a *kitaba*. They were not screened from them."

It is related from Nabhan, the client of Umm Salama, that Umm Salama said to him when he had a *kitaba* from her, "Abu Yahya! Do you have anything left of your *kitaba*?" He said, "Yes." She said, "Pay it to my nephew. He will use it to marry." He wept and said, "I will never pay it to him!" She said, "If it is because you see me, you will not see me. The Messenger of Allah ﷺ said, 'If the slave who has a *kitaba* with you has nothing left of his *kitaba*, veil yourself from him.'"

It is related from Salim Sablan that a slave with a *kitaba* belonged to a man of the Banu Nasr. He used to travel with the wives of the Prophet and they did not veil themselves from him. They did not veil themselves from slaves and slaves with a *kitaba*. Once they were free, then they veiled themselves from them."

Why the Messenger of Allah stayed away from his wives and his giving them a choice

A man came to Jabir and said, "Abu 'Abdullah! 'Urwa ibn az-Zubayr has sent me to you to ask you about why the Messenger of Allah stayed away from his wives." Jabir said, "The Messenger of Allah left us for a day and night and did not even come out for the prayer. We began to go to and fro. We gathered at his door talking so that he would hear us speaking and know we were there. We remained standing but he did not give us permission nor come out to us. We said, 'The Messenger of Allah knows that we are here. If he wants to give us permission, he will give us permission.' So we dispersed and did not disturb him.

"The people dispersed, except for 'Umar ibn al-Khattab who kept on clearing his throat and asking permission until the Messenger of Allah gave him permission. 'Umar said, 'I entered and he had his hand on his cheek so that I knew he was dejected. I said, "O Prophet of Allah, may my father and mother be your ransom, what has disturbed you? People are distressed on account of their not seeing you!" He said, "'Umar, they have asked me for what I do not have," meaning his wives. "That has done what you see to me." I said, "Prophet of Allah, I slapped Jamila bint Thabit with a blow that floored her because she asked me for what I did not have. You, Messenger of Allah, have a promise with your Lord and He will appoint ease after hardship."'

"He said, 'I kept on talking to him until I saw some of that had abated in the Messenger of Allah. I went out and met Abu Bakr as-Siddiq and told him the story.' Abu Bakr went to 'A'isha and said, "You know that the Messenger of Allah does not store up anything, so do not ask him for what he does not have. See what you need and ask me for it."' 'Umar went to Hafsa and mentioned the like of that to her. Then they went to the Mothers of the Believers and began to mention to them the like of that until they went to Umm Salama and mentioned that to her. She said, 'What business have the two of you here? The Messenger of Allah is more entitled to our affair. If he wanted to forbid us, he would forbid us. Who are we to ask if we do not ask the Messenger of Allah? Is there anyone between you and your wives? Do not burden yourselves with this.' So they left her. The wives of the Prophet said to Umm Salama. 'May Allah repay you well when you did what you did. We could not answer him at all!'"

Then Jabir said to Abu Sa'id, "Isn't the *hadith* like that?" He said, "Indeed, and I have some more of it." Jabir said, "I will express that, Allah willing."

Then he went on, "Allah then sent down about that, *'O Prophet, say to your wives, "If it is the life of this world and its finery you desire, then come and I will give you all you need and let you go with kindliness,'* (33:28) meaning the gift accompanying divorce. Letting them go means to divorce them in a good manner. *'But if it is Allah and His Messenger and the abode of the Next World you desire,'* meaning choose Allah and His Messenger and do not marry anyone after him.'

"So the Messenger of Allah went and began with 'A'isha. He said, 'Allah has commanded that I give you a choice between Allah and His Messenger and the Next World, and this world and its finery. I have begun with you. I give you a choice.' She said, 'Prophet of Allah! Did you begin with any of them before me?' He said, 'No.' She said, 'I choose Allah and His Messenger and the Next World. Conceal it for me and do not tell your wives that.' The Messenger of Allah said, 'I will give them a choice.' So the Messenger of Allah ﷺ gave all of them a choice and they chose Allah and His Messenger and the Next World. The choice was that they choose between this world and the Next World. He said, *'But if it is Allah and His Messenger and the abode of the Next World you desire, Allah has prepared, for those among you who do good, an enormous wage.'* (33:29) They chose not to marry after him. Then He said, *'O wives of the Prophet! If any of you commit an act of clear indecency,'* meaning adultery, *'she will get double the punishment,'* i.e. in the Next World. *'That is something easy for Allah. Any of you who is obedient to Allah and His Messenger and acts rightly will be given her wage twice over,'* in the Next World, or the punishment twice over, *'and We have prepared for her generous provision. O wives of the Prophet! You are not like any other women provided you are Godfearing. Do not be soft in your speech in case someone with sickness in his heart becomes desirous. Speak correct and courteous words. Remain in your houses and do not display your beauty as it was displayed in the earlier Days of Ignorance.'* (33:29-33) He said: 'Do not leave your houses nor display yourselves,' i.e. as the people of the Jahiliyya used to do."

It is related that 'Umar ibn al-Khattab asked for permission to enter while there were some women of Quraysh with him who were speaking to him and asking him for more, raising their voices above his voice. When 'Umar ibn al-Khattab asked for permission to enter, they rushed to screen themselves. 'Umar entered and the Messenger of Allah ﷺ was laughing. 'Umar said, "May Allah make you laugh, Messenger of Allah." The Messenger of Allah said, "I am laughing at those women who were with me. When they heard your voice, they rushed behind the curtain." 'Umar said, "O enemies of your selves! Do you fear me and not fear the Messenger of Allah?" They said, "Yes, you are harsher and more severe than the Messenger of Allah." The Messenger of Allah said, "By the One who has my soul in His hand, whenever Shaytan finds you taking a path, he always takes a path other than your path!"

❋✦❋✦❋

Concerning the Two Women who Helped Each Other against the Messenger of Allah

'Abdullah ibn 'Abbas said, "I was eager to ask 'Umar about the two women among the wives of the Prophet ﷺ about whom Allah says, *'If you two turn in repentance to Him, your hearts are indeed so inclined.'* (66:4) I went on *hajj* with him and he went outside, and I went outside with him with a water vessel. He went out for a call of nature and when he came back, I poured some of the water from the vessel on his hands and he did *wudu'*. I said, 'Amir al-Mu'minin, who are the two women about whom Allah says, *"If you two turn in repentance to Him, your hearts are indeed so inclined"*?' He said, 'I am surprised at your question, Ibn 'Abbas. That was 'A'isha and Hafsa.'"

'Umar went on, "I and a neighbour of mine from the Ansar among the Banu Umayya ibn Zayd used to take it in turns to visit the Prophet. He would go one day and I would go the next. When I went,

I would bring him back the news of that day of the revelation and other things. When he went, he did the same. We, the company of Quraysh, used to dominate women, and when we came to the Ansar, they were a people who were dominated by their women. So our women began to adopt the manner of the women of the Ansar. Once I shouted at my wife and she answered me back. I disliked that she should answer me back. She said, 'Do you dislike that I should answer you back? By Allah, the wives of the Prophet answer him back! Some of them might not have anything to do with him for the entire day until night!' That alarmed me, so I said, 'The one among them who has done this will incur a terrible loss!' Then I put on my clothes and visited Hafsa. I said, 'Hafsa! Do any of you sometimes anger the Messenger of Allah for the entire day until night?' She said, 'Yes.' I said, 'She is ruined and lost! Does she feel secure that Allah will not become angry on account of the anger of His Messenger so that she will be destroyed? Do not ask from the Messenger of Allah too much and do not answer him back in anything and do not refuse to speak to him. Ask me what you like. Do not be tempted into being like your neighbour since she is more beautiful than you and more beloved to the Messenger of Allah,' meaning 'A'isha.

"We thought that Ghassan were getting ready to attack us. Once, on a day when it was his turn, my friend went down. He returned in the evening and banged loudly on my door and said, 'Is he here?' I was alarmed and came out to him. He said, 'Something terrible has happened.' I said, 'Has Ghassan attacked?' He said, 'No, something worse still and even more serious. The Messenger of Allah has divorced his wives.' I said, 'Hafsa is ruined and lost!' I used to think that this was about to happen. I got dressed and prayed the *Fajr* prayer with the Prophet. He entered a small upper room of his and withdrew into it. I went to Hafsa and found her weeping. I asked, 'Why are you weeping? Didn't I warn you? Has the Messenger of Allah divorced you all?' She said, 'I do not know. He is in his small upper room.'

"I went to the minbar. A group of people were around it and some of them were weeping. I sat with them a short while and then what I felt overcame me. I went to the small room where he was and I said to a black slave of his, 'Ask permission for 'Umar.' He went in and spoke to the Prophet and then came out and said, 'I mentioned you to him but he was silent.' So I went and sat with the group who were at the minbar. Then what I felt overcame me and I went back again. Then I sat with the group who were at the minbar. Then what I felt overpowered me again and I went to the slave and said, 'Ask permission for 'Umar,' - and the same thing happened. When I turned to go, suddenly the slave called me, saying, 'The Messenger of Allah gives you permission.'

"So I went into him. He was lying down on a woven mat. There was no bedding between him and it and I could see the mark of the mat on his side. He was reclining on a leather cushion stuffed with palm fibre. I greeted him and then I asked while I was standing, 'Have you divorced your wives?' He looked up at me and said, 'No.' I said, 'Allah is greater!' Then I said, sociably while I was standing, 'Messenger of Allah, will you listen to me? We, the company of Quraysh, used to dominate our women. Then we came to a people who were dominated by their women. So our women began to adopt the manner of the women of the Ansar. Once I shouted at my wife and she answered me back. I disliked that she should answer me back. She said, "Do you dislike that I should answer you back? By Allah, the wives of the Prophet answer him back! Some of them might not have anything to do with him for the entire day until night!" I said, "She is ruined and lost! Does she feel secure that Allah will not become angry by the anger of His Messenger so that she will be destroyed?"' The Prophet smiled. Then I said, 'Messenger of Allah, will you listen to me? I visited Hafsa and I said, "Do not be tempted into being like your neighbour since she is more beautiful than you and more beloved to the Messenger of Allah."' The Messenger of Allah smiled again. I sat down when I saw him smile. I raised my eyes to look about the room and, by Allah, I did not see anything of note in it except for three hides. I said, 'Ask Allah to enrich your community. Persia and Byzantium were made rich and were given this world and they did not even worship Allah.' He was reclining and then he said, 'Do you have any doubts, Ibn al-Khattab? Those people were repaid for their good actions in the life of this world.' I said, 'Messenger of Allah, ask forgiveness for me.'

"The Messenger of Allah had withdrawn because of the story which Hafsa divulged to 'A'isha. He had said, 'I will not go to them for a month,' because of the intensity of his anger towards them when Allah rebuked him."

"When twenty-nine days had passed, he went to 'A'isha and began with her. 'A'isha said to him, 'You swore that you would not come to us for a month. Twenty-nine days have passed. I have counted them.' The Prophet said, 'The month is twenty-nine days.' That month was twenty-nine days."

Umm Salama said, "When the Messenger of Allah ﷺ withdrew from his wives in his small room, I began to weep and people came in to me and said, 'Has the Messenger of Allah divorced you?' I said, 'I do not know, by Allah,' until 'Umar came and went in to him and said, 'Have you divorced your wives?' The Messenger of Allah said, 'No.' 'Umar said the *takbir*. We heard it and we were in the rooms. We knew that 'Umar had asked the Messenger of Allah and he had said no. So he said the *takbir* until he brought us the news."

It is related that Sa'id ibn Jubayr said about His words, *"every right-acting man of the believers,"* (66:4) that He means 'Umar ibn al-Khattab.

Ibn 'Abbas said, "Hafsa left her house, and it was the day of 'A'isha. The Messenger of Allah went in with his slavegirl who had her face veiled. Hafsa said to the Messenger of Allah, 'I saw what you did.' The Messenger of Allah said to her, 'Keep quiet about me. She is unlawful.' So Hafsa went to 'A'isha and told her and gave her the good news of the forbidding of the Coptic woman. 'A'isha said, 'It is on my day that he married the Coptic woman. He gave the rest of the wives their days.' So Allah sent down, *'When the Prophet confided a certain matter to one of his wives,'* meaning Hafsa, *'and then when she divulged it Allah disclosed that to him, he communicated part of it and neglected to mention part. When he told her of it, she said, "Who told you of this?" he said, "It was the Knowing, the Aware who told me of it." If the two of you would turn to Allah, for your hearts did deviate...'* meaning Hafsa and 'A'isha. *'But if you support one another against him,'* meaning Hafsa and 'A'isha, *'Allah is his Protector and so is Jibril and every right-acting man of the believers and furthermore the angels too will come to his support. It may well be that if he does divorce you...'* (66:3-4) The Messenger of

Allah left them for 29 nights and then it was revealed, *'O Prophet! Why do you make forbidden what Allah has made lawful for you, seeking the good pleasure of your wives. Allah is Forgiving, Merciful.'* (66:1) So he was commanded and expiated his oath and kept his wives."

It is related from Zayd ibn Aslam that the Prophet ﷺ made the mother of Ibrahim unlawful and said, "She is unlawful for me." He said, "By Allah, I will not go near her." He said, "Then it was revealed, *'Allah has made the expiation of your oaths obligatory for you.'* (66:2)"

Malik ibn Anas said, "So the 'unlawful' is lawful in slavegirls. If a man says to his slavegirl, 'You are unlawful for me,' that has no effect. But if he says, 'By Allah, I will not go near you,' then he owes expiation for the oath."

It is related from ad-Dahhak that the Prophet ﷺ made his slavegirl unlawful. Allah disallowed that and He returned her to him and he expiated his oath.

Jubayr ibn Mut'im said, "Hafsa left her house and the Messenger of Allah sent for his slavegirl and brought her to Hafsa's room. Hafsa came in while she was with him in her room. She said, 'Messenger of Allah! In my room, on my day, on my bed!' The Messenger of Allah said, 'Be quiet. By Allah, I will never go near her. Do not mention it.' Hafsa went and told 'A'isha. Then it was sent down, *'O Prophet! Why do you make forbidden what Allah has made lawful for you.'* (66:1) That making unlawful was that she was lawful. Then he said, *'Allah has made the expiation of your oaths obligatory for you.'* So the Messenger of Allah expiated his path when he denied himself. Then He said, *'Allah disclosed that to him, he communicated part of it and neglected to mention part. When he told her of it,'* meaning Hafsa when Allah told him, *'she said, "Who told you of this?" he said, "It was the Knowing, the Aware who told me of it." If the two of you would turn to Allah, for your hearts did deviate,'* meaning Hafsa and 'A'isha. *'But if you support one another against him,'* Hafsa and 'A'isha, *'Allah is his Protector.'* (66:3-4). The Messenger of Allah ﷺ said, 'I will not visit them for a month!'"

'Urwa ibn az-Zubayr said, "Hafsa went to her father and chatted with him. The Messenger of Allah sent for Maria and remained with her in Hafsa's room. Hafsa returned from her father and saw them and became violently jealous. Then the Messenger of Allah sent his slavegirl away and Hafsa came in. She said, 'I saw who was with you! You have been bad to me.' The Prophet said, 'By Allah, I will please you. I will confide a secret to you, so conceal it for me.' She said, 'What is it?' He said, 'I testify to you that my slavegirl is unlawful for me,' meaning to please Hafsa by doing that. Hafsa and 'A'isha supported each other against the other wives of the Messenger of Allah. Hafsa went and told 'A'isha, 'Good news! Allah has made his slavegirl unlawful for His Messenger.' When she told the secret of the Messenger of Allah, Allah sent down, *'O Prophet! Why do you make forbidden what Allah has made lawful for you, seeking the good pleasure of your wives?'* to *'both previously married women and virgins.'* (66:1-5)"

It is related that al-Qasim said to 'Amra bint 'Abdu'r-Rahman, "Umm Muhammad! Why did the Messenger of Allah stay away from his wives?" 'Amra said, "'A'isha told me that the Messenger of Allah was given a gift while he was in her room. He sent a portion to each of his wives. He sent some to Zaynab bint Jahsh and she was not pleased. Then he gave her more another time and she was not pleased. 'A'isha said. 'She has demeaned you by returning your gift to you!' The Messenger of Allah said, 'I will not visit you all for a month.'"

She said, "He entered his small room. 'Umar ibn al-Khattab had brotherhood with one of the Ansar who did not hear anything without telling him, and whenever 'Umar heard anything, he told him. 'Umar met him that day and he said, 'Do you have any news?' The Ansari said, 'Yes, terrible.' 'Umar said, 'Perhaps al-Harith ibn Shamir has come against us?' The Ansari said, 'It is worse than that.' 'Umar said, 'What is it?' He said, 'I only think that the Messenger of Allah has divorced his wives.' 'Umar said, 'Hafsa is spited! I forbade her to answer back the Messenger of Allah as 'A'isha answers him back!'"

She said, "'Umar went to the mosque and the people were as still as if there had been birds on their heads. He went up the wooden ladder of the Messenger of Allah. There was an Abyssinian boy at the door. He said, 'Peace be upon you, O Prophet, and the mercy of Allah and His blessings. Can I come in?' The Abyssinian put his head inside the room and then indicated no to 'Umar. He waited for a time and then could not bear it so he went up the ladder a second time and said, 'Peace be upon you, O Prophet, and the mercy of Allah and His blessings. Can I come in?' The Abyssinian put his head inside the room and then said, 'Enter.'"

She said, "So 'Umar went in and the Prophet ﷺ was lying down with a leather cushion stuffed with fibre under his head. There was only a mat between him and the floor. The mark of the mat showed on his side. When 'Umar saw that, his eyes flowed with tears. The Messenger of Allah said, 'Why are you weeping, 'Umar?' He said, 'Messenger of Allah, Chosroes and Caesar oppose Allah and they are provided with brocade and silk. You are His Prophet and chosen one and there is nothing between you and the floor except a mat and a cushion stuffed with fibre!' There was some gear near his head which contained a spear. The Messenger of Allah said, 'They have had their good things brought ahead for them.'

"Then 'Umar said, 'Messenger of Allah, have you divorced your wives?' He said, 'No.' 'Umar said a *takbir* which the people of the mosque heard. Then 'Umar said, 'Messenger of Allah, I said to Hafsa, " Do not be tempted by the love of the Messenger of Allah for 'A'isha and her beauty into answering him back as 'A'isha answers him back.'" When he mentioned her beauty, the Messenger of Allah smiled. Then he said, 'Messenger of Allah, if you dislike anything in Hafsa, then divorce her. You and Allah are more beloved to me than my property and my family.' The Messenger of Allah said, "Umar, no one ever believes but that I am more beloved to him than himself.' He said, 'By Allah, Messenger of Allah, you are more beloved to me than myself.' At the end of twenty-nine days, the Messenger of Allah descended from his small room. 'A'isha said, 'May my father and mother be your ransom, Prophet of Allah! You said something which I did not pay any attention to and you became angry with me. Did you not say a month?' He said, "A'isha, the month is such-and-such,' and he pulled in his thumb in the third ten."

In the *hadith*, it is related that when the Ansari met him, he said, "Alas for Hafsa!" Then he went in to visit Hafsa and said, "Perhaps you answered the Prophet back as 'A'isha answers him back. You do not have the precedence of 'A'isha nor the beauty of Zaynab." Then he went to Umm Salama and said, "Umm Salama, do you speak to the Messenger of Allah and answer him back at all?" Umm Salama said, "How extraordinary! What concern is it of yours to meddle with the Messenger of Allah and his wives! By Allah, we speak to him. If he puts up with that, that is more proper for him. If he forbids us, that will be more effective with us than it coming from you!" 'Umar said, "Then I regretted saying what I said to the wives of the Prophet."

It is related that when the Messenger of Allah ﷺ gave his wives a choice, he began with 'A'isha. He said to Abu Bakr, "Help me with her." 'A'isha said, "By Allah, no one will help you against me. Tell me what it is, Messenger of Allah!" He said, "Allah has given you a choice." She said, "I have chosen Allah and His Messenger." She said, "It is a trust with you that you do not inform any of them." The Messenger of Allah said, "I was not sent to pick fights, but I was sent to bring good news. If they ask me, I will tell them." Then he gave Hafsa a choice, and she said, "What did 'A'isha do?" He told her and they all accepted and chose Allah and His Messenger except for the 'Amiri woman. She chose her people and then she used to say later, "I am the wretch."

'A'isha said, "The Messenger of Allah gave his wives a choice and they chose him, and that was not a divorce."

✳✳✳✳✳

Tafsir of the *Ayats* in which the Wives of the Messenger of Allah are mentioned

It is related from 'Urwa that, *"Allah desires to remove all impurity from you, O People of the House, and to purify you completely,"* (33:33) is about the wives of the Prophet. It was revealed in the house of 'A'isha.

Abu Umama ibn Sahl said about His words, *"And remember the signs of Allah, and wise words, recited in your houses,"* (33:34) that the Messenger of Allah ﷺ used to pray voluntary prayers in the houses of his wives, both night and day.

Umm Salama said, "The Messenger of Allah used to pray in the houses of all his wives."

Umm Salama said, "Messenger of Allah, women are not mentioned." Then Allah sent down, *"Muslim men and Muslim women, believing men and believing women,"* to *"an enormous wage."* (33:35)

Qatada said that *,"The signs of Allah, and wise words, recited in your houses,"* (33:34) was the Qur'an and the *Sunna.*

Qatada said, "When the wives of the Prophet ﷺ were mentioned, the women said, 'If there had been any good in us, He would have mentioned us,' so Allah sent down, *'Muslim men and Muslim women ... an enormous wage.'* (33:35)"

It is related from Masruq about *,"The Prophet has closer ties to the believers than their own selves do, and his wives are their mothers,"* (33:6) that he said, "A woman said to 'A'isha, 'O mother!' 'A'isha said, 'I am not your mother. I am the mother of your men.'"

It is related that Umm Salama, the wife of the Prophet, said, "I am the mother of your men and your women."

'Ikrima said, "The earlier days of Ignorance was the time in which Ibrahim was born. The women used to adorn themselves and wear clothes which did not conceal them. The later days of Ignorance are the time in which Muhammad was born. They were a people who were constricted in their way of life in food and drink. So Allah promised His Prophet ﷺ that the earth would be opened for them. He said, 'Say to your wives if they want to display themselves as was done in the earlier days of Ignorance, *"Allah desires to remove all impurity from you, O People of the House, and to purify you completely. And remember the signs of Allah, and wise words, recited in your houses. Allah is All-pervading, All-aware."* (33:33-34)'"

He said, "What was *'recited in your houses'* is the Qur'an. So the women said to the men, 'We became Muslim as you became Muslim, and we did what you did and you are mentioned in the Qur'an and we are not mentioned!' People used to be called Muslims, and when they made the *hijra*, they were called 'believers'. So Allah sent down, *'Muslim men and Muslim women, believing men and believing women, obedient men and obedient women ... fasting men and fasting women,'* (in the month of Ramadan), *'men and women who guard their private parts; men and women who remember Allah repeatedly,'* those who remember the blessings and favours of Allah, *'Allah has prepared for them forgiveness and an enormous wage.'* *(33:35)* When the Messenger of Allah gave them a choice, they chose Allah and His Messenger. So Allah sent down, *'After that no women are lawful to you nor may you exchange them for other wives,'* (33:52). He said that after these nine wives who have chosen you, it is unlawful for you to marry others, *'nor may you exchange them for other wives even though their beauty might be pleasing to you, with the exception of what your right hand owns'*, (33:52) except the nine which you have."

It is related about, *"It is not for you to cause injury to the Messenger of Allah nor ever to marry his wives after him,"* (33:53) that Abu Bakr ibn Muhammad ibn Hazm said, "It was sent down about Talha ibn 'Ubaydullah because he said, 'When the Messenger of Allah dies, I will marry 'A'isha.'"

It is related about, *"Whether you make something known or conceal it,"* (33:54) that Abu Umama ibn Sahl ibn Hunayf said, "If you speak it and say, 'We will marry so-and-so,' being one of the wives of the Prophet, or conceal that in yourselves and do not say it, Allah knows it."

It is related about, *"Any believing woman who gives herself to the Prophet if the Prophet desires to marry her — exclusively for you, not the believers as a whole,"* (33:50) that az-Zuhri said, "The gift is not lawful for anyone after the Messenger of Allah."

It is related about *"And if you desire any you have put off,"* (33:51) ash-Sha'bi said, "There were women who gave themselves to the Messenger of Allah, but he did not consummate the marriage with them nor establish the Veil on them and no one after him married them. One of them was Umm Sharik."

Muhammad ibn 'Umar said, "This is the business known to us."

It is related about, *"There is no restriction on the Prophet in anything Allah assigns to him. The practice of Allah in respect of those who passed away before...,"* (33:38), that Ibn Ka'b al-Qurazi said, "He means that marrying whichever women he wished was his allowance. This was the practice of the Prophets before him. Sulayman ibn Dawud had a thousand wives, seven hundred of whom had a rich dower and three hundred of whom were noble. Da'ud had a hundred wives, including the mother of Sulayman, the wife of Uriah, whom Da'ud married after his test. This is more than the number of wives that Muhammad had."

'Umar, the client of Ghufra, said, "When the Jews saw the Messenger of Allah marrying women, they said, 'Look at this person who is not satisfied by food and, by Allah, he is only interested in women!' They envied him because of the number of his wives and they criticised him for that, saying, 'If he had been a Prophet, he would not have desired women.' The most intense of them in that criticism was Huyayy ibn Akhtab. Allah proved them liars and informed them of the bounty of Allah and His expansion for His Prophet. He said, *'Or do they envy other people for what Allah has given them of His unbounded favour?'* (4:54) By 'people', He means the Messenger of Allah. *'We gave the family of Ibrahim the Book and the Wisdom, and We gave them an immense kingdom.'* (4:54) What Allah gave Sulayman ibn Da'ud was that he had a thousand women, seven hundred of whom had a rich dower and three hundred of whom were noble. Da'ud had a hundred wives, including the mother of Sulayman, the wife of Uriah, whom Da'ud married after the test. This is more than the number of wives that Muhammad had."

❋✲❋✲❋

Concerning Beating Women

'A'isha said, "The Messenger of Allah ﷺ never struck a woman or a servant with his hand, nor did he strike anything except in struggling in the way of Allah. He was not injured by anything and then took revenge on the one who did it, unless the sacred things of Allah were violated, and then he would take revenge for Allah."

'Ali ibn Husayn said, "The Messenger of Allah ﷺ never struck a woman or a servant with his hand, nor did he strike anything except in struggling in the way of Allah."

It is related from al-Qasim ibn Muhammad that the Messenger of Allah forbade striking women. It was said to him, "Messenger of Allah, they are being spoiled." He said, "Beat them, but only the worst of you will beat them."

Umm Kulthum bint Abi Bakr said, "Men were forbidden to hit women and then the men complained about the women to the Messenger of Allah and he allowed them to hit them. Then the Messenger of Allah said, 'In the night seventy women came to the family of Muhammad, all of whom had been beaten. I do not like to see a man with the veins of his neck swelling with anger against his wife, fighting her.'"

Ayyub said, "A woman whose husband had beaten her severely came to the Messenger of Allah. The Messenger of Allah got up and decried that. He said, 'One of you beats his wife like a slave and then embraces her without feeling shame.'"

It is related that the Prophet ﷺ said, "Do not beat women." They stopped beating them and 'Umar came to the Prophet and said, "Messenger of Allah, the women have become refractory towards their husbands." So he gave permission to beat them. The Prophet said, "In the night seventy women came to the family of Muhammad, all of whom complained about their husbands, and those men are not the best of you."

It is related from 'Abdullah ibn Shaddad that the Prophet ﷺ said, "The best of you are the best to their families and I am the best of you towards my family."

'Amra bint 'Abdu'r-Rahman said, "The Messenger of Allah was asked, 'Messenger of Allah, why don't you marry the women of the Ansar? There are some beauties among them.' The Messenger of Allah said, 'They are women with strong jealousy who will not be patient with co-wives. I have co-wives, and I dislike to vex a woman's people regarding her.'"

Concerning the Hajj of the Messenger of Allah with his Wives

Umm Salama said, "When the Messenger of Allah ﷺ went on the Farewell Hajj, all of his wives went on *hajj* with him in howdahs. We reached the Prophet at Dhu'l-Hulayfa at night. 'Abdu'r-Rahman ibn 'Awf and 'Uthman ibn 'Affan were with us."

It is related from Asma' bint Abi Bakr that when the Messenger of Allah ﷺ camped at al-'Araj, he sat in the open area of his camp and 'A'isha came to him and sat down beside him. Abu Bakr came and sat down on the other side of him. Asma' came and sat down beside Abu Bakr. The slave of Abu Bakr came wearing a shirt, and Abu Bakr said to him, "Where is your camel?" He said, "I've lost it." Abu Bakr went to him and began to hit him, saying, "You lose a single camel!" The Messenger of Allah began to smile and say, "Do you see what one in *ihram* does and is prohibited from doing?"

It is related from Ibn 'Abbas that some people disagreed about whether the Prophet fasted on the day of 'Arafa. Umm al-Fadl said, "I know more than you about that. I sent him a cup of milk, and he drank from it while he was speaking."

It is related from 'A'isha that Sawda bint Zam'a asked the Messenger of Allah ﷺ for permission to leave Muzdalifa before the crush of the people. She was a slow woman. He gave her permission, but kept his wives, so that they pushed on with him in the morning. 'A'isha said, "I wish I had asked the Messenger of Allah for permission to go on ahead from Muzdalifa as Sawda bint Zam'a asked permission, wanting to do it with his pleasure."

The mother of 'Imran ibn Abi Anas said, "I went ahead with Sawda, the wife of the Prophet, in his *hajj*. We stoned before dawn."

Ibn 'Abbas said, "I and my mother were among the weak and I was among those who went ahead of the Messenger of Allah on the night of Muzdalifa with his weak wife."

Ibn 'Abbas said, "We, the lads of the Banu 'Abdu'l-Muttalib, went ahead of the Messenger of Allah on the night of Muzdalifa, on red camels. He said, 'O sons, do not stone until the sun rises.'"

145

It is related from 'A'isha that the Prophet ﷺ mentioned Safiyya bint Huyayy and was told that she was menstruating. He said, "Will she detain us?" It was said, "Messenger of Allah, she has done the *Tawaf al-Ifada*." He said, "No, then."

It is related from Abu Hurayra that the Messenger of Allah ﷺ said to his wives on the Farewell *Hajj*, "It is this and then confinement will come." He said, "They all made the *hajj* again except for Sawda bint Zam'a and Zaynab bint Jahsh who both said, 'We will not ride an animal after the Messenger of Allah.'"

It is related from 'Ata' ibn Yasar that the Prophet said to his wives, "Whoever of you fears Allah and does not commit a clearly outrageous action [i.e. fornication] and clings to her confinement, she will be my wife in the Next World."

It is related from the mother of the aunt of Musa ibn Ya'qub az-Zama'i, "Zaynab bint Jahsh did not go on *hajj* after the *hajj* of the Messenger of Allah when she made *hajj* with him, until she died in the khalifate of 'Umar, in 20 AH."

It is related from Abu Ja'far that 'Umar ibn al-Khattab forbade the wives of the Prophet ﷺ to go on *hajj* or *'umra*.

The father of Sa'd said, "When 'Umar ibn al-Khattab went on *hajj* in 23 AH, and it was the last *hajj* that 'Umar made, the wives of the Prophet sent to him to ask permission to go, and he gave them permission and ordered that they be provisioned and carried in howdahs covered by green cloths. He sent 'Abdu'r-Rahman ibn 'Awf and 'Uthman ibn 'Affan with them. 'Uthman travelled on his camel in front of them. He did not let anyone come near them. 'Abdu'r-Rahman travelled on his camel behind them and did not let anyone come near them. They camped with 'Umar whenever he camped."

It is related that 'Abdu'r-Rahman said, "In the year in which he died, 'Umar sent me and 'Uthman with the wives of the Messenger of Allah ﷺ to take them on the *hajj*. 'Uthman went in front of them and did not let anyone come near them nor see them except for the one who looked towards them." 'Abdu'r-Rahman ibn 'Awf went behind them and did the like of that while they were in the howdahs.

They camped with them in the ravines and they spent the middle of the day in the ravines, and they alighted in the ravines and they did not let anyone come near them.

'A'isha said, "'Umar forbade us the *hajj* and *'umra* until the last year when he gave permission and we went on *hajj* with him. When 'Umar died and 'Uthman took charge, I, Umm Salama, Maymuna and Umm Habiba got together and sent to him to ask permission to go on the *hajj*. He said, "Umar did what you saw. I will go on *hajj* with you as 'Umar did. Whoever of you wants to go on *hajj*, I will take her.' 'Uthman made *hajj* with us all except for two women of us. Zaynab had died in the khalifate of 'Umar and 'Umar did not take her on *hajj*, and Sawda bint Zam'a did not leave her house after the death of the Prophet. We were kept well out of sight."

Umm Ma'bad bint Khalid said, "In the khalifate of 'Umar, I saw 'Uthman and 'Abdu'r-Rahman make *hajj* with the wives of the Messenger of Allah. Over their howdahs I saw green shawls. People were denied access to them. Ibn 'Affan went in front of them on his camel shouting whenever anyone came near them, 'Get away! Get away!' Ibn 'Awf was behind them doing the same thing. They camped at Qudayd near my dwelling, separated from the people and they were shielded by trees on every side. I went to them. There were eight of them in total. When I saw them, I sobbed and they said, 'What is making you weep?' I said, 'I remembered the Messenger of Allah.' Then they wept. I said, 'This was where he stopped with me.' They recognised me and greeted me and I had slaughtered some meat for them and provided some milk. They took all of that from me and each woman gave me an onion and said to me, 'When we arrive, Allah willing, and the Amir al-Mu'minin gives out the stipend, then come to us.' I went to them and each woman of them gave me fifty dinars. 'Uthman paid out the register in accordance with how 'Umar had paid it out."

Ibn Abi Nujayh said that the Messenger of Allah said, "The one who will be mindful of my wives is the truthful pious one." 'Abdu'r-Rahman ibn 'Awf travelled with them and set up their camp in the ravine which did not have an outlet and put shawls over their howdahs."

Al-Miswar ibn Makhrama said, "Sometimes I saw a man making his camel kneel on the road in order to repair a saddle or to put some of his gear in order. 'Uthman would meet him when he was in front of the wives of the Prophet. If the road was wide, he took the right or left side and went far from him. If there was no width, he stopped on one side until the man left or finished his task. I saw him meet people coming towards him from Makka on the road and he would say to them, 'Right' or 'Left'. He kept them at their distance until they had passed turning their eyes away as they went."

Al-Miswar said, "'Abdu'r-Rahman ibn 'Awf sold his property at Kaydama to 'Uthman ibn 'Affan for 40,000 dinars. When the money reached him, he called me and he also called 'Abdu'r-Rahman ibn al-Aswad and someone else. He said, 'Collect this property as you see fit. I will begin with the wives of the Prophet ﷺ. So he counted out a thousand dinars for each wife. When that reached them, they prayed for him and said, 'The Messenger of Allah said, "Only a truthful pious one will be mindful of you after me," meaning 'Abdu'r-Rahman ibn 'Awf.' Then he divided up what remained between his relatives and nothing was left for him."

Abu Salama ibn 'Abdu'r-Rahman said, "I said to 'A'isha, "Urwa is superior to us because he can visit you whenever he likes.' She said, 'Whenever you like, sit outside the Screen and ask me whatever you like. We did not find anyone after the Prophet ﷺ more connected to us than your father. The Messenger of Allah said, "Only the truthful pious one will be kind to you." He is 'Abdu'r-Rahman ibn 'Awf.'"

✳✳✳✳✳

Maria, the Mother of Ibrahim, the son of the Messenger of Allah

It is related that 'Abdullah ibn 'Abdu'r-Rahman ibn Abi Sa'sa'a said, "In 7 AH, the Muqawqis, the governor of Alexandria, sent the Messenger of Allah ﷺ Maria and her sister Serene, a thousand *mithqals* of gold, and twenty soft garments, his mule ad-Duldul and his donkey 'Ufayr. Accompanying them was a eunuch called Mabur, an old man who was the brother of Maria. He sent all of that with Hatib ibn Abi Balta'a. Hatib ibn Abi Balta'a offered Islam to Maria and encouraged her to accept it, and she and her sister became Muslim. The eunuch remained a Christian until he became Muslim in Madina later on in the time of the Messenger of Allah. The Messenger of Allah ﷺ liked the mother of Ibrahim. She was fair and beautiful. The Messenger of Allah lodged her in al-'Aliyya in the property which is now called Mashraba Umm Ibrahim. The Messenger of Allah used to visit her there and he set up the Screen for her. He had intercourse with her on the basis that she was his slave. When she became pregnant, she gave birth there and her midwife was Salma, the client of the Messenger of Allah. Abu Rafi', the husband of Salma, came and gave the Messenger of Allah the good news of Ibrahim. He gave him a slave. That was in Dhu'l-Hijja, 8 AH."

'A'isha said, "I was not jealous about a woman except for my jealousy towards Maria. That was because she was beautiful. The Messenger of Allah admired her. When she was first brought to him, he put her in the house of Haritha ibn an-Nu'man. She was our neighbour and the Messenger of Allah spent most of the day and night with her so that we became preoccupied about her. She became alarmed, so he moved her to al-'Aliyya and he used to visit there. It was hard on us. Then Allah gave him a son by her, and we were deprived of that."

Anas ibn Malik said, "Umm Ibrahim was the favourite of the Prophet."

Al-Qasim ibn Muhammad said, "The Messenger of Allah was alone with his slavegirl Maria in Hafsa's room. The Prophet ﷺ came out and she was sitting at the door. She said, 'Messenger of Allah! In my room and on my day!' The Prophet said, 'She is unlawful for me. Restrain yourself from me.' She said, 'I will not accept it without you swearing on oath to me.' So he said, 'By Allah, I will never touch her.'" Al-Qasim considered that the words about her being unlawful were not binding.

Az-Zuhri said, "Maria the mother of Ibrahim, and her sister were given by the Muqawqis to the Prophet. The Prophet ﷺ took the mother of Ibrahim and gave Serene to Hassan ibn Thabit."

Malik said, "The Messenger of Allah ﷺ said, 'Take care of the Copts. They have protection and kinship.'" He said, "Their kinship was that Isma'il ibn Ibrahim was from them and the mother of Ibrahim, the son of the Prophet, was from them."

Anas ibn Malik said, "The mother of Ibrahim, the favourite of the Prophet, was in her upper room and a Copt used to go to her and bring her water and wood. The people talked about that, saying, 'A barbarian visiting a barbarian.' The Messenger of Allah ﷺ heard about that and he sent 'Ali ibn Abi Talib after him. 'Ali found him by a palm tree. When the Copt saw the sword, he was alarmed and threw away the garment he was wearing and exposed himself. He was completely castrated. 'Ali went back to the Prophet and told him. He said, 'Messenger of Allah! Do you think that if you commanded one of us to do something and then he thought something else would be better, he should refer it back to you?' He said, 'Yes.' He told him about the Copt. Maria bore Ibrahim and Jibril came to the Prophet and said, 'Peace be upon you, Abu Ibrahim!' So the Messenger of Allah was put at ease by that."

The like of that is related about 'Ali although the narrator said, "'Ali went out and met him with a pot on his head bringing her some sweet water from a well. When 'Ali saw him, he unsheathed his sword and made for him. When the Copt saw him, he dropped the waterskin and climbed a palm tree and became naked. He was completely castrated. So 'Ali sheathed his sword and then went back to the Prophet and told him the news. The Messenger of Allah said, 'You were right. The witness sees what the one who is not present does not see.'"

Ibn 'Abbas said, "When the mother of Ibrahim gave birth, the Messenger of Allah ﷺ said, 'Her son has freed her.'"

It is related from Ibn 'Abbas that the Messenger of Allah said, "Any slavegirl who gives birth to her master's child is free when he dies unless he frees her before he dies."

There is a *hadith* from 'Abdu'r-Rahman ibn Hassan from his mother, Maria's sister, whose name was Serene and who had been given by the Prophet to Hassan ibn Thabit and who bore him 'Abdu'r-Rahman. She said, "I saw the Prophet ﷺ when Ibrahim was dying and my sister and I were crying out, and he did not forbid us. When he died, he forbade us to cry out and al-Fadl ibn 'Abbas washed him while the Messenger of Allah was sitting down. Then I saw him at the side of the grave and al-'Abbas was beside him. Al-Fadl and Usama ibn Zayd went down into the grave and the sun was eclipsed on that day. The people said, 'It is because of the death of Ibrahim.' The Mes senger of Allah said, 'It is not eclipsed for the death or life of anyone.' The Messenger of Allah saw a gap in the bricks and he ordered that it be blocked up. The Prophet ﷺ was asked about that and he said, 'It does not harm or benefit, but it satisfies the eye of the living. When the slave does an action, Allah likes it to be done well.'"

'Ata' said, "The mother of the child of the Messenger of Allah, Maria, was commanded to observe a waiting-period of three menstrual periods."

It is related that Abu Bakr maintained Maria until his death and then 'Umar maintained her until she died during his khalifate.

Muhammad ibn 'Umar said, "Maria, the mother of Ibrahim, son of the Prophet, died in the month of Muharram, 16 AH. 'Umar ibn al-Khattab gathered the people to attend and prayed over her. Her grave is in al-Baqi'."

✷✸✺✸✷

Concerning the Number of the Wives of the Prophet

Az-Zuhri said, "The first woman that the Messenger of Allah married before prophethood was Khadija bint Khuwaylid. Before him she had been married to 'Atiq ibn 'Abid al-Makhzumi and bore him a girl called Hind. Then after 'Atiq, Khadija married Abu Hala at-Tamimi, the ally of the Banu'd-Dar, and she bore him a son called Hind. Then the Messenger of Allah ﷺ married her when he was 25 and Khadija was 40. She bore him al-Qasim, at-Tahir, who is al-Mutahhir, who both died before he was a Prophet. She also bore him Zaynab, who was married to Abu'l-'As ibn ar-Rabi'. She was the oldest of the daughters of the Prophet. Then there was Ruqayya, who married 'Utayba ibn Abi Lahab and he divorced her before consummating the marriage. Then 'Uthman ibn 'Affan married her after prophethood. Then Khadija bore Umm Kulthum, whom 'Uthman married after Ruqayya. Then she bore Fatima, and 'Ali ibn Abi Talib married her. Khadija died on the 10th of Ramadan, in the tenth year of prophethood, three years before the *hijra,*when she was 65.

"Then after her the Messenger of Allah ﷺ married Sawda bint Zam'a al-'Amiriyya. She had been married to as-Sakran ibn 'Amr, the brother of Suhayl ibn 'Amr. They had emigrated together to Abyssinia and then returned to Makka where he died. The Messenger of Allah married Sawda bint Zam'a in Ramadan in the tenth year of prophethood, before he came to Madina. Then she was brought to Madina in Ramadan, in the tenth year of prophethood.

"Then after her he married 'A'isha bint Abi Bakr as-Siddiq in Makka when she was six in Shawwal, in the tenth year of prophethood. He consummated the marriage with her in Madina when she was nine in Shawwal, at the beginning of the eighth month of the *hijra.* He died when she was 18.

"Then he married Hafsa bint 'Umar ibn al-Khattab. Before him she had been married to Khunaysh ibn Hudhafa as-Sahmi. He died on his return from Badr and she did not bear him any children. The Messenger of Allah married her in Sha'ban at the beginning of the thirtieth month of the *hijra,* two months before Uhud.

"Then he married Umm Salama, the daughter of Abu Umayya ibn al-Mughira. Before him she had been married to Abu Salama ibn 'Abdu'l-Asad. From him she had 'Umar, Salama, Zaynab, and Barra. Abu Salama died in Madina after Uhud. The Messenger of Allah married her at the end of Shawwal, 4 AH.

"Then he married Juwayriyya bint al-Harith ibn Abi Dirar of the Banu'l-Mustaliq. Before him she had been married to her cousin, Safwan Dhu'sh-Shafr, ibn Malika. He was killed in the Battle of al-Muraysi' in Sha'ban, 5 AH.

"Then he married Zaynab bint Jahsh al-Asadiyya. Her mother was Umayma bint 'Abdu'l-Muttalib. Before him she was married to Zayd ibn Haritha, and she did not have any children from him. The Messenger of Allah married her in Dhu'l-Qa'da, 5 AH.

"Then he married Zaynab bint Khuzayma al-Hilaliyya, who is the Mother of the Poor. She died while married to him. Before him she had been married to at-Tufayl ibn al-Harith ibn al-Muttalib.

"Then he married Rayhana bint Zayd ibn 'Amr an-Nadriyya. Before him she had been married to a man of the Banu'n-Nadir called al-Hakam. Al-Hakam died. Rayhana died while the Messenger of Allah was still alive. The expedition against the Banu Qurayza occurred in Dhu'l-Qa'da or Dhu'l-Hijja, 5 AH.

"Then he married Umm Habiba, the daughter of Abu Sufyan ibn Harb, during the truce while she was in Abyssinia. He sent word to the Negus to marry him to her and he did so. Her guardian on the day of her marriage was Khalid ibn Sa'id ibn al-'As. Before the Messenger of Allah she had been married to 'Ubaydullah ibn Jahsh. He had become Muslim and emigrated to Abyssinia with the Muslims who emigrated. Then he apostatised and became a Christian. He died there as a Christian.

"Then he married Safiyya bint Huyayy ibn Akhtab. She was his property and then he set her free and married her. Before him she had been married. Her husband divorced her and she married Kinana ibn ar-Rabi' ibn Abi'l-Huyayq. He was killed on the Day of Khaybar. She did not bear them any children. She was captured from al-Qamus. The Messenger of Allah consummated the marriage with her at as-Sabha' in Jumada al-Akhira, 7 AH.

"Then he married Maymuna bint al-Harith al-Hilaliyya in Dhu'l-Qa'da, 7 AH. It was the year of the Fulfilled 'Umra. Before him she had been married to Abu Ruhm ibn 'Abdu'l-'Uzza al-'Amiri. He died and she did not bear him any children.

"He married Fatima bint ad-Dahhak ibn Sufyan al-Kilabiyya and she sought refuge from him and he parted from her. She used to visit the wives of the Prophet ﷺ and say, 'I am the wretch.' It is also said that he divorced her because of some white leprosy she had. He married her in Dhu'l-Qa'da, 8 AH, when he left al-Ji'rana, and she died in 60 AH.

"He married Asma' bint an-Nu'man al-Jawniyya and did not consummate the marriage with her. She is the one who sought refuge from him. He married her in Rabi' al-Awwal, 9 AH, and she died in the khalifate of 'Uthman ibn 'Affan with her family at Najd.

"They reject all that is mentioned about the Messenger of Allah marrying other than these women. They reject Qutayla bint Qays, the sister of al-Ash'ath ibn Qays. They reject the Kinana woman and other women whom he is said to have married other than those mentioned at the beginning of this account. They said, 'The Messenger of Allah ﷺ married fourteen women, six of whom were Qurayshi without a doubt: Khadija bint Khuwaylid ibn Asad ibn 'Abdu'l-'Uzza, 'A'isha bint Abi Bakr of the Banu Taym, Sawda bint Zam'a of the Banu 'Amir ibn Lu'ayy, Umm Salama bint Abi Umayya of the Banu Makhzum, Umm Habiba bint Abi Sufyan ibn Umayya of the Banu Umayya, and Hafsa bint 'Umar ibn al-Khattab of the Banu 'Adi ibn Ka'b. Among the Arabs he married Zaynab bint Jahsh al-Asadiyya, Maymuna bint al-Harith al-Hilaliyya, Juwayriyya bint al-Harith of al-Mustaliq, Asma' bint an-Nu'man al-Jawniyya, whose marriage was not consummated, Fatima bint ad-Dahhak al-Kilabiyya, and Zaynab bint Khuzayma al-Hilaliyya, the Mother of the Poor. He married Rayhana bint Zayd of the Banu'n-Nadir, who was part of the booty Allah gave him, and he married Safiyya bint Huyayy ibn Akhtab who was part of the booty Allah gave him.'"

'Amir said, "The Messenger of Allah married fourteen women."

It is related from Muhammad ibn Ka'b al-Qurazi, 'Umar ibn al-Hakam, and 'Abdullah ibn 'Ubaydullah, "The Messenger of Allah married thirteen women." Then they named all the wives of the Messenger of Allah mentioned in the first *hadith* except for Rayhana bint Zayd.

Muhammad ibn Huyayy said, "The Messenger of Allah ﷺ married fifteen women." He named the fourteen in the *hadith* and said, "He married a woman of the Banu Layth called Mulayka bint Ka'b." Muhammad ibn 'Umar said, "Abu Ma'shar mentioned that the Messenger of Allah married Mulayka bint Ka'b."

Muhammad ibn 'Umar said, "What is agreed upon is that the Messenger of Allah married fourteen women who are named in the first hadith. Of them he divorced the Jawni and Kilabi women. Those who died in his lifetime were Khadija bint Khuwaylid, Zaynab bint Khuzayma al-Hilaliyya and Rayhana bint Zayd an-Nadiriyya. The Messenger of Allah ﷺ died leaving nine wives. There is no disagreement about them. They are: 'A'isha bint Abi Bakr as-Siddiq, Hafsa bint 'Umar ibn al-Khattab, Umm Salama bint Abi Umayya, Umm Habiba bint Abi Sufyan ibn Harb, Sawda bint Zam'a, Zaynab bint Jahsh, Maymuna bint al-Harith al-Hilaliyya, Juwayriyya bint al-Harith al-Mustaliqiyya, and Safiyya bint Huyayy ibn Akhtab."

It is related that 'Urwa ibn az-Zubayr was asked whether the wives of the Messenger of Allah observed the waiting-period after his death. He said, "Yes, they observed a waiting period of four months and ten days." He was asked, "Abu 'Abdullah, why did they observe the waiting period when they were not lawful for anyone? The waiting period is for making free [of pregnancy]." 'Urwa became angry and said, "Perhaps you have taken His words, *'O wives of the Prophet! You are not like any other women.'* (33:32) They observed the waiting-period by the Book."

Ja'far ibn 'Abdullah ibn Abi'l-Hakam said, "The term of the wives of the Messenger of Allah ﷺ was four months and ten days. They visited one another and did not spend the night away from their houses. They were out of action until they were like nuns. Not one day or two or three passed by them except that each woman was heard sobbing."

Chapter Ten:
Qurayshi Women, their Allies, their Clients and Foreign Arab Women

Fatima bint Asad ibn Hashim

Her mother was Fatima bint Qays. She was the daughter of the uncle of Za'ida ibn al-Asamm, the grandfather of Khadija bint Khuwaylid, the wife of the Messenger of Allah on the mother's side. Fatima bint Asad was the wife of Abu Talib ibn 'Abdu'l-Muttalib. She bore him Talib, 'Aqil, Ja'far, 'Ali, Umm Hani', Jumana, and Rayta. Fatima bint Asad became Muslim. She was a righteous woman. The Messenger of Allah used to visit her and spend midday in her house.

❋❋❋❋❋

Ruqayqa bint Sayfi ibn Hashim

Her mother was Hala, or Tumadir bint Kalda ibn 'Abdu Manaf. She was married to Nawfal ibn Uhayb ibn 'Abdu Manaf. She bore him Makhrama, Safwan and Umayya.

Ruqayqa bint Sayfi said, "I can recall my uncle Shayba (meaning 'Abdu'l-Muttalib) and I was still a girl that day. Al-Muttalib ibn 'Abd Manaf visited us and I was the first to run to him. I clung to him and told my family he was there." On that day she was older than 'Abdu'l-Muttalib. She became Muslim and joined the Messenger of Allah ﷺ and she was the harshest of people towards her son, Makhrama, before he became Muslim.

It is related that Ruqayqa bint Sayfi, the mother of Makhrama ibn Nawfal, warned the Messenger of Allah ﷺ saying, "Quraysh has gathered together intending to come at you during the night." Al-

Miswar said, "The Messenger of Allah ﷺ left his bed and 'Ali ibn Abi Talib spent the night in it."

＊＊＊＊＊

Umm Ayman, who is Baraka, the client and nursemaid of the Prophet

The Messenger of Allah ﷺ inherited her from his father along with five camels and some sheep. The Messenger of Allah freed Umm Ayman when he married Khadija bint Khuwaylid, and she married 'Ubayd ibn Zayd of the Banu al-Harith ibn al-Khazraj. Umm Ayman bore him Ayman. He was a Companion of the Prophet and was killed as a martyr at Hunayn. Zayd ibn Haritha al-Kalbi was the client of Khadija bint Khuwaylid. She gave him to the Messenger of Allah who freed him and he married Umm Ayman after prophethood and she bore him Usama ibn Zayd.

It is related that the Messenger of Allah ﷺ said to Umm Ayman, "O mother," and when he looked at her, she said, "This is a remnant of the people of my House."

'Uthman ibn al-Qasim said, "When Umm Ayman emigrated, she was detained at al-Munsarif below ar-Rawha'. She became thirsty but did not have any water. She was fasting. Thirst was hard for her and then a bucket of water descended from heaven with a white feather. She took it and drank from it until she was quenched. She used to say, 'No thirst afflicted me after that. I had been known for thirst when fasting among the emigrants, but after that drink I was not thirsty; even when I fasted on a hot day I was not thirsty.'"

Sufyan ibn 'Uqba said, "Umm Ayman used to be kind to the Prophet and care for him. The Messenger of Allah ﷺ said, 'Whoever is happy to marry a woman of the Garden should marry Umm Ayman,' So Zayd ibn Haritha married her and she bore him Usama ibn Zayd."

It is related from Mujahid that the Prophet ﷺ said, "Cover yourself with your head-covering, Umm Ayman."

Muhammad ibn Qays said, "Umm Ayman went to the Prophet and said, 'Give me a mount.' He said, 'I will mount you on the offspring of the she-camel.' She said, 'Messenger of Allah, it will not be able to support me and I do not want it.' He said, 'I will only mount you on the offspring of the she-camel.' He was intending to joke with her. The Messenger of Allah used to joke, but he only spoke the truth. All camels are the offspring of she-camels."

It is related that when Umm Ayman visited the Prophet, she said, "Peace, not on you," and so the Messenger of Allah allowed her to simply say, 'Peace.'

It is related from Abu'l-Huwayrith that Umm Ayman said [about those who fled] on the Day of Hunayn, "May Allah stop your feet!" The Prophet ﷺ said, "Be quiet, Umm Ayman. You are harsh-tongued."

It is related from Anas ibn Malik from the Prophet ﷺ that a man had set aside some palm trees for him. When the Qurayza and an-Nadir were defeated, he returned that. Anas said, "My family told me to go to the Prophet and ask him for that which he had to give or some of it. The Prophet ﷺ had given it to Umm Ayman. She said, 'I asked the Prophet and he gave them to me.' Umm Ayman came and put a cloth on my neck and began to say, 'No, by the One who is the only God, I will not give them to you! He gave them to me.' The Prophet of Allah ﷺ said, 'You will have such-and-such.' She said, 'No, by Allah!' He said, 'You will have the like', of what he gave her. I reckon that he said ten times like it or about that."

Muhammad ibn 'Umar said, "Umm Ayman was at Uhud and she was bringing water and treating the wounded, and she was at Khaybar with the Messenger of Allah."

Az-Zuhri said, "While Harmala, the client of Usama ibn Zayd, was sitting with 'Abdullah ibn 'Umar, al-Hajjaj ibn Ayman entered and prayed a prayer in which he did not complete his bowing or his prostration. Ibn 'Umar called him when he said the *salam*. He said, 'Brother, do you reckon that you have prayed? You have not prayed. Repeat your prayer.'" He said, "When al-Hajjaj turned away,

'Abdullah ibn 'Umar said to me, 'Who is this?' I replied, 'Al-Hajjaj ibn Ayman, the son of Umm Ayman.' Ibn 'Umar said, 'If the Messenger of Allah ﷺ had seen this man, he would have loved him.' Then he mentioned his love for the offspring of Umm Ayman. She was the nursemaid of the Prophet."

Tariq ibn Shihab said, "When the Prophet ﷺ died, Umm Ayman wept. It was said to her, 'Why are you weeping?' She said, 'I am weeping for the [stoppage of the] news of heaven.'"

It is related from Anas that Umm Ayman wept when the Prophet died. She was asked, "Why are you weeping?" She said, "By Allah, I knew that the Messenger of Allah would die, but I am weeping for the revelation since it has been cut off from us from heaven."

Tariq ibn Shihab said, "When 'Umar was murdered, Umm Ayman wept and said, 'Today! When Islam is dominant!'" Qabisa said in his variant, "Umm Ayman wept when the Prophet died and she was asked about that and she said, 'I am weeping for the [stoppage of the] news of heaven.'"

Muhammad ibn 'Umar said, "Umm Ayman died at the beginning of the khalifate of 'Uthman."

Muhammad ibn 'Umar said, "There was a dispute between Ibn Abi'l-Furtat, the client of Usama ibn Zayd and al-Hasan ibn Usama. In the course of the discussion, Ibn Abi'l-Furat said to him, 'Son of Baraka!' meaning Umm Ayman. Al-Hasan said, 'Bear witness!' The business was taken to Abu Bakr ibn Muhammad ibn 'Amr ibn Hazm, who was the Qadi of Madina at that time, or the governor of 'Umar ibn 'Abdu'l-'Aziz. The story was recounted to him and Abu Bakr said to Ibn Abi'l-Furat, 'What did you mean by your words, "Son of Baraka"?' He said, 'I have named him by her name.' Abu Bakr said, 'You meant by this to belittle her in spite of her position in Islam and her position with the Messenger of Allah who said to her, "O mother," and "O Umm Ayman." Allah will not release me if I release you.' He had him beaten with 70 lashes."

✳✶✳✶✳

Salma, the client of the Messenger of Allah

I have heard it said that she was the client of Safiyya bint 'Abdu'l-Muttalib. Salma was the wife of Abu Rafi', the client of the Messenger of Allah and the mother of his children. She is the one who was the midwife of Khadija bint Khuwaylid when she bore the children of the Messenger of Allah. She would prepare what was needed in advance. She was the midwife of Maria, the mother of Ibrahim when she bore Ibrahim. She went to her husband, Abu Rafi', and informed him that Maria had given birth to a boy. Abu Rafi' gave the Messenger of Allah the good news. The Messenger of Allah gave him a slave. Salma was present with the Messenger of Allah at Khaybar.

Khadija bint al-Husayn ibn al-Harith

She became Muslim and gave allegiance to the Messenger of Allah. The Messenger of Allah assigned her and her sister Hind a hundred *wasqs* from Khaybar.

Hind bint al-Husayn ibn al-Harith

She became Muslim and gave allegiance to the Messenger of Allah. The Messenger of Allah assigned her and her sister Khadija a hundred *wasqs* from Khaybar.

Umm Rimtha

Or Umm Rumaytha bint 'Amr ibn Hashim. She became Muslim and gave allegiance to the Messenger of Allah ﷺ. The Messenger of Allah assigned her forty *wasqs* of dates from Khaybar and five *wasqs* of barley. She was the mother of Hakim, Abu'l-Qa'qa' ibn Hakim.

Buhayna

Her name is 'Abda bint al-Harith. Her mother was Umm Sayfi bint al-Aswad ibn al-Muttalib ibn Asad. She married Malik, a man of Azd, their ally, and bore him 'Abdullah and Jubayr. She accompanied the Prophet. Buhayna became Muslim and gave allegiance to the Messenger of Allah. The Messenger of Allah assigned her 30 *wasqs*.

Hind bint Uthatha ibn 'Abbad

Her mother was Umm Mistah bint Abi Ruhm ibn al-Muttalib. She became Muslim and gave allegiance to the Messenger of Allah ﷺ. The Messenger of Allah assigned her and her brother, Mistah ibn Uthatha, thirty *wasqs* from Khaybar. Hind emigrated with Abu Jundub and bore him Rayta.

Umm Mistah bint Abi Ruhm ibn al-Muttalib

Her mother was Rayta bint Sakhr. Uthatha ibn 'Abbad married her and she bore him Mistah, one of the people of Badr, and Hind. Umm Mistah became a good Muslim and was one of the strongest of people against Mistah when he spoke with the people of the Lie about 'A'isha, may Allah be pleased with her.

❊❊❊❊❊

Arwa bint Kurayz ibn Rabi'a

Her mother was Umm Hakim al-Bayda' bint 'Abdu'l-Muttalib. She married 'Uthman ibn Abi'l-'As and bore him 'Uthman and Amina. Then she married 'Uqba ibn Abi Mu'ayt and bore him al-Walid, 'Ammara, Khalid, Umm Kulthum, Umm Hakim and Hind. Arwa bint Kurayz became Muslim and emigrated to Madina after her daughter, Umm Kulthum bint 'Uqba and gave allegiance to the Messenger of Allah. She remained in Madina until she died during the khalifate of 'Uthman ibn 'Affan.

'Abdullah ibn Ka'b, the client of the family of 'Uthman, said that 'Abdullah ibn Hanzala said, "We were there when the mother of

'Uthman ibn 'Affan died. We buried her at al-Baqi'. He returned and led the people in the prayer in the mosque. 'Uthman prayed alone in the mosque, and I prayed beside him." He said, "I heard him say in prostration. 'O Allah, have mercy on my mother!' or 'O Allah, forgive my mother!' That was during his khalifate."

'Isa ibn Talha said, "I saw 'Uthman ibn 'Affan carrying the bed of his mother between the two pillars from the house of Ghutaysh until he put her down at the place of funeral prayers." He said, "After she was buried, I saw him standing at her grave making supplication for her."

✻✻✻✻✻

Umm Kulthum bint 'Uqba ibn Abi Mu'ayt

Her mother was Arwa ibn Kurayz. She became Muslim in Makka and gave allegiance before the *hijra*. She was the first woman to emigrate after the Messenger of Allah ﷺ emigrated to Madina. We do not know of any Qurayshi woman who left her parents as a Muslim to emigrate to Allah and His Messenger except for Umm Kulthum bint 'Uqba. She left Makka alone and accompanied a man of Khuza'a and arrived in Madina after the Truce of al-Hudaybiyya. Her brothers, al-Walid and 'Ammara, the sons of 'Uqba, set out after her. They arrived in Madina the day after she had arrived. They said, "O Muhammad, fulfil for us our precondition and that on which we concluded the treaty." Umm Kulthum said, "Messenger of Allah! I am a woman and the state of women is among those who are weak as you know. If you return me to the unbelievers, they will test me in my *deen* and I may not have endurance." So Allah broke the contract regarding women in the Truce of al-Hudaybiyya and sent down the test about them and gave a judgement about that which pleased all of them. He sent down about Umm Kulthum, *"Submit them to a test. Allah has best knowledge of their belief."* (60:10) So the Messenger of Allah tested her and tested the women after her, saying, "By Allah, is it only love of Allah and His Messenger and Islam which has brought you out, or have you not left for a husband or for money?" When they said that, they were kept and not returned to their families. The Messenger of Allah ﷺ said to al-Walid and 'Ammara,

"Allah has broken the treaty regarding women by what you know, so leave." Umm Kulthum did not have a husband in Makka. When she came to Madina , she married Zayd ibn Haritha al-Kalbi and she bore him children. He was killed on the Day of Mu'ta and then she married az-Zubayr ibn al-'Awwam and bore him Zaynab.

Maymun said, "Umm Kulthum bint 'Uqba ibn Abi Mu'ayt was married to az-Zubayr ibn al-'Awwam. He had some harshness towards women and she disliked him. So she asked him for a divorce. He refused her until he divorced her unwittingly. Once she pestered him while he was doing *wudu'* for the prayer and he divorced her with a single divorce. Then she left and gave birth. One of his family met him and told him that she had given birth. He said, 'She tricked me, may Allah trick her!' He went to the Prophet ﷺ and mentioned that to him and he said, 'The Book of Allah has decided regarding her position, so propose to her again.' He said, 'She will never come back to me.'"

Muhammad ibn 'Umar said, "Then she married 'Abdu'r-Rahman ibn 'Awf and bore him Ibrahim and Hamid. 'Abdu'r-Rahman then died while she was married to him. Then she married 'Amr ibn al-'As and she died while married to him."

❋✶❋✶❋

Umama bint Abi'l-'As ibn ar-Rabi'

Her mother was Zaynab, the daughter of the Messenger of Allah.

Abu Qatada said, "While we were at the door of the Messenger of Allah, he came out to us carrying Umama bint Abi'l-'As. Her mother was Zaynab, daughter of the Messenger of Allah. She was a child." He said, "The Messenger of Allah prayed with her on his shoulder and put her down when he bowed and put her back on his shoulder when he stood up until he finished the prayer."

It is related from 'Ali ibn Zayd that the Messenger of Allah ﷺ visited his family with an onyx necklace. He said, "I will give it to the one among you for whom I have the most compassion." They said, "He will give it to the daughter of Abu Bakr." He called the daughter of Abu'l-'As by Zaynab and he held her by the hand and there was some secretion from her eye which he wiped off with his hand.

It is related from 'A'isha that the Negus gave the Messenger of Allah ﷺ some jewellery which included a gold ring. He took it and turned away from it and then sent it to his granddaughter, the daughter of his daughter Zaynab. He said, "Adorn yourself with it, girl."

Muhammad ibn 'Umar said, "'Ali ibn Abi Talib married Umama bint Abi'l-'As after Fatima the daughter of the Messenger of Allah. He was killed while married to her and she did not bear him any children. Then she married al-Mughira ibn Nawfal."

✳✳✳✳✳

Umm Khalid bint Khalid

She is Ama bint Khalid ibn Sa'id ibn al-'As. Her mother was Humayma bint Khalaf of Khuza'a. Khalid ibn Sa'id emigrated to Abyssinia with his wife Humayma bint Khalaf and there she bore him Ama bint Khalid. She remained in Abyssinia until they came in the two boats. Ama had reached puberty and had discernment.

Umm Khalid bint Khalid said, "On the day we left, I heard the Negus say to his the people of the two boats, 'All of you convey my greeting to the Messenger of Allah.'" Ama said, "I was one of those who conveyed the greeting of the Negus to the Messenger of Allah." She related *hadiths* from the Messenger of Allah ﷺ.

Umm Khalid bint Khalid said, "The Messenger of Allah was brought some clothes which included a small black wrap. He said, 'Who do you think I should give this wrap to?' The people were silent. He said,' Bring me Umm Khalid.' I was carried to the Messenger of Allah. He put it on me with his hand. He said, 'Wear it until it is worn out,' two or three times. He began to look at a yellow or red border of the wrap. He said 'This is *sana*, Umm Khalid. This is *sana*, Umm Khalid.' He pointed with his finger at the border." "*Sana*" means "beautiful" in Abyssinian.

Ishaq said, "A woman of my people said that she saw the wrap with Umm Khalid."

Ibrahim ibn 'Uqba said, "I listened to Umm Khalid bint Khalid ibn Sa'd. She was a very old woman who had been born in Abyssinia. I said to her, 'Did you hear anything from the Messenger of Allah?' She said, 'I heard the Messenger of Allah ﷺ seeking refuge from the punishment of the grave.'"

Muhammad ibn 'Umar said, "Az-Zubayr ibn al-'Awwam married Ama bint Khalid and she bore him 'Umar and Khalid. Ama was therefore called Umm Khalid.

❊✳❊✳

Hind bint 'Uqba ibn Rabi'a

Her mother was Safiyya bint Umayya. Hind married Hafs ibn al-Mughira of Makhzum and bore him Aban.

'Abdu'l-Malik ibn Nawfal, a shaykh of the people of Madina from the Banu 'Amir ibn Lu'ayy, said, "Hind said to her father, 'I am a woman with control over my affairs. Do not give me in marriage to a man until you have let me consider him first.' He said to her, 'You have that.' Then one day he said to her, 'Two men of your people have asked to marry you. I will not tell you their names until I have described them to you. The first has nobility and noble lineage which will distract you from his foolish haste and heedlessness. His nobility atones for his nature. He is good company and has a ready reply. If you follow him, he will follow you. If you make a decision, he will be with you. You can compel him as you like in his property and not bother about his weakness. The other man is the paragon of his clan in his noble lineage and intelligent opinion. He disciplines his family and they do not discipline him. If they follow him, it is easier for them. If they contend with him, he is hard on them. He has great jealousy, and is swift in regaining his composure and is strong in defending his home. If he is hungry, he does not importune; and if someone contends with him, he is not defeated. So the state of both of them is clear to you.' She said, 'As for the first, he is a master who wastes his noble woman, respecting her when she may be pliant after her refusal. She wastes herself. If she brings him a child, she is foolish. If she begets noble sons, it is from error. Do not bother to mention this man and do not name him. As for the other one, he is the proper husband of a noble free woman. I admire his character and I accept him. I will accept the discipline of my husband and I will cling to my tent and care little. Our child is worthy of defending the women of his clan and protecting its cohesion in adversity. Who is he?' He said, 'That is Abu Sufyan ibn Harb.' She said, 'Marry me to him and do not give me to him in an obsequious manner. Ask Allah above for the best and He will choose for you by His knowledge of the decree.'"

Muhammad ibn Sharahil al-'Abdari said, "When Abu Sufyan ibn Harb consummated the marriage with Hind ibn 'Uqba ibn Rabi'a, 'Uqba ibn Rabi'a sent his son, al-Walid, to the Banu Abu'l-Huqayq and borrowed their jewellery. Al-Walid gave himself as the pledge along with a group of the Banu 'Abdu Shams. He took the jewellery and was absent for a month and then they returned it in full and they released the pledge."

'Abdullah ibn az-Zubayr said, "On the Day of the Conquest, Hind bint 'Uqba became Muslim as did the other women. They went to the Messenger of Allah while he was at al-Abtah to give him allegiance. Hind spoke and said, 'Messenger of Allah, praise belongs to Allah who has given victory to the *deen* which He chose for Himself so that I benefit by your mercy. Muhammad, I am a woman who believes in Allah and confirms His Messenger.' Then she removed her veil and said, 'I am Hind bint 'Uqba.' The Messenger of Allah said, 'Welcome to you.' She said, 'By Allah, there was no one on the earth of the people of any land whom I wanted to abase more than your land. Now there is no one on the earth whose land I would want to be more exalted than your land.' The Messenger of Allah said, 'And more.' He read the Qur'an to them and took their allegiance. Hind spoke out among them, 'Messenger of Allah, do we take your hand?' He said, 'I do not shake hands with women. My word to a hundred woman is like my word to one woman.'"

Muhammad ibn 'Umar said, "When Hind became Muslim, she began to strike an idol in her house with an axe until she smashed it to pieces, saying, 'We were deluded about you!'"

'A'isha said, "Hind went to the Messenger of Allah and said, 'Messenger of Allah, Abu Sufyan is a stingy man who does not give what is adequate for me and my children unless I take it from his money without him knowing.' He said, 'Take what is enough for you and your child in a correct manner.'"

It is related from Maymun ibn Mahran that some women including Hind, the daughter of 'Utba ibn Rabi'a and the mother of Mu'awiya, came to the Prophet ﷺ to give him allegiance. When he said, "Do not associate anything with Allah and do not steal," Hind said, "Messenger of Allah, Abu Sufyan is a stingy man. Is there anything held against me if I take some of his food without his permission?" He said that the Messenger of Allah ﷺ sanctioned that in fresh food but did not allow it in dry food. He said, "Do not fornicate." She said, "Does a free woman fornicate?" He said, "Do not kill your children." She said, "Have you left us a child that you did not kill at Badr?" He said, "Do not disobey me in anything correct." Maymun said, "Allah did not give His Prophet obedience from them except in what is correct, and what is correct is obedience to Allah Almighty."

It is related that ash-Sha'bi was heard to mention that when the women gave allegiance, the Messenger of Allah ﷺ said, "Give allegiance on the basis that you do not associate anything with Allah." Hind said, "We say that." "Nor should you steal." Hind said, "I took something from the property of Abu Sufyan." Abu Sufyan said, "What you took of my property is lawful for you." He said, "You should not commit fornication." Hind said, "Does a free woman fornicate?" He said, "You should not kill your children." Hind said, "You have killed them."

※✳※✳※

Umm Kulthum bint 'Uqba ibn Rabi'a

Her mother was the daughter of Haritha ibn al-Awqas. She married 'Abdu'r-Rahman ibn 'Awf and bore him Salim the elder before Islam.

※✳※✳※

Fatima bint 'Uqba ibn Rabi'a

Her mother was Safiyya bint Umayya. She married Quraza ibn 'Abd 'Amr ibn Nawfal and bore him al-Walid, Hisham, Ubayy, 'Utba, and Muslim, who was killed in the Battle of the Camel, and Fatikha. Then she was married to 'Abdullah ibn 'Amir. They said, "Then Abu Hudhayfa ibn 'Utba married Fatima bint 'Uqba to Salim, the client of Abu Hudhayfa. She became Muslim and gave her allegiance."

Ibn Abi Mulayka said, "'Aqil ibn Abi Talib married Fatima bint 'Uqba. She had sizeable wealth and said, 'I will marry you provided that you are responsible for my property and I pay you.' He married her. When he went in to her, she used to say, 'Where is 'Utba ibn Rabi'a? Where is Shayba ibn Rabi'a?' One day he went in to her when he was annoyed. She said, 'Where is 'Utba ibn Rabi'a? Where is Shayba ibn Rabi'a?' He replied, 'On your left when you enter the Fire.' She tightened her garment around her and said, 'My head and yours will never be joined!' She went to 'Uthman and he sent Mu'awiya and Ibn 'Abbas. Ibn 'Abbas said, 'By Allah, I will not part them.' Mu'awiya said, 'I would not part two elders of the Banu 'Abdu Manaf.' They went and brought them together and put things right between them."

It is related from 'Ikrima that 'Uthman, who sent Ibn 'Abbas and Mu'awiya, said, "If you think that you can join them, then join them. If you think they should separate, then separate them." That was about Fatima bint 'Uqba and 'Aqil ibn Abi Talib. He said, "She was recalcitrant towards 'Aqil."

✳✳✳✳

Ramla bint Shayba ibn Rabi'a

Her mother was Umm Shirak bint Waqdan of the Banu 'Amir ibn Lu'ayy. Ramla married 'Uthman ibn 'Affan and bore him 'A'isha, Umm Aban, and Umm 'Amr. Abu'z-Zinad, whose name is 'Abdullah ibn Dhakwan, was the client of Ramla bint Shayba. Ramla became Muslim and gave her allegiance to the Prophet.

Umayna bint Abi Sufyan ibn Harb

Her mother was Sufayya bint Abi'l-'As. She married Huwaytib ibn 'Abdu'l-'Uzza of the Banu 'Amir ibn Lu'ayy. She bore him Abu Sufyan. Then she was married to Safwan ibn Umayya and she bore him 'Abdu'r-Rahman.

Juwayriyya bint Abi Sufyan ibn Harb

Her mother was Hind bint 'Utba. She married as-Sa'ib ibn Abi Hubaysh and after him 'Abdu'r-Rahman ibn al-Harith.

Umm Hakam bint Abi Sufyan ibn Harb

Her mother was Hind bint 'Utba. She married 'Abdullah ibn 'Uthman of Thaqif and bore him 'Abdu'r-Rahman. He was called Ibn Umm al-Hakam.

Hind bint Abi Sufyan ibn Harb

Her mother was Safiyya bint Abi 'Amr. She married al-Harith ibn Nawfal and bore him 'Abdullah, Muhammad the elder, Rabi'a, 'Abdu'r-Rahman, Ramla, and Umm az-Zubayr who was the mother of al-Mughira and Zhurayba.

Sakhra bint Abi Sufyan ibn Harb

Her mother was Safiyya bint Abi 'Amr. She married Sa'id ibn al-Akhnas and bore him children.

Maymuna bint Abi Sufyan ibn Harb

Her mother was Lubaba bint Abi'l-'As. She married 'Urwa ibn Mas'ud ath-Thaqafi and bore him children and then she was married to al-Mughira ibn Shu'ba ath-Thaqafi.

Hamna bint Jahsh ibn Rithab

Her mother was Umayma bint 'Abdul-Muttalib. Jahsh ibn Rithab was the ally of Harb ibn Umayya. Hamna was married to Mus'ab ibn 'Umayr and bore him a daughter. He was killed in the Battle of Uhud.

Muhammad ibn 'Abdullah ibn Jahsh said, "When the Messenger of Allah returned from Uhud, the women went to ask people about their folk. They did not get any information until they went to the Prophet ﷺ and when any woman asked him, he informed her. Hamna bint Jahsh came to him and he said, 'Hamna, expect that your brother, 'Abdullah ibn Jahsh, will be rewarded.' She said, *'We belong to Allah and to Him we return.* (2:156) May Allah have mercy on him and forgive him.' Then he said, 'Hamna, expect that your uncle, Hamza ibn 'Abdu'l-Muttalib will be rewarded.' She said, *'We belong to Allah and to Him we return.* May Allah have mercy on him and forgive him.' Then he said, 'Hamna, expect that your husband, Mus'ab ibn 'Umayr, will be rewarded.' She said, 'O loss!' The Prophet said, 'The man has a place in the woman which nothing else has.'"

Muhammad ibn 'Umar said about the *hadith*, "The Prophet ﷺ said to her, 'Why do you say about Mus'ab what you do not say about others?' She said, 'Messenger of Allah, I remembered that his children are orphans.'" He said, "She was present at Uhud giving water to the thirsty and treating the wounded. The Messenger of Allah assigned her thirty *wasqs* from Khaybar. After that she married Talha ibn 'Ubaydullah and she bore him Muhammad ibn Talha as-Sajjad and 'Imran ibn Talha.

❈❈❈❈❈

Habiba, or Umm Habib bint Jahsh ibn Rithab

Her mother was Umayma bint 'Abdu'l-Muttalib. Habiba was the woman who had constant bleeding. Some of the people of *hadith* switch her name about and say, Umm Habiba. She is Umm Habib and her name was Habiba.

It is related from 'A'isha that Umm Habiba bint Jahsh had constant bleeding for seven years. She was married to 'Abdu'r-Rahman ibn 'Awf. She asked the Messenger of Allah about that and the Messenger of Allah said, "This is a vein. It is not menstruation. Do a *ghusl* and pray." She said, "She used to do a *ghusl* for every prayer."

Muhammad ibn 'Umar said, "Some of them err and relate that the woman with constant bleeding was Hamna bint Jahsh and believe that her *kunya* was Umm Habiba. The matter is as we have stated. She is Habiba, Umm Habib bint Jahsh. She did not bear 'Abdu'r-Rahman ibn 'Awf any children."

✳✳✳✳✳

Umm Qays bint Mihsan

She is the sister of 'Ukkasha ibn Mihsan, of the people of Badr, the allies of Harb ibn Umayya. She related from the Messenger of Allah ﷺ. She became Muslim early on in Makka and emigrated to Madina with the people of her house.

It is related that Umm Qays bint Mihsan, the sister of 'Ukkasha ibn Mihsan, said, "I went to the Messenger of Allah ﷺ with a son of mine who had not yet eaten food. He put him on his lap and he urinated on the garment of the Messenger of Allah. He called for water and sprinkled it on and did not wash it."

✳✳✳✳✳

Amina bint Ruqaysh ibn Rithab

She is the sister of Yazid ibn Ruqaysh, one of the people of Badr. She became Muslim early on in Makka and emigrated to Madina with the people of her house.

Judhama bint Jandal al-Asadiyya

She became Muslim early on in Makka and gave allegiance and emigrated to Madina with her family.

It is related that 'Uthman al-Jahshi said, "The Banu Ghanim were the allies of Harb ibn Umayya, the people of Islam. They became Muslim at Makka and were all moved to emigrate, both their men and women. Among the women who left on *hijra* were Zaynab, Habiba, and Hamna, the daughters of Jahsh, and Judhama bint Jandal, Umm Qays bint Mihsan, Amina bint Ruqaysh and Umm Habib bint Nabbata."

Muhammad ibn 'Umar said, "Judhama bint Jandal was married to Unays ibn Qatada who was present at Badr and was killed as a martyr at Uhud. Judhama related *hadith* from the Messenger of Allah."

It is related from 'A'isha, the wife of the Prophet, that Judhama bint Jandal informed her that she heard the Messenger of Allah say, "I wanted to forbid the *ghila* and then I remembered that the Greeks and Persians used to do that and it did not harm their children."

Malik ibn Anas said, "*Ghila* is that a man has intercourse with his wife while she is breast-feeding."

✳✳✳✳✳

Umm Habiba bint Nabbata al-Asadiyya

She became Muslim and gave allegiance to the Messenger of Allah and emigrated to Madina with those of her people who emigrated.

✳✳✳✳✳

Nafisa bint Umayya ibn Ubayy of Tamim

Her mother was Munya bint Jabir. Munya was the paternal aunt of 'Utba ibn Ghazwan. They were all allies of al-Harith ibn Nawfal ibn 'Abdu Manaf. Nafisa bint Umayya became Muslim and she is the one who arranged things between the Messenger of Allah and Khadija until the Messenger of Allah married her.

✳✳✳✳✳

Al-Hawla' bint Tuwayt ibn Habib

She became Muslim and gave allegiance to the Messenger of Allah after the *hijra*.

✻✻✻✻✻

Fatima bint Abi Hubaysh

She married 'Abdullah ibn Jahsh and bore him Muhammad.

It is related that 'A'isha said, "Fatima bint Abi Hubaysh came to the Prophet ﷺ and said, 'Messenger of Allah, I am a woman who has constant bleeding. I do not become pure. Do I abandon the prayer?' The Messenger of Allah said, 'That is a vein and not menstruation. When menstruation comes, leave the prayer, and when menstruation finishes, then wash the blood from yourself and pray."

✻✻✻✻✻

Busra bint Safwan ibn Nawfal

Her mother was Salima bint Umayya ibn Haritha. Her half-brother was 'Uqba ibn Abi Mu'ayt. Busra was married to al-Mughira ibn Abi'l-'As and bore him Mu'awiya ibn al-Mughira who was killed when the Messenger of Allah left Uhud. He is the grandfather of 'Abdu'l-Malik ibn Marwan. 'Abdu'l-Malik's mother was 'A'isha bint Mu'awiya ibn al-Mughira.

It is related that Marwan ibn al-Hakam heard Busra bint Safwan say that she heard the Messenger of Allah ﷺ say, "When one of you touches his penis, he should do *wudu'*."

✻✻✻✻✻

Baraka bint Yasar

She is the sister of Abu Tajra, the client of the Banu 'Abdu'd-Dar. They said, "We are from the Yemen from Azd, the allies of the Banu 'Abdu'd-Dar." Baraka became Muslim in Makka early on and gave *bay'a* and emigrated to Abyssinia in the second emigration with her husband, Qays ibn 'Abdullah al-Asadi. Yasar has the *kunya* of Abu Fukayha.

Fukayha bint Yasar

She was Baraka's sister. She became Muslim in Makka early on and gave her allegiance and emigrated to Abyssinia in the second emigration with her husband, Hattab ibn al-Harith.

✳✳✳✳✳

Barra bint Abi Tajra ibn Abi Fukayha

Barra related from the Messenger of Allah.

It is related that Barra bint Abi Tajra said, "When Allah wanted to honour the Messenger of Allah ﷺ and his prophethood began, when he went out for the call of nature, he went far so that no house could be seen and he went to ravines and the bottoms of valleys. He did not pass by a stone or a tree but that it said, 'Peace be upon you, Messenger of Allah.' He turned to his right and left and behind him without seeing anyone."

✳✳✳✳✳

Habiba bint Abi Tajra

She was Barra's sister. She related *hadith* from the Messenger of Allah.

'Ata' ibn Abi Rabah said, "Safiyya bint Shayba related to me from a woman called Habiba bint Abi Tajra who said, 'We entered the house of Abu Husayn with some women of Quraysh.' The Prophet ﷺ went around until his garment went in a circle, saying to his Companions, 'Strive. Allah Almighty has written striving for you.'"

✳✳✳✳✳

'Atika bint 'Awf

She is the full sister of 'Abdu'r-Rahman ibn 'Awf. Their mother was ash-Shifa bint 'Awf. She married Makhrama ibn Nawfal and bore him al-Miswar, Safwan the elder, and Umm Safwan. 'Atika bint 'Awf became Muslim as did her mother, and they gave allegiance to the Messenger of Allah ﷺ.

Ash-Shifa bint 'Awf

Her mother was Salma bint 'Amir of Khuza'a. She married 'Awf ibn 'Abdu 'Awf and bore him 'Abdu'r-Rahman who was present at Badr; al-Aswad, who became Muslim and emigrated before the Conquest; 'Atika, and Ama. Ash-Shifa bint 'Awf and her daughter, 'Atika bint 'Awf, became Muslim and they gave allegiance to the Messenger of Allah. Ash-Shifa was one of the women emigrants. About her has come the *sunna* about setting free on behalf of a dead person. She died during the lifetime of the Messenger of Allah. 'Abdu'r-Rahman ibn 'Awf said, "Messenger of Allah, can I set free on behalf of my mother." The Messenger of Allah ﷺ said, "Yes," and he freed on her behalf.

*****

Khalida bint al-Aswad ibn 'Abdu Yaghuth

Her mother was Amina bint Nawfal of Zuhra. Khalida bint al-Aswad became Muslim in Madina and gave allegiance to the Messenger of Allah. She married 'Abdullah ibn al-Arqam.

It is related about His words, *"Who extracts the living from the dead and extracts the dead from the living?"* (10:31) that az-Zuhri said, "The Messenger of Allah visited one of his wives and there was a woman of beautiful appearance there. He said, 'Who is this?' She said, 'One of your maternal aunts.' He said, 'My aunts in this land are foreigners. Which of my aunts is this?' They replied, 'Khalida bint al-Aswad ibn 'Abdu Yaghuth.' He said, 'Glory be to Allah who brings out the living from the dead!'" She was a righteous woman and her father died an unbeliever.

Muhammad ibn 'Umar said that the commentary of *"Who extracts the living from the dead"* means the believer from the unbeliever.

*****

Umm Farwa bint Abi Quhafa

Abu Quhafa is 'Uthman ibn 'Amir. Her mother was Hind bint Nuqayd. Abu Bakr as-Siddiq gave her in marriage to al-Ash'ath ibn

Qays al-Kindi and she bore him Muhammad, Ishaq, Isma'il, Hubaba, and Qurayba.

Qurayba bint Abi Quhafa

Her mother was Hind bint Nuqayd. She married Qays ibn Sa'd ibn 'Ubada as-Sa'idi but did not bear him any children.

Umm 'Amir bint Abi Quhafa

Her mother was Hind bint Nuqayd. She married 'Amir ibn Abi Waqqas and bore him Du'ayfa.

✴✴✴✴✴

Asma' bint Abi Bakr as-Siddiq

Her mother was Qutayla bint 'Abdu'l-'Uzza of the Banu 'Amir ibn Lu'ayy. She was the full sister of 'Abdullah ibn Abi Bakr. She became Muslim early on in Makka and gave allegiance to the Messenger of Allah. She is "the one with the two belts". She took her belt and tore it in two and used one of them for the provisions of the Messenger of Allah and the other to tie his waterskin on the night when the Messenger of Allah and Abu Bakr went out to the Cave. She was called "She of the two belts." She married az-Zubayr ibn al-'Awwam and bore him 'Abdullah, 'Urwa, al-Mundhir, 'Asim, al-Muhajir, Khadija, Umm al-Hasan and 'A'isha.

Asma' said, "I prepared the provision-bag of the Prophet ﷺ in the house of Abu Bakr when he wanted to emigrate to Madina. We did not find anything with which to tie his bag or waterskin. I said to Abu Bakr, 'By Allah, I cannot find anything to tie it with except my belt.' He said, 'Tear it in two and tie the waterskin with one and the bag with the other.'" She did that and so she was called "She of the two belts".

It is related from 'Urwa that the people of Syria were fighting Ibn az-Zubayr and shouting at him, "Son of the woman of the two belts!" Ibn az-Zubayr said, "That is a fault whose blame is far from you."

Asma' said to him, "So they reproach you by it?" He said, "Yes." She said, "By Allah, it is true."

Asma' bint Abi Bakr said, "When I married az-Zubayr, he had neither property nor slave nor any possession in the earth other than his horse. I used to graze his horse, provide fodder for it, and look after it, as well as grinding date-stones. I also used to graze the camel, give it water, patch our leather bucket, and knead the bread. I was not good at making bread, and so my neighbours of the Ansar used to make bread for me. They were sincere women. I used to bring date-stones on my head from the land of az-Zubayr which the Messenger of Allah had granted to him. It was a distance of about two miles. One day I came with the date-stones on my head and I met the Messenger of Allah. There was a group of his Companions with him. He called me and said, 'Come on! Come one!' so that I could ride behind him. I was too shy to travel with the men and I remembered az-Zubayr and his jealousy. He was one of the most jealous of people. The Messenger of Allah saw that I was shy and he went on. I went to az-Zubayr and said, 'The Messenger of Allah met me while I was carrying the date-stones on my head. There was a group of his Companions with him. He made his camel kneel so that I could ride with him, but I was too shy and I know your jealousy.' He said, 'By Allah, the thought of you carrying the date-stones is harder for me than your riding with him.' Later Abu Bakr sent a slave who looked after the horse for me and it was as if he had set me free."

It is related from 'Ikrima that Asma' bint Abi Bakr was married to az-Zubayr ibn al-'Awwam. He was hard on her and she went to her father and complained about that to him. He said, "My daughter, be patient. When a woman has a righteous husband and he dies and she does not remarry after him, they will be re-united in the Garden."

It is related from 'Abbas ibn 'Abdullah ibn az-Zubayr from Asma' bint Abi Bakr that she went to the Prophet ﷺ and said, "O Prophet of Allah! There is nothing in my house except what az-Zubayr brings me. Is there anything wrong in my giving away some of what he brings me?" He said, "Spend what you can. Do not hoard, or Allah will withhold from you."

It is related from 'Ubayd ibn 'Umayr that Asma' had a swelling on her neck and the Prophet ﷺ began to stroke it, saying. "O Allah, preserve her from his excess and harm."

It is related from Ibn Abi Mulayka that Asma' bint Abi Bakr used to get headaches and she would put her hand on her head and say, "My body, and what Allah forgives is much!"

It is related from Fatima bint al-Mundhir that Asma' bint Abi Bakr fell ill and she set free every slave she had.

It is related from Fatima about Asma', "She used to say to her daughters and family, 'Spend and give *sadaqa* and do not wait for a surplus. If you wait for a surplus, you will not have any surplus. If you give *sadaqa*, you will not experience loss."

It is related from Muhammad ibn al-Munkadir that the Messenger of Allah ﷺ said to Asma' bint Abi Bakr, "Do not hoard, or Allah will withhold from you." She was a woman with a generous heart.

It is related that 'Abdullah ibn az-Zubayr said, "Qutayla bint 'Abdu'l-'Uzza came to her daughter, Asma' bint Abi Bakr. Abu Bakr had divorced her in the Jahiliyya. She had brought some dates, ghee, and mimosa leaves, but she refused to accept her gift or to let her enter her house. She sent to 'A'isha, 'Ask the Messenger of Allah.' He said, 'She should let her enter and accept her gifts.' Allah sent down, *'Allah does not forbid you, in respect of those who have not fought you in the deen '* to *'those, they are the wrongdoers.'* (60:8-9)"

Ar-Rukayn ibn ar-Rubayyi' said, "I visited Asma' bint Abi Bakr when she was a very old blind woman. I found her praying. There was someone with her and she was instructing him, 'Stand. Sit. Do this.'"

It is related that al-Mundhir ibn az-Zubayr came from Iraq and sent Asma' bint Abu Bakr a dress made of thin fine soft cloth after she had gone blind. He said, "She touched it with her hand and then said, 'Uff! Return his garment to him!' That was hard on him and he said, 'Mother, it is not transparent!' She said, 'If it is not transparent, it is translucent.'" He said, "Then he bought for her soft comfortable garments, and she accepted them. She said, 'I will wear the like of this.'"

Abu Waqid al-Laythi, the Companion of the Prophet who was present at Yarmuk, said, "Asma' bint Abi Bakr was with az-Zubayr. I heard her say to az-Zubayr, 'O Abu 'Abdullah! By Allah, a man of the enemy passed by running and then his foot hit the loop of my tent rope, and he fell down dead on his face without being hit by a weapon!'"

It is related that in the time of Sa'id ibn al-'As, Asma' bint Abi Bakr took a dagger to use against thieves who were rife in Madina, and she put it under her head.

It is related that 'Ikrima said, "Asma' bint Abi Bakr was asked whether any of the *Salaf* fainted from fear. She said, 'No, but they used to weep.'"

Mus'ab ibn Sa'd said, "'Umar allotted the stipends, and he allotted Asma' bint Abi Bakr a thousand dirhams."

It is related from Hisham ibn 'Urwa that az-Zubayr divorced Asma' and took 'Urwa who was young at that time.

It is related from Hisham ibn 'Urwa that Asma' wore clothes dyed with safflower when she was in *ihram* and the dye did not contain any saffron.

It is related that Fatima bint al-Mundhir said, "I only saw Asma' wearing garments dyed with safflower until she met Allah. She used to wear outer garments that had been dyed with safflower."

It is related from al-Qasim ibn Muhammad ath-Thaqafi that Asma' went to al-Hajjaj with her girls after she had gone blind. She said, "Where is al-Hajjaj?" They said, "He is not here." She said, "Inform him that I heard the Messenger of Allah ﷺ say, 'There are two men in Thaqif: a liar and a destroyer.'"

It is related from Abu's-Siddiq an-Naji that al-Hajjaj went to Asma' bint Abi Bakr and said to her, "Your son has deviated in this House and Allah has made him taste a painful punishment and has done for him." She said to him, "You lie. He was dutiful to his parents, and fasted and prayed, but by Allah, the Messenger of Allah informed us that two liars would emerge from Thaqif, one of them worse than the first, who is a destroyer."

It is related that Asma' bint Abi Bakr commanded, "When I die, wash me and shroud me and perfume me but do not leave any perfume on my shroud and do not follow me with fire."

It is related from Fatima bint al-Mundhir that Asma' bint Abi Bakr said, "Fumigate my clothes over the clothes stand and use *hanut* perfume on me, but do not leave any of it on my clothes."

They said, "Asma' bint Abi Bakr died some nights after her son, 'Abdullah ibn az-Zubayr had been killed. He was killed on Tuesday, 17th Jumada al-Ula in 73."

✳✴✳✴✳

Rayta bint al-Harith ibn Hubayla of Taym

Her mother was Zaynab bint 'Abdullah ibn Sa'ida. She was the sister of Subayha ibn al-Harith. She became Muslim in Makka early on and gave allegiance and emigrated to Abyssinia in the second emigration with her husband, al-Harith ibn Khalid. There she bore him Musa, 'A'isha, and Zaynab. Musa died in Abyssinia and Rayta bint al-Harith died on the journey back.

✳✴✳✴✳

Umayma bint Ruqayqa

She is the one from whom Muhammad ibn al-Munkadir transmitted. She related from the Prophet ﷺ the *hadith* about him receiving the allegiance of the women. She is Umayma bint 'Abdullah. Her mother was Ruqayqa bint Khuwaylid, the sister of Khadija bint Khuwaylid, the wife of the Prophet. Umayma went to a foreigner and married Habib ibn Ku'ayb ath-Thaqafi. She bore him an-Nahdiyya. Her daughter, Umm 'Umays and Zunnira became Muslim in Makka early on. They were among those who were tortured for Allah. Abu Bakr as-Siddiq bought them and set them free. His father, Abu Quhafa said to him, "My son, you devote yourself to this man and leave your people and purchase those weaklings!" He said to him, "O father, I know best what I am doing."

When he purchased an-Nahdiyya she had some flour she had

ground for her mistress or some date-stones she had milled. Abu Bakr said to her, "Return her flour or stones." She said, 'Not until I have milled it for her." That was after she had sold her and Abu Bakr had set her free. Zunnira was afflicted in her sight and went blind. It was said to her, "Al-Lat and al-'Uzza have afflicted you!" She said, "No, by Allah, they have not afflicted me. This is from Allah." Allah restored her sight and Quraysh said, "This is some of the magic of Muhammad."

✳✳✳✳✳

Jariyya bint 'Amr

She became Muslim in Makka early on. She was one of those tortured for Allah. Before he became Muslim, 'Umar ibn al-Khattab is the one who used to torture her to make her abandon Islam. He tortured her until he flagged and then he called her and said, "By Allah, I have only left you out of boredom." She said, "That is what your Lord will do to you. "

✳✳✳✳✳

Barira, the client of 'A'isha bint Abi Bakr

Ayman said, "She visited 'A'isha and said to her, 'Umm al-Mu'minin! I belonged to 'Utba ibn Abi Luhayb, and his wife and sons will sell me provided that they have the *wala'*. So whose client am I?' She said, 'Barira has come to me and she has a freedom-contract (*kitaba*). She said, "Buy me," and I said, "Yes." Then she said, "They will not sell me unless they impose the precondition of keeping the *wala'*." I said, "I have no need of you." The Messenger of Allah heard that and said, "What is the matter with Barira?" and I told him. He said, "Buy her and set her free and give them the condition they want." So I bought her and set her free. The Messenger of Allah said, "The *wala'* belongs to the one who sets free, even if a hundred preconditions are made.""

'A'isha said, "The Prophet ﷺ got up and made a speech when 'A'isha set Barira free after her people had made the precondition of keeping the *wala'*. He said, 'Why is it that some men make conditions which are not in the Book of Allah? Any condition which is not in the Book of Allah is invalid even if it is stipulated a hundred times. The decision of Allah is more binding and the condition of Allah is firmer.'"

It is related from Ibn 'Abbas that the husband of Barira was a black slave called Mughith. The Prophet ﷺ made four judgements regarding her: her owners stipulated that they should keep the *wala'* and he judged that the *wala'* belongs to the one who sets free; she was given a choice and she chose herself and the Prophet ordered her to observe the waiting-period. He said, "I used to see him (meaning her husband) following her in the streets of Madina with his eyes fixed on her." In another case, she was given *sadaqa* and she gave some of it to 'A'isha. She mentioned that to the Prophet, and he said, 'It is *sadaqa* for her and a gift for us.'"

It is related from 'A'isha that Barira was set free, and she had a husband. The Messenger of Allah ﷺ gave her a choice of remaining with him or separating from him. Barira was given some meat as *sadaqa* and they cut it up and they offered the Messenger of Allah some food which consisted of condiments without meat. He said, "Didn't I see you had some meat?" They replied, "Messenger of Allah, it is meat which was given as *sadaqa* to Barira." The Messenger of Allah ﷺ said, "It is *sadaqa* for Barira and a gift for us." Barira went to 'A'isha to ask for her help in her freedom-contract from her people. 'A'isha said, "If your people agree, I will buy you and pay your price all at once." Barira went to her people and told them that. They said, "And we will have your *wala'*." Barira went to 'A'isha and said that they had said that they would have the *wala'*. The Messenger of Allah said, "Buy her. What they said will not harm you. The *wala'* belongs to the one who sets free."

'Ata' said, "The husband of Barira was a slave called Mughith belonging to the Banu'l-Mughira. When she was freed, the Messenger of Allah gave her a choice. He said that Ibn Abi Layla thought that there was a choice in the case of a slave, but not in the case of a free man."

It is related from Muhammad that the Messenger of Allah ﷺ gave Barira a choice. The Messenger of Allah spoke to her and she said, "Messenger of Allah, is it something obligatory for me?" He said, "No. Rather I am interceding for him." She said, "I have no need of him."

It is related from Ibn 'Abbas that the husband of Barira on the day that she was set free was a black slave of the Banu'l-Mughira. He said, "By Allah, I used to see him in the roads of Madina following her, weeping and trying to appease her, but she refused."

Ayyub said, "I do not know of anyone of the people of Madina and Makka who disagrees that he was a slave," i.e. Barira's husband.

Ibn 'Abbas said, "Barira's husband on the day when she was given a choice was a black slave of the Banu'l-Mughira called Mughith. I can see him now following her in the streets of Madina, with his tears running down into his beard. She was saying, 'I have no need of you.'"

It is related from 'A'isha [and others] that Barira's husband was a free man on the day she was given a choice."

✳✱✳✱✳

Fatima bint al-Walid ibn al-Mughira of Makhzum

Her mother was Hantama bint Shaytan (who is 'Abdullah ibn 'Amr). She married al-Harith ibn Hisham and bore him 'Abdu'r-Rahman and Umm Hakim.

'Abdullah ibn az-Zubayr said, "On the day of the Conquest, Fatima bint al-Walid ibn al-Mughira became Muslim and went to the Messenger of Allah ﷺ and gave him allegiance.

✳✱✳✱✳

Umm Hakim bint al-Harith ibn Hisham

Her mother was Fatima bint al-Walid ibn al-Mughira.

It is related that 'Abdullah ibn az-Zubayr said, "On the day of the Conquest, Umm Hakim bint al-Harith, the wife of 'Ikrima ibn Abi Jahl, became Muslim and went to the Messenger of Allah ﷺ and gave him allegiance.

Juwayriyya bint Abi Jahl ibn Hisham

Her mother was Arwa bint Abi'l-'Is ibn Umayya. She became Muslim and gave allegiance. She married 'Attab ibn Usayd ibn Abi'l-'Is. Then she married Aban ibn Sa'id ibn al-'As but did not bear him any children. Juwayriyya was the woman to whom 'Ali ibn Abi Talib proposed. The Banu'l-Mughira went to the Messenger of Allah ﷺ to consult him about that. He did not give them permission to marry him. He said, "Fatima is a part of me. What harms her harms me."

Al-Hunfa' bint Abi Jahl ibn Hisham

Her mother was Arwa bint Abi'l-'Is ibn Umayya. She became Muslim and gave allegiance. She married Suhayl ibn 'Amr of the Banu 'Amir ibn Lu'ayy and bore him Hind. They also say that Usama ibn Zayd ibn Haritha married her.

✳✳✳✳✳

Qurayba bint Abi Umayya ibn al-Mughira

Her mother was 'Atika bint 'Utba ibn Rabi'a. She was the half-sister of Umm Salama bint Abi Umayya, the wife of the Prophet. She became Muslim and gave allegiance. She married 'Abdu'r-Rahman ibn Abi Bakr and bore him 'Abdullah, Umm Hakim, and Hafsa.

Ibn Abi Mulayka said, "'Abdu'r-Rahman ibn Abi Bakr married Qurayba bint Abi Umayya, the sister of Umm Salama. There was some harshness in his character. One day she said to him, 'By Allah, I was warned about you!' He said, 'Your case is in your hands.' She said, 'I will not prefer anyone over the son of the Siddiq.' He stayed with her and it was not a divorce."

✳✳✳✳✳

Fatima bint al-Aswad ibn 'Abdu'l-Asad

She became Muslim and gave allegiance. She is the one who stole, and the Prophet ﷺ cut off her hand.

It is related from Habib ibn Abi Thabit that Fatima bint al-Aswad ibn 'Abdu'l-Asad stole some jewellery in the time of the Messenger of Allah. More than one person interceded on her behalf with the Messenger of Allah. They asked Usama ibn Zayd to speak to the Messenger of Allah as the Messenger of Allah used to accept his intercession. When Usama came and the Prophet saw him, he said, "Usama, do not speak to me. When the *hudud* are violated, there is no alternative. If the daughter of Muhammad had stolen, I would have cut off her hand."

Muhammad ibn Sa'd said, "This is a transmission about Fatima bint al-Aswad. Included in the transmission of the people of Madina and other people of Makka is that the one who stole and whose hand was cut off by the Messenger of Allah was Umm 'Amr bint Sufyan. Her mother was the daughter of 'Abdu'l-'Uzza ibn Qays, the sister of Huwaytib ibn 'Abdu'l-'Uzza. She went out in the night during the Farewell *Hajj* and came upon a camp of travellers. She took a bag of theirs and the people seized her and bound her. In the morning, they brought her to the Prophet صلى الله عليه وسلم. She sought refuge with Umm Salama, the wife of the Prophet. He ordered her to let go of her and said, 'By Allah, if Fatima, the daughter of Muhammad had stolen, I would cut off her hand.' Then he ordered that her hand be cut off and she left with her hand dripping blood and went to the wife of Usayd ibn Hudayr, the brother of the Banu 'Abdu'l-Ashhal. She recognised her and took her in and made some hot food for her. Usayd ibn Hudayr came from the Prophet. Before he entered the house, he called to his wife, 'Do you how what has happened to Umm 'Amr bint Sufyan?' She said, 'She is here with me.' Usayd ibn Hudayr went back and told the Prophet صلى الله عليه وسلم who said, 'She has had mercy on her. May Allah have mercy on you.' When she went back to her father, he said, 'Take her to the Banu 'Abdu'l-'Uzza. She resembles them.' They state that Huwaytib ibn 'Abdu'l-'Uzza took her in. He was her uncle."

✻✻✻✻✻

Sumayya bint Khubbat, the client of Abu Hudhayfa

She was the mother of 'Ammar ibn Yasar. She became Muslim early on in Makka. She was one of those who was tortured for Allah to make her leave her *deen*. She did not do that, but remained steadfast until Abu Jahl passed by her one day and stabbed her with a spear in her private parts and she died. She was the first to be martyred in Islam. She was a very old and frail woman. When Abu Jahl was killed in the Battle of Badr, the Messenger of Allah ﷺ said to 'Ammar ibn Yasar, "Allah has killed your mother's killer. "

It is related that Mujahid said, "The first person martyred in Islam was Sumayya, the mother of 'Ammar. Abu Jahl went to her and stabbed her with a spear in her private parts."

✳✶✳✶✳

'Atika bint Zayd ibn 'Amr

Her mother was Umm Kurz bint al-Hadrami. She became Muslim, gave allegiance, and emigrated.

It is related that 'Atika bint Zayd ibn 'Amr was married to 'Abdullah ibn Abi Bakr as-Siddiq. He gave her part of his property provided that she would not re-marry after him. He died and 'Umar sent to 'Atika, "You have made unlawful for yourself what Allah has made lawful for you. Therefore return the property which you have taken to its people and re-marry." She did that. 'Umar proposed to her and she married him.

It is related from 'Ali ibn Zayd that 'Atika bint Zayd ibn 'Amr was married to 'Abdullah ibn Abi Bakr. He died and he imposed on her that she should not re-marry after him. She remained celibate and did not re-marry. Men began to propose to her and she rejected them. 'Umar said to her guardian, "Mention me to her." He was mentioned to her and she also rejected 'Umar. 'Umar said, "Marry her to me." He married him to her and 'Umar went to her and went in where she was and contended with her until he overcame her and she carried out the marriage to him. When he finished, he said ," Bother! Bother! Bother! I say 'Bother!' to her!" Then he left her and left her alone and did not go to her. She sent a client of hers, saying to him, "Come, and I will prepare for you."

It is related from Khalid ibn Salama that 'Atika bint Zayd was married to 'Abdullah ibn Abi Bakr. He loved her and assigned her part of his lands provided that she would not re-marry after him.

'Umar ibn al-Khattab married her and 'A'isha sent to tell her to return the lands to them. When 'Abdullah ibn Abi Bakr died, 'Atika said:

"I vow that my soul will remain in sorrow over you
and my skin will continue to be dusty."

When 'Umar ibn al-Khattab married her, 'A'isha said:

"I vow that my eye will remain fixed on you
and my skin will continue to be yellow.

Return our land to us."

It is related that Yahya ibn 'Abdu'r-Rahman ibn Hatib said, "Rabi'a ibn Umayya went to 'Umar ibn al-Khattab and said, 'I had a dream that Abu Bakr died and after him I sent to this celibate woman and married her. I went in to her as her bridegroom and at your door was a basket of trefoil.' She was 'Atika bint Zayd ibn 'Amr. She had been married to 'Abdullah ibn Abi Bakr. He had been killed on the Day of Ta'if, and he assigned her part of his property provided that she did not re-marry after him. 'Umar said, 'You are disappointed! There is no way to this woman.' Then Abu Bakr died and 'Umar took his place. He sent to 'Atika, 'You have made unlawful for yourself what Allah has made lawful. Return the property to its people and marry.' She did that and 'Umar proposed to her and she married him. Rabi'a ibn Umayya came and asked permission to visit 'Umar while he was her bridegroom. He said, 'O Allah, do not delight him!' He gave him permission and he entered and he began to look at the basket of trefoil at his door."

It is related from 'Umar's grandson that 'Atika bint Zayd was married to 'Umar ibn al-Khattab and that she kissed him while he was fasting, and he did not forbid her to do it.

It is related from Yahya ibn Sa'd that 'Atika bint Zayd was the wife of 'Umar ibn al-Khattab and that she used to kiss 'Umar's head while he was fasting and he did not forbid her to do it.

It is related from Hamid ibn 'Abdu'r-Rahman ibn 'Awf that 'Atika bint Zayd, the wife of 'Umar ibn al-Khattab, used to ask permission to go to the mosque. When she asked for permission, 'Umar used to say to her, "You know that I want you to stay." She said, "I will not cease to ask your permission." 'Umar did not restrain her when she asked permission. 'Umar was stabbed while in the mosque.

*****

Fatima bint al-Khattab

She was the sister of 'Umar ibn al-Khattab. Her mother was Hantama bint Hashim. She married Sa'id ibn Zayd. She and her husband became Muslim before 'Umar ibn al-Khattab and before the Messenger of Allah ﷺ entered the house of al-Arqam. She is also called Umm Jamil bint al-Khattab.

Layla bint Hathma ibn Hudhayfa

Her mother was an *umm walad* from Tanukh among the captives of the Arabs. She became Muslim early on, gave allegiance, and emigrated to Abyssinia in both emigrations with her husband, 'Amir ibn Rabi'a, the ally of al-Khattab ibn Nufayl. She bore children to 'Amir ibn Rabi'a. 'Amir's child married into the Banu 'Adi.

'Amir ibn Rabi'a said, "No woman came to Madina before Layla bint Hathma. I came with her in the *hijra*."

Ash-Shifa bint 'Abdullah ibn 'Abdu Shams

Her mother was Fatima bint Wahb. Ash-Shifa became Muslim early on before the *hijra* and gave allegiance to the Prophet ﷺ. She married Abu Hathma ibn Hudhayfa and bore him Sulayman ibn Abi Hathma. She also bore Masruq ibn Hudhayfa. He was a noble. Ash-Shifa emigrated to Madina.

Ramla bint Abi 'Awf ibn Subayra

Her mother was Umm 'Abdullah, who is Surma' bint al-Harith. Ramla became Muslim early on in Makka before the Messenger of Allah ﷺ entered the house of al-Arqam. She gave allegiance and emigrated to Abyssinia in the second emigration with her husband, al-Muttalib ibn Azhar. There she bore him 'Abdullah ibn 'Amr.

Rayta bint Munabbih ibn al-Hajjaj

Her mother was from Khath'am. She married 'Amr ibn al-'As as-Sahmi and bore him 'Abdullah ibn 'Amr.

'Abdullah ibn az-Zubayr said, "On the Day of the Conquest, Rayta bint Munabbih became Muslim. She is the mother of 'Abdullah ibn 'Amr ibn al-'As. She went to the Messenger of Allah and gave him her allegiance.

Zaynab bint 'Uthman ibn Maz'un

Nafi' said, "'Abdullah ibn 'Umar married Zaynab bint 'Uthman ibn Maz'un after her father had died. Her uncle, Quddama ibn Maz'un, gave her in marriage to him. The girl's mother said to the girl, 'Do not permit it.' The girl disliked the marriage, and she and her mother told that to the Messenger of Allah. So the Messenger of Allah ended her marriage and al-Mughira ibn Shu'ba married her."

At-Taw'ama bint Umayya ibn Khalaf

Her mother was Layla bint Habib ibn 'Amr of Banu Tamim. At-Taw'ama went abroad with 'Asim ibn al-Ja'd al-Fizari and bore him children. At-Taw'ama and her sister were twins, which is the origin of the name [*taw'ama* means twin].

It is related from Sulayman ibn Yasar that at-Taw'ama bint Umayya was divorced irrevocably and she asked 'Umar ibn al-Khattab about it and he made it a single divorce.

❊❊❊❊❊

Sahla bint Suhayl ibn 'Amr

Her mother was Fatima bint 'Abdu'l-'Uzza. She became Muslim early on in Makka and gave allegiance and emigrated to Abyssinia in both emigrations with her husband, Abu Hudhayfa ibn 'Utba. There she bore him Muhammad. After Abu Hudhayfa she married 'Abdullah ibn al-Aswad and bore him Salit. Then after him she married Shammakh ibn Sa'id and bore him 'Amir. Then she married 'Abdu'r-Rahman ibn 'Awf and bore him Salim. Sahla bint Suhayl had adopted Salim, the *mawla* of Abu Hudhayfa, and he used to visit her. The Messenger of Allah ﷺ allowed her to give him five drinks of her milk.

It is related that Sahla bint Suhayl, the wife of Abu Hudhayfa, asked the Messenger of Allah, "Messenger of Allah, we used to consider Salim to be our son, and he visits me when I am lightly dressed and he sees some of me." The Messenger of Allah said, "Give him five drinks of your milk and then he can visit you."

Az-Zuhri said, "'A'isha used to take this line. Salim informed me that he visited Umm Kulthum bint Abi Bakr so that she could give him five drinks of milk so that he could visit 'A'isha and listen to her. She gave him two or three drinks and then she became ill and he did not visit her."

Umm Salama said, "The wives of the Prophet ﷺ refused to accept this and said, "This is a special allowance from the Messenger of Allah for Sahla bint Suhayl."

It is related from 'Amra bint 'Abdu'r-Rahman that the wife of Abu Hudhayfa ibn 'Utba mentioned Salim, the client of Abu Hudhayfa, to the Messenger of Allah and the fact that he came in where she was. The Messenger of Allah ﷺ commanded her to give him some of her milk, and she did so although he was old and had been present at Badr.

Az-Zuhri said, "She used to put milk in a vessel or a cup with her milk and Salim drank it for five consecutive days. Then he used to visit her when she was uncovered. It was an allowance which the Messenger of Allah made for Sahla bint Suhayl."

✳✳✳✳✳

Umm Kulthum bint Suhayl ibn 'Amr

Her mother was Fakhita bint 'Amir ibn Nawfal. She became Muslim early on in Makka, gave allegiance and emigrated to Abyssinia in the second emigration with her husband, Abu Sabra ibn Abi Ruhm. Umm Kulthum bore Abu Sabra Muhammad and 'Abdullah.

Fatima, who is Umm Jamil bint al-Mujallil

Her mother is Umm Habib bint al-'As, the sister of Abu Uhayha Sa'id ibn al-'As. Fatima became Muslim early on in Makka, gave allegiance and emigrated to Abyssinia in the second emigration with her husband, Hatib ibn al-Harith. Their sons, Muhammad and al-Harith, were with them in the emigration.

Fatima, who is Umm Qihtam bint 'Alqama

Her mother was 'Atika bint As'ad of Khuza'a. She became Muslim early on in Makka and gave allegiance and emigrated to Abyssinia in the second emigration with her husband, Salit ibn 'Umar, and bore him Salit ibn Salit.

✳✶✳✶✳

Fatima bint Qays, the sister of ad-Dahhak ibn Qays

Her mother was Umayma bint Rabi'a of Kinana.

It is related from Fatima bint Qays that Abu Amr ibn Hafs divorced her irrevocably when he was away. His agent sent her some barley and she exasperated him. He said, "By Allah, you will have nothing from us!" She went to the Messenger of Allah and he said, "You have no maintenance from him." He commanded that she observe her waiting-period in the house of Umm Sharik. Then he said, "That is a woman whom my Companions visit. Observe the waiting-period in the house of Ibn Umm Maktum. He is a blind man and you can remove your garments. Inform me when you become lawful." She said, "When I was lawful, I told him that Mu'awiya ibn Abi Sufyan ibn Harb and Abu Jahm ibn Hudhayfa had proposed to me. The Messenger of Allah said, 'As for Mu'awiya, he is destitute with no property. Abu Jahm does not take his staff from his shoulder [meaning he is always travelling]. Rather marry Usama.' I disliked him and he said, 'Marry Usama.' So I married him and Allah put good in him and I was envied for it."

Abu Salama said, "Fatima bint Qays visited me. She said, 'I went to the Messenger of Allah desiring lodging and maintenance. He said, "Fatima, lodging and maintenance are owed by a husband who can take his wife back. Go to Umm Sharik and do not fail to inform me about yourself." Then he said, "Umm Sharik is visited by her brothers among the Muhajirun. Go to Ibn Umm Maktum, He is a blind man."' When her term came to an end, Mu'awiya, Abu Jahm ibn Hudhayfa, and Usama asked to marry her. The Messenger of Allah said, 'Mu'awiya is destitute without property. Abu Jahm does not take his staff from off his shoulder. What is your position with Usama?' It seemed that her family disliked that. She said, 'I will only marry the one whom the Messenger of Allah says.'"

It is related that ash-Sha'bi said that he was informed by Fatima bint Qays that she was married to one of the Banu Makhzum and that he sent her word of her divorce on the road from one of the expeditions on which he went to Yemen. She asked his family for maintenance and lodging and they refused. They said, "He did not send us any of that." She said, "I went to the Messenger of Allah ﷺ and said, 'I am a daughter of the family of Khalid and my husband has sent me word of my divorce. I asked his family for maintenance and lodging and they refused me.' They said, 'Messenger of Allah, he sent three divorce pronouncements to her.' The Messenger of Allah ﷺ said, 'Lodging and maintenance are owed by a husband who can take his wife back.'"

Chapter Eleven:
Non-Qurayshi Emigrant Muslim Women

Umm Ruman bint 'Amir ibn 'Umaymir

Umm Ruman was the wife of al-Harith ibn Sakhbara of Azd and bore him at-Tufayl. Al-Harith ibn Sakhbara came from as-Sara to Makka with his wife, Umm Ruman, and his son by her. He formed an alliance with Abu Bakr as-Siddiq. Then al-Harith died in Makka and Abu Bakr married Umm Ruman and she bore him 'Abdu'r-Rahman and 'A'isha, the wife of the Prophet. Umm Ruman became Muslim in Makka early on and gave allegiance and emigrated to Madina with the family of the Messenger of Allah and her children when the family of Abu Bakr made the *hijra*. Umm Ruman was a righteous woman. She died in the time of the Prophet ﷺ in Madina in Dhu'l-Hijja, 6 AH.

Muhammad ibn al-Qasim said, "When Umm Ruman was lowered into her grave, the Messenger of Allah ﷺ said, 'Whoever is pleased to look at a woman of the houris should look at Umm Ruman.'" 'Affan said that the Messenger of Allah went down into her grave.

✳✳✳✳✳

Umm al-Fadl

She is Lubaba the elder, bint al-Harith ibn Hazm. Her mother was Hind, who is Khawla bint 'Awf, who are related to Himyar, and her mother was 'A'isha bint al-Muhazzam. Umm al-Fadl was the first woman to become Muslim in Makka after Khadija bint Khuwaylid. The Messenger of Allah ﷺ used to visit her and he was welcomed in her house. The sisters of Umm al-Fadl included her full sister, Maymuna bint al-Harith, the wife of the Prophet; Lubaba the younger, who is al-'Asma' bint al-Harith, the mother of Khalid ibn al-Walid, her half-sister by her father; 'Izza bint al-Harith, her half-sister by the father; Huzayla bint al-Harith, her half-sister by the father; and her brothers and sisters by the mother: Mahmiyya ibn Jaza' az-Zubaydi, the Companion of the Messenger of Allah, 'Awn, Asma' and Salma, the children of 'Umays. Umm al-Fadl married al-'Abbas ibn 'Abdu'l-Muttalib and bore him al-Fadl, 'Abdullah, 'Ubaydullah, Ma'bad, Qutham, 'Abdu'r-Rahman and Umm Habib. 'Abdullah ibn Yazid al-Hilali said:

> A noblewoman did not bear from a master
> any like the six which came from Umm al-Fadl.

It is related from Kurayb that Maymuna bint al-Harith, Umm al-Fadl bint al-Harith and her sisters, Lubaba the younger, Huzayla, 'Izza, Asma' and Salma, the two daughters of 'Umays were mentioned, and the Messenger of Allah said, "The sisters are believers."

Ibn 'Abbas said, "My mother constantly used to fast on Monday and Thursday."

Muhammad ibn 'Umar said, "Umm al-Fadl bint al-Harith emigrated to Madina after al-'Abbas ibn al-Muttalib became Muslim. The Messenger of Allah ﷺ used to visit her and he went to her house a lot."

Zayd ibn 'Ali ibn Husayn said, "After prophethood, the Messenger of Allah did not place his head in the room of a woman nor was it lawful for him, except for Umm al-Fadl. She used to delouse him and put kohl in his eyes. One day while she was putting the kohl on, a teardrop fell from her eye onto his cheek. He raised his head to her and said, 'What is wrong with you?' She said, 'Allah has announced your death to us. If you were to command who should succeed you, then the business would be in us or in other than us.' He said, 'You will be defeated and victimised after me.'"

Umm al-Fadl, the wife of Al-'Abbas ibn 'Abdu'l-Muttalib, said, "Messenger of Allah, I dreamt that one of your limbs was in my house." He said, "You have had a good dream. Fatima will bear a boy and you will nurse him with the milk of your son, Qutham." She gave birth to al-Husayn and Umm al-Fadl looked after him. She said,

"I took him to the Messenger of Allah ﷺ and he bounced him up and down and kissed him, and he urinated on the Messenger of Allah. He said, 'Umm al-Fadl, take my son. He has urinated on me.' I took him and pinched him and it made him cry. I said, 'You have annoyed the Messenger of Allah! You have urinated on him!' When the child wept, he said, 'Umm al-Fadl, you harm me in my son by making him weep!' Then he called for water and poured it on him. Then he said, 'When it is a boy then pour water. If it is a girl, then wash it completely.'"

Qabus ibn al-Makhariq said, "Umm al-Fadl had a dream of the Messenger of Allah in her house. She went to the Prophet ﷺ and told him and he said, 'It is good, Allah willing. Fatima will give birth to a son and you will nurse him with the milk of your son Qutham.' She gave birth to Husayn and he gave him to her and she nursed until he moved. She took him to the Prophet, and he sat him on his lap and he urinated. She struck her hand between his shoulders and he said, 'You have caused pain to my son, may Allah put you right - or may Allah have mercy on you.' She said, 'Remove your wrapper and put on another while I wash it.' He said, 'The urine of a boy is sprinkled and that of a girl is washed.'"

It is related from Salim Abu'n-Nadr that Umm al-Fadl bint al-Harith sent a cup of milk to the Prophet on the Day of 'Arafa while he was on his camel and he drank it.

✳✳✳✳✳

Layla the Younger

She is al-'Asma' bint al-Harith ibn Hazm. Her mother was Fakhita bint 'Amr. She married al-Walid ibn al-Mughira in Makka and bore him Khalid ibn al-Walid, the Sword of Allah. Then she became Muslim after the *hijra* and gave allegiance to the Messenger of Allah ﷺ.

✳✳✳✳✳

Huzayla bint al-Harith ibn Hazm

She became Muslim after the *hijra* and gave allegiance to the Messenger of Allah ﷺ.

✳✳✳✳✳

'Izza bint al-Harith ibn Hazm

She married 'Abdullah ibn Malik and bore him Ziyad, 'Abdu'r-Rahman, and Barza. Barza bore Yazid to al-Asamm al-Baka'i, the companion of 'Abdullah ibn al-'Abbas. Another transmission has that Barza, the mother of Yazid ibn al-Asamm was the half-sister of 'Izza bint al-Harith, and that her mother was the daughter of 'Amir ibn Mu'attib, and that 'Izza bint al-Harith was married to a man of Banu Kilab to whom she bore children.

✳✳✳✳✳

Asma' bint 'Umays

Her mother was Hind, who is Khawla bint 'Awf.

It is related that Asma' bint 'Umays became Muslim after the Messenger of Allah ﷺ had entered the house al-Arqam in Makka. She gave allegiance and emigrated to the land of Abyssinia with her husband, Ja'far ibn Abi Talib. There she bore him 'Abdullah, Muhammad, and 'Awn. Ja'far was killed at Mu'ta as a martyr in Jumada al-Ula, 8 AH.

It is related that when Asma' bint 'Umays came from Abyssinia, 'Umar said to her, "O Abyssinian, we have done *hijra* before you!" She said, "By my life, you spoke the truth. You were with the Messenger of Allah who was feeding your hungry ones and teaching your ignorant ones while we were far away and banished. By Allah, I will go to the Prophet and mention that to him." He said, "The people have one *hijra*, and you have two *hijras*."

Asma' bint 'Umays said, "Messenger of Allah, some men are boasting over us and claim that we are not among the first Muhajirun." The Messenger of Allah said, "Rather you have two *hijras*. You emigrated to Abyssinia when we were in custody in Makka, and then you emigrated after that." They came from Abyssinia during Khaybar.

'Amir said, "The first to suggest the bier for the woman was Asma' bint 'Umays when she came from Abyssinia. She had seen the Christians doing that there."

It is related from Asma' bint 'Umays, "On the morning in which Ja'far and his companions were killed, the Messenger of Allah ﷺ came to me. I had tanned forty skins, and I was kneading my bread. I took my sons and washed their faces and oiled them. Then the Messenger of Allah came to me and said, 'Asma', where are the sons of Ja'far?' I brought them to him, and he embraced them and smelt them and then his eyes overflowed with tears and he wept. I said, 'Messenger of Allah, perhaps some news has reached you about Ja'far?' He said, 'Yes, he was killed today.' I began to shout and the women gathered round me. The Messenger of Allah began to say, 'Asma', do not say rash words nor strike your chest.' The Messenger of Allah went out and went to his daughter Fatima, who was saying, 'O uncle!' The Messenger of Allah ﷺ said, 'For one like Ja'far, let the weeper weep.' Then the Messenger of Allah said, 'Prepare some food for the family of Ja'far. They are distracted today.'"

Muhammad ibn 'Umar said, "Abu Bakr as-Siddiq married Asma' bint 'Umays after Ja'far ibn Abi Talib died and she bore him Muhammad ibn Abi Bakr, and then Abu Bakr died."

It is related from Sa'id ibn al-Musayyab that Asma' bint 'Umays was bleeding after the birth of Muhammad ibn Abi Bakr at Dhu'l-Hulayfa when they were intending to make the Farewell Hajj. Abu Bakr commanded her to have a *ghusl* and then begin the *hajj*."

It is related that Asma' bint 'Umays gave birth to Muhammad ibn Abi Bakr at al-Bayda' and Abu Bakr mentioned that to the Messenger of Allah who said, "Let her have a *ghusl* and then go into *ihram*."

It is related from Jabir that when they were at Dhu'l-Hulayfa, he prayed there and Asma' bint 'Umays gave birth to Muhammad ibn Abi Bakr. She sent to the Messenger of Allah who commanded her to bind up her private parts with a cloth and then have a *ghusl* and then begin.

Qays ibn Abi Hazim said, "I visited Abu Bakr with my father He was a thin white man. I saw the hand of Asma' was tattooed."

It is related from Abu Bakr ibn Hafs that Abu Bakr left instructions that Asma' bint 'Umays should wash him when he died. He adjured her to do it when she was not fasting because she would be better able to cope. She remembered his oath at the end of the day and she called for water and drank it. She said, "By Allah, today I will not let a broken oath follow him."

It is related from al-Qasim that Abu Bakr as-Siddiq left a will that his wife Asma' should wash him. If she was unable to accomplish it, their son Muhammad should help her. Muhammad said, "This is weak."

'Ata' said, "Abu Bakr left a will that his wife, Asma' bint 'Umays, should wash him and that if she was unable, then 'Abdu'r-Rahman ibn Abi Bakr should help her." Muhammad ibn 'Umar said, "This is established. How could her son Muhammad help her when he was born at Dhu'l-Hulayfa in the Farewell Hajj, 10 AH and so he was only around three years old on the day that Abu Bakr died?"

It is related from 'A'isha that Asma' washed Abu Bakr.

It is related from 'Abdullah ibn Abi Bakr that Asma' bint 'Umays, the wife of Abu Bakr as-Siddiq, washed Abu Bakr when he died. Then she went out and asked those of the Muhajirun who were present, "I am fasting and this is a very cold day. Do I have to do a *ghusl?*" They said, "No."

It is related that 'Ata' said, "She washed him on a cold morning and she asked 'Uthman whether she had to do a *ghusl*. He said no. 'Umar heard that and did not object."

It is related that 'Umar allotted Asma' bint 'Umays a stipend of 1000 dirhams.

Muhammad ibn 'Umar said, "Then after Abu Bakr, Asma' bint 'Umays married 'Ali ibn Abi Talib and bore him Yahya and 'Awn."

'Amir said, "'Ali ibn Abi Talib married Asma' bint 'Umays. Her sons, Muhammad ibn Ja'far and Muhammad ibn Abi Bakr were rivalling in boasts, each of them saying, 'I am nobler than you! My father was better than your father!' 'Ali said to her, 'Settle things between them, Asma'.' She said, 'I have not seen any youth among the Arabs better than Ja'far, and I have not seen any mature man better than Abu Bakr.' 'Ali said, 'You have not left us anything! If you had said other than what you said, I would have hated you.' Asma' said, 'Of the three, you are least of them to choose.'"

*****

Salma bint 'Umays

Her mother was Hind, who is Khawla bint 'Awf. She and her sister Asma' became Muslim early on. She married Hamza ibn 'Abdu'l-Muttalib and bore him his daughter 'Umara. She is the one who was in Makka whom 'Ali ibn Abi Talib brought out in the Fulfilled *'Umra*. 'Ali, Zayd ibn Haritha and Ja'far ibn Abi Talib quarrelled about which one should take her. The Messenger of Allah decided that Ja'far ibn Abi Talib would care for her because her aunt, Asma' bint 'Umays, was married to him. The Messenger of Allah said, "A woman is not married along with her aunt." Hamza ibn 'Abdu'l-Muttalib was killed at Uhud as a martyr and Salma bint 'Umays became a widow. Then she married Shaddad ibn al-Had al-Laythi and bore him 'Abdullah ibn Shaddad. He is the half-brother of Hamza and the son of the maternal aunt of al-'Abbas by Umm al-Fadl, and the son of the aunt of Khalid ibn al-Walid.

*****

Humayna bint Khalaf ibn As'ad

She became Muslim early on in Makka and emigrated to Abyssinia in the second emigration with her husband, Khalif ibn Sa'id ibn al-'As, and his mother, Bint Khalid. His mother married az-Zubayr ibn al-'Awwam and bore him 'Amr and Khalid.

Harmala bint 'Abd of Khuza'a

She became Muslim early on in Makka and gave allegiance and emigrated to Abyssinia in the second emigration with her husband, Jahm ibn Qays. Harmala died there in Abyssinia. She bore him Hurmayla, 'Abdullah and 'Amr. She was called Umm Hurmayla. Her mother was a slave of 'Amr ibn 'Abdu Shams.

Fatima bint Safwan ibn Muhrith

She became Muslim early on in Makka and gave allegiance and emigrated to Abyssinia in the second emigration with her husband, 'Amr ibn Sa'id ibn al-'As.

Hasana, Umm Sharahbil

She became Muslim early on in Makka and gave her allegiance and emigrated to Abyssinia in the second emigration with her son, Sharahbil ibn Hasana.

Khirniq bint al-Husayn of Khuza'a

She became Muslim and gave her allegiance to the Messenger of Allah and related *hadith* from him.

✶✶✶✶✶

Subay'a bint al-Harith al-Aslamiyya

She was married to Sa'd ibn Khawla, but she was widowed.

It is related that Subay'a al-Aslamiyya gave birth some days after the death of her husband. She went to the Messenger of Allah ﷺ and asked for permission to marry and he gave her permission and she married.

'Ubaydullah ibn 'Abdullah ibn 'Utba said, "Abu's-Sanabil ibn Ba'kak reproved Subay'a bint al-Harith and she told him that she had gone to the Messenger of Allah and he had told her to marry."

It is related from Abu Salama ibn 'Abdu'r-Rahman that when he and Ibn 'Abbas argued about the *hadith* of Subay'a al-Aslamiyya, Ibn 'Abbas said to his slave, Kurayb, "Go to Umm Salama and ask her." She said, "Subay'a bint al-Harith al-Aslamiyya gave birth twenty days after the death of her husband, and the Messenger of Allah commanded her to marry. Abu's-Sanabil was one of those who proposed to her."

✶✶✶✶✶

Umm Ma'bad

Her name was 'Atika bint Khalid of Khuza'a. She was married to her cousin, who is called Tamim ibn 'Abdu'l-'Uzza. She lived at Qudayd. She is the one with whom the Messenger of Allah ﷺ stopped when he emigrated to Madina.

It is related that Quraysh did not know where the Messenger of Allah ﷺ had gone when he left the Cave at the end of Monday or Tuesday night before dawn making for Qudayd. They heard a voice coming from the bottom of Makka which the slaves, and women and children followed until they reached the top of Makka, but no one could be seen:

Allah the Lord of the people, has given his best repayment
to two companions who spent midday in the tents of Umm Ma'bad.

Umm Ma'bad said, "Four people on two mounts came up to us and stopped. I brought the Messenger of Allah a sheep intending to slaughter it. It had milk. I brought it up to him and he touched its udder and said 'Do not slaughter it.' So I released it and brought another and slaughtered it. I ground for him and he and his companions ate." Hisham said, "Who was with him?" She said, "The son of Abi Quhafa, the client of Ibn Abi Quhafa, and Ibn Urayqit." She said, "The Messenger of Allah ﷺ and his companions ate and took as much provision from it as their bags would hold, and we still had some meat, or more than it. We kept the sheep whose udder the Messenger of Allah had touched until the Year of Drought, in the time of 'Umar ibn al-Khattab in 18 AH. We used to milk it in the morning and evening, whether there was a little or a lot in the land." Umm Ma'bad was a Muslim then.

Muhammad ibn 'Umar and others said, "Rather she came later and became Muslim and gave her allegiance."

✳✳✳✳✳

Umm 'Abdullah ibn Mas'ud

She is Umm 'Abd bint 'Abdu Wudd. Her mother was Hind bint 'Abd. She became Muslim and gave her allegiance to the Prophet.

It is related that 'Umar allotted Umm 'Abdullah a stipend of 1000 dirhams.

*****

Rayta bint 'Abdullah

She was the wife of 'Abdullah ibn Mas'ud and mother of his child. She was a craftswoman. She said, "Messenger of Allah, I am a woman with work which I sell and neither me nor my husband nor child have anything." She asked him about maintenance for them and he said, "You will have a reward for what you spend on them."

*****

Zaynab bint Abi Mu'awiya ath-Thaqafiyya

She was the wife of Abdullah ibn Mas'ud. She became Muslim and gave allegiance and related *hadith* from the Messenger of Allah.

It is related from Busr ibn Sa'id that the Messenger of Allah said to Zaynab ath-Thaqafiyya, the wife of Abdullah ibn Mas'ud, "When you go out for the *'Isha'* prayer, do not put on perfume."

*****

The daughter of Khabbab ibn al-Aratt

She became Muslim, met the Messenger of Allah ﷺ and transmitted from him.

Khabbab's daughter said, "Khabbab went out on an expedition and the Messenger of Allah ﷺ undertook to come to us and milk a goat for us in a bowl of ours. He used to milk it until it was overflowing. When Khabbab returned, its milk decreased."

The daughter of Khabbab ibn al-Aratt said, "My father went out on a raid and only left us a sheep. He said, 'When you want to milk it, take it to the People of the Suffa.' We took it while the Messenger of Allah ﷺ was sitting there. He took it and hobbled it and milked it. Then he said, 'Bring me the largest vessel you have.' I went and could only find a bowl in which we kneaded bread. I brought it, and he milked until the bowl was full. He said, 'Go and drink and give some to your neighbours. When you want to milk it, bring it to me.'

We used to take it to him and we had plenty until my father came and took it and hobbled it. My mother went to its milk and said, 'Our sheep is closed to us.' He said, 'How is that?' She said, 'Its milk used to fill this bowl.' He said, 'Who used to milk it?' She said, 'The Messenger of Allah.' He said, 'And you make me equal with him! By Allah! His hand has more blessing than mine.'"

✳✳✳✳

Ku'ayba bint Sa'd al-Aslamiyya

She gave allegiance after the *hijra*. She was the one who had a tent in the mosque where she used to treat the sick and wounded. When Sa'd ibn Mu'adh was wounded in the Battle of the Ditch, she treated his wound until he died. Ku'ayba was present with the Messenger of Allah ﷺ at Khaybar.

Umm Muta' al-Aslamiyya

She became Muslim after the *hijra* and gave allegiance and was present with the Messenger of Allah ﷺ at Khaybar.

✳✳✳✳

Umm Sinan al-Aslamiyya

She became Muslim after the *hijra* and gave her allegiance.

Umm Sinan al-Aslamiyya said, "When the Messenger of Allah wanted to go out to Khaybar, I went to him and said, 'Messenger of Allah, I will go out with you to sew the waterskins and treat the sick and wounded, if there are any, and see to the camels.' The Messenger of Allah said, 'Go with the blessing of Allah. Your companions who have spoken to me, and I have given them leave, are both from your people and from others. If you wish, go with your people, or if you wish, go with us.' I said, 'With you.' He said, 'You can be with Umm Salama, my wife.' So I was with her."

Umm Sinan al-Aslamiyya was present at the conquest of Khaybar with the Messenger of Allah ﷺ . She said, "We used not to go out to *Jumu'a* and the *'Ids* until we despaired of finding husbands."

✳✳✳✳

Umayya bint Qays ibn Abi's-Salt al-Ghifariyya

She became Muslim and gave her allegiance and was present at Khaybar with the Messenger of Allah.

Umayya bint Qays ibn Abi's-Salt al-Ghifariyya said, "I went to the Messenger of Allah ﷺ with some women of the Banu Ghifar. We said, 'Messenger of Allah, we wish to go out with you to Khaybar to treat the wounded and help the Muslims as much as we can.' The Messenger of Allah said, 'With the blessing of Allah.' We went out with him. I was still a young girl, so the Messenger of Allah put me behind the back of the saddle of his camel. He dismounted for *Subh* and made the camel kneel and I saw that the back of the saddle I had been on had a trace of blood from me. It was the first time I menstruated. I clung to the camel and was embarrassed. When the Messenger of Allah saw what I was doing and saw the blood, he said, 'Perhaps you have menstruated?' I said, 'Yes.' He said, 'Attend to yourself and then take a vessel of water and put some salt in it, and then wash the blood which is on the saddle and come back.' I did that. When Allah let us conquer Khaybar, he gave us some gifts from the booty but did not give us an actual share. He took this necklace which you see on my neck and gave it to me and put it on my neck with his own hands. By Allah, it will never leave me." It remained on her neck until she died, and she left instructions for it to be buried with her. Whenever she purified herself, she put salt in her water and she left instructions that salt be put in her *ghusl* water when she was washed.

✳✳✳✳✳
Umm Hufayd al-Hilaliyya

She became Muslim and gave allegiance to the Messenger of Allah after the *hijra*. She is the one who gave a lizard to the Messenger of Allah.

Umm Sunbula al-Malikiyya

She became Muslim and gave allegiance to the Messenger of Allah after the *hijra*.

'A'isha, the wife of the Prophet, said, "When we came to Madina, the Messenger of Allah ﷺ forbade us to accept gifts from the bedouins. Umm Sunbula al-Aslamiyya came with some milk and brought it to us but we refused to accept it. We were like that until the Messenger of Allah and Abu Bakr came. He said, 'What is this?' I said, 'Messenger of Allah, this is Umm Sunbula who has given us some milk and you forbade us to accept anything from the bedouins.' The Messenger of Allah ﷺ said, 'Take it. When they become Muslim, they are not bedouins. They are the people of our desert and we are the people of their towns. When we call them, they answer. When we ask for their help, they give it. Pour it, Umm Sunbula!' She poured it and he said, 'Give it to Abu Bakr.' He drank and he said, 'Pour it,' and she poured and the Messenger of Allah drank. Then he said 'Pour it,' and she poured and he gave it to 'A'isha who drank it." 'A'isha said, "How cool it is on the liver!"

✳✳✳✳✳

Umm Kurz al-Khuza'iyya

She went to the Messenger of Allah ﷺ on the Day of al-Hudaybiyya when he was dividing the meat of the sacrificial camels and became Muslim. She transmitted from the Messenger of Allah.

Umm Kurz al-Khuza'iyya said, "I asked the Messenger of Allah about the *'aqiqa* and he said, 'It is two sheep for a boy and one sheep for a girl.'"

Umm Ma'qil al-Asadiyya

She became Muslim, gave allegiance to the Messenger of Allah and transmitted from him.

Umm Ma'qil said, "Messenger of Allah, I want to go on *hajj*, and my camel is old. What do you command me?" He said, "Do *'umra* in Ramadan. *'Umra* in Ramadan is equal to *hajj*."

Umm Subayya Khawla bint Qays al-Jahmiyya

She became Muslim and gave allegiance after the *hijra* and related *hadiths* from the Messenger of Allah.

Umm Subayya said, "My hand and the hand of the Messenger of Allah ﷺ alternated in the same *wudu'* vessel."

Umm Subayya Khawla bint Qays al-Jahmiyya said, "I used to listen to the *khutba* of the Messenger of Allah on Jumu'a while I was at the back of the women and listen to him recite *Qaf* on the minbar while I was at the back of the mosque."

It is related from Sawda bint Abi Dubays al-Jahmiyya who met the Prophet that Umm Subayya Khawla bint Qays said, "In the time of the Prophet and Abu Bakr and the beginning of the khalifate of 'Umar, we women in the mosque used to socialise. Sometimes we spun and sometimes some of us would work with palm leaves." 'Umar said, 'I will make you become free women [i.e. make you stay at home].' So we left it although we used to attend the prayers at their times. 'Umar used to go out when he had prayed the final *'Isha'* prayer and go around with his whip to anyone who was in the mosque. He would look at them and note their faces and check up on them and ask them whether they had prayed *Isha'*, or he would take them out and give them supper."

✳✳✳✳✳

Sawda bint Abi Dubays al-Jahmiyya

She became Muslim and gave allegiance after the *hijra* and her father was a Companion.

Umayma, or Umama bint Sufyan ibn Wahb

Of Kinana. Her mother was Umm 'Abdullah. Umayma was the wife of Abu Sufyan ibn Harb. She became Muslim on the Day of the Conquest and gave her allegiance. It is also said that it was shortly after that.

Barza bint Mas'ud ibn 'Amr ath-Thaqafiyya

Her mother was Ama bint Khalaf ibn Wahb. She married Safwan ibn Umayya and bore him 'Abdullah the elder. He is at-Tawil who was killed with 'Abdullah ibn az-Zubayr. She also bore Safwan Hisham the elder, Umayya and Umm Habib. Barza became Muslim and gave allegiance to the Messenger of Allah in the Farewell Hajj.

Al-Baghum bint al-Mu'adhdhil

She is the mother of 'Abdullah the younger, son of Safwan, and Safwan ibn Safwan and 'Amr ibn Safwan. Al-Baghum became Muslim and gave her allegiance to the Messenger of Allah ﷺ in the Farewell Hajj. It is also reported that she became Muslim earlier than that, on the Day of the Conquest of Makka.

'Abdullah ibn az-Zubayr said, "On the Day of the Conquest, al-Baghum bint al-Mu'adhdhil of Kinana became Muslim. She was the wife of Safwan ibn Umayya and she went to the Messenger of Allah and gave him allegiance.

Umm Hakim bint Tariq al-Kinaniyya

She became Muslim and gave her allegiance to the Messenger of Allah in the Farewell Hajj.

Qutayla bint 'Amr al-Kinaniyya

She became Muslim and gave her allegiance to the Messenger of Allah in the Farewell Hajj.

✳✳✳✳✳

Tumadir bint al-Asbagh ibn 'Amr of Kalb

Her mother was Juwayriyya bint Wabra of Kalb.

It is related from Ibrahim ibn 'Abdu'r-Rahman that the Prophet sent 'Abdu'r-Rahman ibn 'Awf to Kalb. He said, "If they respond to you, then marry the daughter of their king or the daughter of their chief." When 'Abdu'r-Rahman arrived, he called them to Islam and they responded. He established the *jizya*. Then 'Abdu'r-Rahman ibn 'Awf married Tumadir bint al-Asbagh, the daughter of their king, and brought her to Madina. She was the mother of Abu Salama ibn 'Abdu'r-Rahman.

Muhammad ibn 'Umar, said, "She was the first Kalbite woman to marry a Qurayshi. She only bore Abu Salama to 'Abdu'r-Rahman.

It is related that Tumadir had some bad qualities and there were two divorce pronouncements against her. When 'Abdu'r-Rahman became ill, some words passed between him and her and he said to her, "By Allah, if you ask me for a divorce, I will divorce you!" She said, "By Allah, I ask you!" Then he said, "Inform me when you have menstruated and become pure." When she had menstruated and become pure, she sent word to inform him. Her messenger passed one of his family and he called him and said, "Where are you going?" He said, "Tumadir has sent me to 'Abdu'r-Rahman to inform me that she has menstruated and become pure." He said, "Go back to her and tell her not to do it. By Allah, he will not take back his oath." He went back to her and she said, "By Allah, I will never take back my oath! Go and tell him." He went to him and informed him and he divorced her.

Umm Kulthum said, "When 'Abdu'r-Rahman ibn 'Awf divorced his Kalbite wife Tumadir, he gave her a black slavegirl. He said that he gave her the use of her."

It is related from Talha ibn 'Abdullah that 'Uthman ibn 'Affan let Tumadir bint al-Asbagh al-Kalbiyya inherit from 'Abdu'r-Rahman as he had divorced her in his final illness. It was her final divorce.

It is related from Sa'd ibn Ibrahim that 'Abdu'r-Rahman divorced Tumadir three times and 'Uthman let her inherit from him after the end of the waiting-period." Sa'd said, "Abu Salama's mother was Tumadir bint al-Asbagh."

Muhammad ibn 'Umar said, "Then az-Zubayr ibn al-'Awwam married Tumadir bint al-Asbagh al-Kalbiyya after 'Abdu'r-Rahman ibn 'Awf. She was only married to him a short time before he divorced her."

It is related that when az-Zubayr ibn al-'Awwam divorced Tumadir bint al-Asbagh al-Kalbiyya, she had been with him for seven days. He did not delay divorcing her and she used to say to the women, "When one of you marries, she should not be deceived by seven days after what az-Zubayr has done to me."

✳✦✳✦✳

Asma' bint Mukharraba ibn Jandal of Tamim

Her mother was al-'Inaq bint al-Jabbar. She married Hisham ibn al-Mughira and bore him Abu Jahl and al-Harith. Then Hisham died and after him she married his brother, Abu Rabi'a ibn al-Mughira, and bore him 'Ayyash, 'Abdullah and Umm Hujayr. Asma' became Muslim and gave her allegiance and went to Madina and remained until the khalifate of 'Umar ibn al-Khattab or after it.

Ar-Rubayyi' bint Mu'awwidh said, "I went with some Ansar women to visit Asma' bint Mukharraba, Umm Abi Jahl, in the time of 'Umar ibn al-Khattab. Her son 'Abdullah ibn Rabi'a used to send her some perfume from Yemen and she used to sell it. We used to buy it from her. When she put some for me in my bottle and weighed it for me as she weighed it for her friends, she said, 'Write for me what you owe me.' I said, 'Yes, I will write for her against ar-Rubayyi' bint Mu'awwidh.' Asma' said, 'Get away! You are the daughter of someone who killed his master.' I said, 'No, but the daughter of someone who killed his slave.' She said, 'By Allah, I will never sell you anything!' I said, 'And, by Allah, I will never buy anything from you! By Allah, it is neither good nor fragrant.' By Allah I have never smelt a perfume better than it, but I was angry."

✳✦✳✦✳

Asma' bint Salama of Tamim

Her mother was Salma bint Zuhayr. She became Muslim early on in Makka, gave her allegiance, and emigrated to Abyssinia in the second emigration with her husband, 'Ayyash ibn Abi Rabi'a and there she bore him 'Abdullah ibn 'Ayyash.

Umm Saba'

Umm Saba' asked the Messenger of Allah, "Messenger of Allah, is there an *'aqiqa* for our children?" He said, "Yes, two sheep for a boy, and one sheep for a girl. "

Mawiya, the client of Hujayr ibn Abi Ihab

She is the woman in whose house Khubayb ibn 'Adi was impris-
oned in Makka until the end of the sacred months when they killed
him. She used to recount his story and then she became a good
Muslim.

She said, "By Allah, I never saw a better person that Khubayb. I
looked at him through a crack in the door while he was in irons at a
time when I did not know of any grapes in the land which could be
eaten. In his hand was a bunch of grapes the size of a man's head
which he was eating. It was only the provision of Allah. Khubayb
used to do *tajahhud* prayers, and the women would listen to him and
weep and feel compassion for him. I said to him, 'Khubayb, do you
need anything?' He said 'No, other than you giving me fresh water to
drink and not giving me to eat what was been sacrificed to idols, and
telling me when you mean to kill me.' At the end of the sacred
months, they agreed to kill him, and I went to him and told him. By
Allah, he did not seem bothered by that. He said, 'Send me something which I can use.' I sent him a razor with my son, Abu Husayn.
(She used to care for him although he was not her natural son.) When
the boy had left, I said, 'By Allah, the man will have his revenge!
What have I done? I have sent the boy with the weapon and he will
kill him and say, "A life for a life."' When my son brought him the
implement, he took it from him and then joked with him, 'By my
father, you are bold! Doesn't your mother have any fear of my
treachery so that she sends you with an implement when you are
intending to kill me!'" Mawiya said, "I was listening to that and I
said, 'Khubayb, I trusted you by the security of Allah and gave to
you by your God. I did not give to you so that you would kill my
son.' Khubayb said, 'I would not kill him. We do not consider treachery lawful in our *deen*.' Then I told him that they would take him out
and kill him the following day. They took him out in irons until they
reached at-Tan'im. The children, women and slaves and a group of
the people of Makka went out with him. No one stayed behind. They
were either someone seeking revenge, and hoping to quench the
desire for revenge by being present, or someone who was not seeking
revenge, but was opposed to Islam and its people. Then they took

him to at-Tan'im along with Zayd ibn ad –Dathima. They ordered that a tall piece of wood be set up. When they were about to put Khubayb on it, he said, 'Will you let me pray two *rak'ats*?' They said, 'Yes.' So he prayed two perfect *rak'ats* without making them long."

***** *****

Umm Tariq, the client of Sa'd

Umm Tariq, the client of Sa'd, said, "The Prophet ﷺ went to Sa'd and asked for permission to enter. Sa'd was silent for three times. Then the Prophet left and Sa'd sent me after him to say, 'Nothing prevented us from giving you permission but that we wanted more from you.'" She said,"I heard a voice at the door asking permission to enter, but I did not see anything. The Prophet ﷺ said, 'Who is it?' She said, 'I am Umm Maldam.' He said, 'You have no welcome! Are you going to give to the people of Quba?' She said, 'Yes.' He said, 'Then go to them.'"

***** *****

Umm Farwa, the grandmother of al-Qasim ibn Ghannam

It is related from Umm Farwa, who gave her allegiance to the Prophet, that she listened to the Messenger of Allah ﷺ when a man asked him about the best action. The Messenger of Allah said, "The prayer at the beginning of its time."

***** *****

Maymuna bint Kardam

Maymuna bint Kardam, the client of Yazid ibn Miqsam, said, "I was riding behind my father and I heard him ask the Prophet ﷺ, 'Messenger of Allah, I have vowed to sacrifice at Buwana.' He said, 'Is it an idol or a false deity which is worshipped?' He said, 'No.' He said, 'Then fulfil your vow.'"

Maymuna bint Kardam said, "I saw the Messenger of Allah at Makka while he was on a camel. I was with my father. The Messenger of Allah was holding a whip resembling a scribe's whip. I heard the bedouins and the people saying, 'The whip! The whip!' My father went up to him and took hold of his foot, and the Messenger of Allah stopped for him. I have not forgotten the length of his second toe over the rest of his toes. My father said to him, 'I was present in an army which was involved in some fighting.' The Messenger of Allah knew about that army. He said, 'Tariq ibn al-Murr said, "Who will give me a spear with its garment?" I said, "What is its garment?" He said, "I will marry him to the first daughter I have." So I gave him my spear and then left him until he had a daughter and she had come of age. Then I went to him and said, "Prepare my wife for me." He said, "No, by Allah, I will not prepare her until you give me a new dower other than that." I swore that I would not do it.' The Messenger of Allah ﷺ said, 'What sort of woman is she?' He said, 'She has begun to go grey.' The Messenger of Allah said, 'Let her be. She will have no good for you.' That alarmed me and I looked at him. The Messenger of Allah said, 'You have no wrong action and your companion has no wrong action.'"

She said, "My father said to him in that place, 'I vowed to slaughter a number of sheep.' I think that he said, 'fifty sheep at the beginning of Buwana.' The Messenger of Allah said, 'Are there any idols there?' He said, 'No.' The Messenger of Allah said, 'Then fulfil the vow you have made to Allah.' My father collected them and began to slaughter them. One sheep slipped away from him and he went after it, saying, 'O Allah, fulfil my vow for me!' until he caught it and slaughtered it."

✳✳✳✳✳

Maymuna bint Sa'id, the client of the Prophet

Maymuna, the client of the Prophet, said, "The Messenger of Allah ﷺ said, 'Maymuna, seek refuge with Allah from the punishment of the grave.' I said, 'Messenger of Allah, is it true?' He said, 'Yes, Maymuna, the worst punishment on the Day of Rising will be for slander and urine.'"

✳✳✳✳✳

Umm al-Husayn al-Ahmasiyya

Umm al-Husayn said, "I saw the Messenger of Allah ﷺ when he was addressing the people at Mina. He was wrapped in his garment and the muscle of his arm was quivering. He was saying, 'O people! Fear Allah and hear and obey him. If an Abyssinian slave is put in charge of you, then obey him as long as he acts in accordance with the Book of Allah.'"

Umm al-Husayn said, "I saw the Messenger of Allah ﷺ while he was on his camel and saddle, and Husayn was in my lap. He had put his garment under his armpit and was saying, 'O people! Fear Allah and obey the one who is in charge of you, even if he is an Abyssinian, even if he is a mutilated Abyssinian slave. Obey him as long as he acts in accordance the Book of Allah.'"

✼✼✼✼✼

Umm Jundub al-Azdiyya

She is Umm Sulaym ibn 'Amr ibn al-Ahwas. She became Muslim and gave allegiance to the Messenger of Allah and related from him.

It is related from her son that she saw the Prophet ﷺ stoning the Jamra al-'Aqaba at the bottom of the valley. He threw seven pebbles the size of fruit stones, saying, "O people! Do not kill one another." There was a man behind him shielding him from people's stones. She asked about him and was told, "It is al-'Abbas ibn 'Abdu'l-Muttalib." He threw seven pebbles and then left. A woman went to him and said, "Messenger of Allah, My son is ill." He said, "Bring me some water from those tents." She brought him some water in a stone vessel. He drank from it and spat in it. He said, "Have your son drink it and Allah will heal him." He gave it to him to drink and her son was cured.

Umm Jundub said, "I saw the Messenger of Allah ﷺ throwing stones at the Jamra al-'Aqaba on his mule. Behind him was a man who was shielding him from the stones. I said, 'Who is this behind the Messenger of Allah?' It was said, 'This is al-Fadl ibn al-'Abbas.'

I heard the Messenger of Allah ﷺ say, 'O people, be calm when you stone, and throw pebbles the size of fruit-stones.'"

*****

Umm Hakim bint Wida' al-Khuza'iyya

She became Muslim and related a number of *hadiths* from the Messenger of Allah.

Umm Hakim bint Wida' said, "I said to the Prophet, 'How do the poor repay the rich?' He replied, 'With good advice and supplication.'"

Umm Muslim al-Ashja'iyya

She became Muslim and transmitted a *hadith* from the Prophet.

Umm Muslim al-Ashja'iyya said, "The Messenger of Allah ﷺ came to me while I was in a leather tent of mine. He said, 'How excellent it would be if it were not carrion!' I began to examine it."

Umm Kabsha, a woman of Quda'a

She became Muslim and transmitted a *hadith* from the Messenger of Allah.

It is related about Umm Kabsha, a woman of Quda'a, that she asked permission from the Messenger of Allah ﷺ to go on a raid with him. He said, "No." She said, "Messenger of Allah, I will treat the wounded and attend to the sick." The Messenger of Allah said, "Stay. People will not say that Muhammad went on a raid with a woman."

*****

Umm as-Sa'ib

She met the Messenger of Allah ﷺ and became Muslim.

It is related that the Prophet ﷺ visited Umm as-Sa'ib when she was trembling with fever. He said, "What is the matter with you?" She said, "Fever, may Allah disgrace it." He said, "No, do not curse it! It removes the wrong actions of the Muslims as the bellows removes the dross of iron."

*****

Qutayla bint Sayfi al-Juhaniyya

She became Muslim and transmitted a *hadith* from the Prophet.

Qutayla bint Sayfi said, "One of the rabbis came to the Prophet and said, 'Muhammad, you would be the best of people were it not that you associate.' The Prophet said to him, 'How is that?' He said, 'One of you says, "No, by the Ka'ba."' The Prophet said, 'Whoever takes an oath, should say, "By the Lord of the Ka'ba."' He said, 'Muhammad, you would be the best of people were it not that you appoint an equal with Allah.' He said, 'How is that?' He said, 'One of you says, "What He wills and I wish."' The Prophet ﷺ said, 'The one of you who says it should say, "What Allah wills, and then what I wish."'"

*****

Salama bint al-Hurr

She became Muslim and transmitted a *hadith* from the Prophet.

Salama bint al-Hurr said, "I heard the Messenger of Allah ﷺ say, 'A time will come upon people when they stand for a time and do not find an Imam to lead them in prayer.'"

*****

Busayra, the grandmother of Humayda bint Yasir

She became Muslim and transmitted a *hadith* from the Prophet.

Busayra, who was one of the women Muhajirun, said, "The Messenger of Allah ﷺ said, 'Women of the believers! You must say "*la ilaha illa' llah*,"-"Glory be to Allah," and glorify Allah and do not neglect it so that you forget mercy. Use your fingers to count. They will questioned and will be asked to speak.'"

*****

Sarra' bint Nabhan al-Ghanawiyya

She became Muslim and transmitted *hadith* from the Prophet.
Sarra' bint Nabhan, who was the owner of a house in the Jahiliy-ya, said that she heard the Prophet ﷺ say on the day they call "heads" [i.e. when the sacrifices are eaten] which is the day after the Day of Sacrifice, "What day is this?" They said, "Allah and His Messenger know best." He said, "This is the middle of the Days of *Tashriq*." He said, "Do you know what land this is?" They said, "Allah and His Messenger know best." He said, "This is the Sacred Landmark." Then he said to 'Ali, "I will not instruct you the year after this. Your blood, your property, and your honour are sacred to one another, like the sacredness of this day in this land. Let those of you who were near convey to those of you who are far until you meet your Lord and He asks you about your actions." She said, "Then he went to Madina and only remained for some days until he died, may the blessing of Allah and His mercy and blessing be upon him."

✳✳✳✳✳

Ruzayna, the servant of the Messenger of Allah

She became Muslim and transmitted *hadith* from the Messenger of Allah about fasting, 'Ashura', the Dajjal and other things.

✳✳✳✳✳

Qayla, Umm Bani Anmar

She related *hadith* from the Messenger of Allah.
Qayla, Umm Bani Anmar, said, "The Messenger of Allah ﷺ came to Marwa to perform his duty in the *'umra*. I came leaning on a staff and sat down by him. I said, 'Messenger of Allah, I am a woman who buys and sells. Sometimes I want to buy goods and I offer less for them than I want to pay and then I increase and increase until I take them for what I want to pay for them. Sometimes I want to sell goods and I offer them for more than what I take for them for and then I go lower and lower until I sell them for what I want to sell them for.' The Messenger of Allah said to me, 'Do not do that, Qayla. If you want to buy something, then offer what you want to

pay for it for and it can be taken or refused. If you want to sell something, then name what you want to sell it for and it can be taken or refused.'"

✻✻✻✻✻

Qayla bint Makhrama at-Tamimiyya

She was married to Habib ibn Azhar, the brother of the Banu Janab and bore him girls. Then he died at the beginning of Islam and their uncle, Athub ibn Azhar, took her daughters from her. She went out to find companions to go to the Messenger of Allah ﷺ at the beginning of Islam. She accompanied Hurayth ibn Hassan ash-Shaybani, the delegation of Bakr ibn Wa'il, to the Messenger of Allah. She went with him to the Messenger of Allah and questioned him. She listened to him and prayed with him as 'Abdullah ibn Hassan transmits in the *hadith* of Qayla. Qayla had a son called Hizam and it is mentioned that he fought with the Prophet on the Day of ar-Rabadha. Then he went to collect grain in Khaybar and fell ill with a fever and died, leaving daughters.

✻✻✻✻✻

The aunt of al-'As ibn 'Amr at-Tafawi

She related *hadith* from the Prophet.

Al-'As ibn 'Amr at-Tafawi said that he heard his aunt say that she went to the Prophet ﷺ with some of her people. She said to him, "O Prophet of Allah, relate to me a *hadith* by which Allah will benefit me." He told her, "Beware of the evil of the ear. Beware of the evil of the ear. Beware of the evil of the ear."

✻✻✻✻✻

Umm Walad Shayba

It is related from Umm Walad Shayba that she saw the Messenger of Allah ﷺ running between Safa and Marwa, saying, "Only cross the valley fast."

Safiyya bint 'Uthman said, "I looked at the Messenger of Allah while I was in the doorway of Abu Husayn, running between Safa and Marwa. He had raised his waist-wrapper so that I could see his knees. He said, 'The valley is only crossed fast,' running on the flat of the valley."

*****

Khulayda bint Qays ibn Thabit

She married al-Bara' ibn Ma'rur of the Banu Salama, who was one of the chiefs, and bore him Bishr. He was present at Badr. He is the one who ate some of the poisoned sheep with the Messenger of Allah ﷺ. Khulayda Umm Bishr became Muslim and gave *bay'a* to the Messenger of Allah and related from him.

Umm Bishr ibn al-Bara' said to the Messenger of Allah, "Messenger of Allah, do the dead recognise one another?" He said, "May your hands be dusty! The good soul is a green bird in the Garden. The birds recognise each other at the tops of the trees. They recognise one another."

Umm Bishr ibn al-Bara' said, "I heard the Messenger of Allah say to his Companions, 'Shall I inform you of the best of people?' They said, 'Yes, indeed, Messenger of Allah.' He threw his hand towards the west and said, 'A man who takes the reins of his horse waiting to attack or be attacked. Shall I tell you of the best of people after him?' They said, 'Yes indeed, Messenger of Allah.' He threw his hand towards the Hijaz and said, 'A man among his sheep who establishes the prayer and pays the *zakat* and knows that Allah has a right over him in his property. He has withdrawn from the evils of people.'"

'A'isha said, "Umm Bishr ibn al-Bara' ibn Ma'rur visited the Messenger of Allah ﷺ in his final illness when he had a fever. She touched him and said, 'I have not felt the like of your fever in anyone!' The Messenger of Allah said, 'As the reward is doubled for us, so the affliction is doubled for us. What are people saying?'" She said, "I said, 'People are claiming that the Messenger of Allah has pleurisy.' He said, 'It is not for Allah to give it power over me. It is a touch from shaytan. Rather, it is from the food which I and your son ate on the Day of Khaybar. It has afflicted me a number of times until this and now it cuts my aorta.' The Messenger of Allah ﷺ died a martyr."

Chapter Twelve:
The Muslim Ansar Women of Aws

The Names of Women of the Banu 'Abdu'l-Ashhal

Ar-Rabab bint an-Nu'man ibn Imru'l-Qays

Her mother was Mu'adha bint Anas ibn Qays. They were the Banu Hudhayla. Ar-Rabab bint an-Nu'man was the aunt of Sa'd ibn Mu'adh. Ar-Rabab bint an-Nu'man married Zurara ibn 'Amr and bore him Mu'adh. He is Abu Abi Namla, the Companion of the Messenger of Allah. Then she married Ma'rur ibn Sakhr of Khazraj and she bore him al-Bara', one of the twelve chiefs. Al-Bara' died before the Messenger of Allah emigrated to Madina. The Messenger of Allah went to his grave and prayed over him. Ar-Rabab bint an-Nu'man became Muslim and gave her allegiance to the Messenger of Allah.

'Iqrab bint Mu'adh ibn an-Nu'man

Her mother was Kabsha bint Rafi'. She was the full sister of Sa'd ibn Mu'adh. 'Iqrab married Yazid ibn Kurz and bore him Rafi' and Hawwa'. Then 'Iqrab married Qays ibn al-Khutaym and bore him Yazid, from whom Qays takes his *kunya*, and Thabit. Yazid was killed on the Day of the Bridge of Abu 'Ubayd. 'Iqrab became Muslim and gave her allegiance to the Messenger of Allah.

Hind bint Simak

Her mother was Umm Jundub bint Rifa'a. She is the paternal aunt of Uzayd ibn Hudayr. Hind married Sa'd ibn Mu'adh and bore him

'Umar and 'Abdullah. Hind was also married to Aws ibn Mu'adh, the brother of Sa'd ibn Mu'adh, and bore him al-Harith who was present at Badr. Hind became Muslim and gave allegiance to the Prophet.

Umama bint Simak

Her mother was Umm Jundub bint Rifa'a. She was also the paternal aunt of Uzayd ibn Hudayr. Umama married Sharik ibn Anas and bore him 'Abdullah, Umm Sakhr, Umm Sulayman, and Habiba. Umama bint Simak became Muslim and gave her allegiance to the Prophet.

Hawwa' bint Rafi' ibn Imru'l-Qays

That is how her lineage is given by Muhammad ibn 'Umar. He names her among the women who gave allegiance, but we do not find Rafi' ibn Imru'l-Qays in the lineage of the Ansar except for a single daughter whose name is as-Sa'ba. Her mother was Khuzayma bint 'Adi. As-Sa'ba is the sister of Abu'l-Haysar Anas ibn Rafi'.

Umm Iyas bint Anas ibn Rafi'

Her mother was Umm Sharik bint Khalid of Khazraj. Umm Iyas married Abu Sa'd ibn Talha. Umm Iyas became Muslim and gave her allegiance to the Messenger of Allah.

Umm al-Hakim

She is Wadda bint 'Uqba ibn Rafi'. Her mother was Umm al-Banin bint Hudhayfa of Quda'a. She is the paternal aunt of Mahmud ibn Labid. Umm al-Hakim married Qays ibn Makhrama and bore him children. She became Muslim and gave allegiance to the Prophet.

Umm Sa'd bint 'Uqba ibn Rafi'

Her mother was Salma bint 'Amr. She is also the paternal aunt of Mahmud ibn Labid. Qays ibn Makhrama married her after her sister,

Wadda bint 'Uqba. Umm Sa'd bint 'Uqba became Muslim and gave her allegiance to the Messenger of Allah.

Khawla bint 'Uqba ibn Rafi'

Her mother was Salma bint 'Amr. She is the paternal aunt of Mahmud ibn Labid. Khawla married al-Harith ibn as-Simma and bore him Sa'd. Then she was married to 'Abdullah ibn Qatada and bore him 'Amr. Khawla bint 'Uqba became Muslim and gave her allegiance to the Messenger of Allah.

'Amira bint Yazid ibn as-Sakan

Her mother was Umm Sa'd bint Khuzaym. 'Amira married Manzur ibn Labid and bore him al-Harith and 'Uthayra. 'Amira bint Yazid became Muslim and gave allegiance to the Messenger of Allah.

Umm 'Amir al-Ashhaliyya

Her name is Fukayha. She is also called Asma' bint Yazid. Her mother was Umm Sa'd bint Khuzaym. Umm 'Amir became Muslim and gave allegiance to the Messenger of Allah.

Umm 'Amir bint Yazid brought a meaty bone to the Prophet ﷺ and he took it while he was in the mosque of the Banu 'Abdu'l-Ashhal and then got up and prayed without doing *wudu'*.

Umm 'Amir al-Ashhaliyya said, "When the Messenger of Allah looked over our houses and said, 'What good is in these houses! These are the best of the people of the Ansar!'"

Umm 'Amir Asma' bint Yazid said, "I saw the Messenger of Allah ﷺ pray *Maghrib* in our mosque. I went to my house and brought him a meaty bone and some loaves of bread and said, 'By my father and mother, have supper.' He said to his Companions, 'Eat in the name of Allah.' So he and his Companions who had come with him and those of the people of the house who were present ate. By the One who has my soul in His hand, I saw that some of the meaty bone had not been eaten and most of the bread remained although there were forty men. Then he drank some water from a waterskin and left. I took that waterskin and oiled it and rolled it up, and we used to let the sick drink from it and we would drink from it hoping for blessing."

It is related that Asma' bint Yazid said, "The Prophet ﷺ passed by me while I was with some other women.He greeted us and we returned the greeting to him."

Ar-Rabab bint Ka'b ibn 'Adi

She married al-Yaman ibn Jabir al-'Abasi, their ally, and bore him Hudhayfa, Sa'd, Safwan, Mudlij, and Layla. Ar-Rabab bint Ka'b became Muslim and gave her allegiance to the Messenger of Allah.

Umm Niyar bint Zayd ibn Malik

She is the sister of Sa'd ibn Zayd al-Ashhali. Sa'd was present at 'Aqaba and Badr. Muhammad ibn 'Umar says she is one of those who gave allegiance, but we do not find her mentioned in the *Book of the Lineage of the Ansar.*

Umm 'Amr bint Salama

Her mother was Salma bint Salama. She is the full sister of Salama ibn Salama. He was present at al-'Aqaba and Badr. Umm 'Amr bint Salama married Muhammad ibn Maslama and bore him children. Umm 'Amr bint Salama became Muslim and gave her allegiance to the Messenger of Allah.

Na'ila bint Salama

Her mother is Umm 'Amr bint 'Atik. She is the half sister of Salama ibn Salama. Na'ila married 'Abdullah ibn Simak of Ghassan, the ally of the Banu Mu'awiya ibn Malik of Aws and bore him children. Then she was married to Ka'b ibn al-Qayn of Aws and bore him Sahl who was martyred at Uhud. Na'ila became Muslim and gave her allegiance to the Messenger of Allah.

'Iqrab bint Salama

Her mother was Suhayma bint 'Abdullah. She was the half sister of Salama ibn Salama. 'Iqrab married Rafi' ibn Yazid and bore him Usayd. 'Iqrab became Muslim and gave her allegiance to the Messenger of Allah.

Al-Muhayya bint Silkan

Her mother was Umm Sahl bint Rumi. She became Muslim and gave her allegiance to the Messenger of Allah.

Muhammad ibn 'Umar said, "She is 'Ubada bint Abi Na'ila Silkan ibn Salama. Silkan only had one daughter, but they disagree about her name."

Umm Hanzala bint Rumi

Her mother is Suhayma bint 'Abdullah ibn Rifa'a. She married Tha'laba ibn Anas and bore him children. Umm Hanzala became Muslim and gave her allegiance to the Messenger of Allah.

Umm Sahl bint Rumi

Her mother was Suhayma bint 'Abdullah. She married Silkan ibn Salama and bore him children. Umm Sahl became Muslim and gave her allegiance to the Messenger of Allah.

Umama bint Bishr ibn Waqsh

Her mother was Fatima bint Bishr of Khazraj. She was the sister of 'Abbad ibn Bishr who was present at Badr and all the battles with the Messenger of Allah. He was killed as a martyr in the Battle of

Yamana. Umama bint Bishr married Mahmud ibn Maslama and bore him children. Muhammad ibn 'Umar mentioned that Umama bint Bishr was the mother of 'Ali ibn Asad al-Hadli, and al-Hadl are the brethren of Qurayza. 'Abdullah ibn Muhammad said, "She is Umm 'Ali ibn Asad ibn 'Ubayd al-Hadli. Umm 'Ali is the daughter of Salama ibn Waqsh." Umama became Muslim and gave her allegiance to the Messenger of Allah.

Hawwa' bint Zayd ibn Sakan

Her mother was 'Iqrab bint Mu'adh. She was the sister of Rafi' ibn Yazid who was present at Badr. She married Qays ibn al-Khutaym and bore him Thabit.

She became Muslim early on in Makka before the *hijra* and was a good Muslim. The Messenger of Allah ﷺ heard about it. Qays ibn al-Khutaym went to Dhu'l-Mijaz, one of the markets of Makka. The Messenger of Allah went to him and called him to Islam earnestly. Qays said, "How excellent is that to which you call! That to which you call is good but war has distracted me from this news." The Messenger of Allah began to press him and said, "Abu Yazid, I am calling you to Allah." Qays repeated what he had said the first time. The Messenger of Allah said, "Abu Yazid, I have heard that you have treated your wife Hawwa' badly since she left your *deen*. Fear Allah and guard her for me and do not oppose her." He said, "Yes, I will do what you want and I will only treat her well." Qays had behaved very badly towards her before that. Then Qays came to Madina and said, "Hawwa', I met your companion Muhammad and he asked me to take care of you for him. By Allah, I will fulfil the undertaking I gave him, and you must attend to yourself. By Allah, you will never receive any harm from me." So Hawwa' made public the Islam she had been concealing and Qays did not oppose her. People talked about that and said to him, "Abu Yazid, your wife is following the *deen* of Muhammad!" Qays said, "I have promised Muhammad that I will not harm her and will look after her for him."

Umayma bint 'Amr ibn Sahl

She became Muslim and gave allegiance to the Messenger of Allah according to Muhammad ibn 'Umar.

Hind bint Sahl ibn Zayd

She became Muslim and gave her allegiance to the Messenger of Allah according to Muhammad ibn 'Umar.

Mulayka bint Sahl ibn Zayd

She became Muslim and gave allegiance to the Prophet. She was the wife of Abu'l-Haytham ibn at-Tayhan and bore him children.

As-Sa'ba bint Sahl ibn Zayd

She became Muslim and gave her allegiance to the Messenger of Allah according to Muhammad ibn 'Umar.

Umayma bint Abi'l-Haytham

Her mother was Mulayka bint Sahl ibn Zayd. She became Muslim and gave her allegiance to the Messenger of Allah according to Muhammad ibn 'Umar.

Fatima bint al-Yaman

The sister of Hudhayfa ibn al-Yaman al-'Abasi. They are the allies of the Banu'l-Ashhal. She became Muslim and gave her allegiance to the Messenger of Allah.

Fatima said, "I visited the Messenger of Allah with some women and there was a waterskin hanging with some water dripping on him due to the intensity of the heat of his fever. We said, 'Messenger of Allah, if you were to ask Allah, He would remove this from you.' He said, 'The people with the most severe affliction are the Prophets, and then those who follow them and then those who follow them.'"

The sister of Hudhayfa, who had sisters who met the Prophet, said, "The Messenger of Allah addressed us and said, 'Company of women, do you not have silver with which you can adorn yourselves? There is no woman among you who openly adorns herself with gold but that she will be punished by it.'"

Mansur said, "I mentioned that to Mujahid and he said, 'I met them and one of them would make her sleeve long so as to cover her ring.'"

✳✳✳✳✳

The Women of the Banu Haritha ibn Al-Khazraj, descendants of Malik ibn Al-Aws

Umama bint Khadij ibn Rafi'

The sister of Rafi' ibn Khadij. She is mentioned by Muhammad ibn 'Umar.

Umama bint Rafi'

She became Muslim and gave allegiance to the Messenger of Allah. Her mother was Halima bint 'Urwa of Khazraj. She married Usayd ibn Zhuhayr of Aws and bore him Thabit, Muhammad, Umm Kulthum, and Umm al-Hasan.

'Amira bint Zuhayr

Her mother was Fatima bint Bishr. She married Mirba' ibn Qayzi of Aws and bore him Zayd, Surara, 'Abdu'r-Rahman, and 'Abdullah who were both killed on the Day of the Bridge as martyrs without children. 'Amira became Muslim and gave *her* allegiance to the Messenger of Allah.

Layla bint Nahik

Her mother was Umm 'Abdullah bint Aslam. Layla married Sahl ibn ar-Rabi'. Layla became Muslim and gave allegiance to the Prophet.

Thubayta bint ar-Rabi' ibn 'Amr

Her mother was Sahla bint Imru'l-Qays. She married Aws ibn Qayzi and bore him 'Abdullah, Kubbatha, and 'Urraba. Thubayta bint ar-Rabi' became Muslim and gave allegiance to the Prophet.

Jamila bint Sayfi ibn 'Amr

Her mother was an-Nuwwar bint Qays. Jamila was the half-sister of Ghulba ibn Zayd. Jamila married 'Atik ibn Qays. Jamila became Muslim and gave allegiance to the Messenger of Allah.

Umayma bint 'Uqba ibn 'Amr

Her mother was Umm 'Umayr bint 'Amr. Umayma married Sahl ibn 'Atik. Umayma became Muslim and gave allegiance to the Prophet.

Umm 'Amir bint Sulaym

Her name was Habbaba. Her mother was Su'ad bint 'Amir. She married Usayd ibn Sa'ida and bore him Yazid. Umm 'Amir became Muslim and gave allegiance to the Messenger of Allah.

Jamila bint Sinan ibn Tha'laba

She married 'Ubayd as-Sahham ibn Sulaym and bore him Thabit. Jamila became Muslim and gave allegiance to the Prophet.

'Amira bint Abi Hathma

Her mother was Umm ar-Rabi' bint Aslam. She married Yazid ibn Usayd and then she was married to Yazid ibn Bardha'. 'Amira became Muslim and gave her allegiance to the Messenger of Allah.

Umm Suhayl bint Abi Hathma

Her mother was Hujja bint 'Umayr. She married Yazid ibn al-Bara' ibn 'Azib and bore him Mukhallid. Umm Suhayl became Muslim and gave her allegiance to the Messenger of Allah.

Umayma bint Abi Hathma

Her mother was Hujja bint 'Umayr. She married Hilal ibn al-Harith and then later married Abu Sindar ibn al-Husayn al-Aslami. Umayma became Muslim and gave her allegiance to the Prophet.

'Amira bint Sa'd ibn 'Amir

Her mother was Umm 'Amir bint Sulaym. She married Kabbatha ibn Aws. 'Amira became Muslim and gave allegiance to the Prophet.

Al-Waqsa' bint Mas'ud ibn 'Amir

Her mother was Kabsha bint Aws. She married an-Nu'man ibn Malik. Al-Waqsa' became Muslim and gave allegiance to the Prophet.

An-Nuwwar bint Qays ibn al-Harith

She married Zayd ibn Nuwayra and bore him 'Azib. An-Nuwwar became Muslim and gave allegiance to the Messenger of Allah.

Umm 'Abdullah bint 'Azib bint al-Harith

She was the full sister of al-Bara' ibn 'Azib. Their mother was Umm Habiba bint Abi Habiba, and it is also said that their mother was Umm Khalid bint Thabit. Umm 'Abdullah became Muslim and gave her allegiance to the Messenger of Allah ﷺ.

Umm 'Abs bint Maslama ibn Salama

Her mother was Umm Sahm. Her name was Khulayda bint Abi 'Ubayd. She was the full sister of Muhammad and Mahmud ibn Salama. She married Abu 'Abs ibn Jabr and bore him children. Umm 'Abs became Muslim and gave allegiance to the Messenger of Allah.

Hind bint Mahmud ibn Maslama

Her mother was ash-Shamus bint 'Amr. She married 'Amr ibn Sa'd ibn Mu'adh. Hind became Muslim and gave her allegiance to the Messenger of Allah.

Umm Manzur bint Mahmud ibn Maslama

Her mother was ash-Shamus bint 'Amr. She married Labid ibn 'Uqba and bore him Mahmud ibn Labid al-Faqih, Manzur, and Maymuna. Umm Manzur became Muslim and gave her allegiance to the Messenger of Allah.

Umm 'Amr bint Mahmud ibn Maslama

Her mother was Umama bint Bishr. She married 'Abdullah ibn Muhammad ibn Maslama and bore him 'Amr and Humayd. Then she married Zayd ibn Sa'd. Umm 'Amr became Muslim and gave her allegiance to the Messenger of Allah.

Umm ar-Rubayyi' bint Aslam

Her mother was Su'ad bint Rafi'. She was the full sister of Salama ibn Aslam, one of the people of Badr. She married Abu Hathma ibn Sa'ida and bore him Sahl, 'Amira, and Umm Damra. Umm ar-Rubayyi' became Muslim and gave allegiance to the Prophet.

Suhayma bint Aslam ibn Harish

Her mother was Su'ad bint Rafi'. She was the full sister of Salama ibn Aslam, one of the people of Badr. She married Muhayyisa ibn Mas'ud. Suhayma became Muslim and gave her allegiance to the Messenger of Allah.

Lubaba bint Aslam ibn Harish

Her mother was Su'ad bint Rafi'. She was the full sister of Salama ibn Aslam, one of the people of Badr. She married Zayd ibn Sa'd. Lubaba became Muslim and gave allegiance to the Prophet.

Umm 'Abdullah

She is Salma bint Aslam. Her mother was Umm Khalid bint Khalid. She was the half sister of Salama ibn Aslam. She married

Nahik ibn 'Adi. Umm 'Abdullah became Muslim and gave her allegiance to the Messenger of Allah.

Salama bint Mas'ud ibn Ka'b

Her mother was Adam bint al-Jamuh. She was the full sister of Huwaysa, Muhayyisa and al-Ahwas, the sons of Mas'ud ibn Ka'b. Salama married Murshida ibn Jabr and bore him children. Salama bint Mas'ud became Muslim and gave allegiance to the Prophet.

Lubna bint Qayzi ibn Qays

Her mother was Umm Habib bint Qurad. She married Abu Thabit, and then she was married to Abu Ahmad ibn Qays. Lubna became Muslim and gave her allegiance to the Messenger of Allah.

Layla bint Rafi'

Her mother was Umm al-Bara' bint Salama She married Jabr ibn 'Amr and bore him Abu 'Abs, one of the people of Badr. Layla became Muslim and gave allegiance to the Messenger of Allah.

Asma' bint Murshida ibn Jabr

Her mother was Salama bint Mas'ud. She married ad-Dahhak ibn Khalifa and bore him Thabit, Abu Jubayra, Abu Bakr, 'Umar, Thubayta who married Muhammad ibn Maslama, Bakra, Hammada, and Safiyya. Asma' became Muslim and gave her allegiance to the Messenger of Allah.

'Amira bint Murshida ibn Jabr

Her mother was Salama bint Mas'ud. She married Suwayd ibn an-Nu'man. 'Umayra became Muslim and gave her allegiance to the Messenger of Allah ﷺ. He said, "Some of the Ansar said that Murshida ibn Jabr went on one of the Prophet's expeditions."

Umm ad-Dahhak bint Mas'ud al-Harithiyya

She became Muslim and gave allegiance to the Messenger of Allah. She was present at Khaybar with the Messenger of Allah.

*****

The Women of the Banu Zafar, descendants of Malik ibn al-Aws

Layla bint al-Khutaym

She was the sister of Qays ibn al-Khutaym. Her mother was Sharqat ad-Dar bint Haysha. In the Jahiliyya she married Mas'ud ibn Aws and bore him 'Amra and 'Amira. He died when the Messenger of Allah came to Madina. Layla was the first woman to give allegiance to the Messenger of Allah ﷺ accompanied by her two daughters and her daughters' two daughters. She gave herself to the Prophet. Then the Banu Zafar told her to ask to be released, and he released and divorced her because of her jealousy. She is called "the one who was eaten by the lion."

Lubna bint al-Khutaym

Her mother and the mother of Qays ibn al-Khutaym was Qurayba bint Qays. She married 'Abdullah ibn Nahik and bore him children. She became Muslim and gave allegiance to the Messenger of Allah.

Umm Sahl bint an-Nu'man ibn Zayd

She is the full sister of Qatada ibn an-Nu'man, one of the people of Badr. Umm Sahl became Muslim and gave allegiance to the Prophet.

Habiba bint Qays ibn Zayd

Her mother was 'Amira bint Mas'ud ibn Aws. She married Mu'adh ibn al-Harith and bore him 'Ubaydullah. Then she married

Abu Fadala ibn Thabit and bore him Kharija. Habiba bint Qays became Muslim and gave allegiance to the Messenger of Allah.

'Amra bint Mas'ud ibn Aws

Her mother was Layla bint al-Khutaym. She married Muhammad ibn Maslama and bore him 'Abdullah. 'Amra bint Mas'ud became Muslim and gave allegiance to the Messenger of Allah.

'Amira bint Mas'ud ibn Aws

Her mother was Layla bint al-Khutaym. She married Qays ibn Zayd and bore him Habiba who gave allegiance, and Umm Jundub who married Thabit ibn Qays. 'Amira bint Mas'ud became Muslim along with her mother, Layla bint al-Khutaym, and gave allegiance to the Messenger of Allah.

Suhayma bint Mas'ud ibn Aws

Her mother was ash-Shamus bint 'Amr. She married her cousin, Jabir ibn 'Abdullah and bore him 'Abdu'r-Rahman and Umm Habib. Suhayma became Muslim and gave allegiance to the Prophet.

Umm Salama bint Mas'ud ibn Aws

Her mother was ash-Shamus bint 'Amr. She married Aws ibn Malik and bore him al-Harith. Umm Salama became Muslim and gave her allegiance to the Messenger of Allah.

Habiba bint Mas'ud ibn Aws

Her mother was ash-Shamus bint 'Amr. She married Sinan ibn 'Amr, their ally, and bore him al-Muqanna' and Umm al-Harith. Habiba became Muslim and gave her allegiance to the Messenger of Allah.

Umm Jundub bint Mas'ud ibn Aws

Her mother was ash-Shamus bint 'Amr. She married Nasr ibn al-Harith and bore him al-Harith. Umm Jundub bint Mas'ud became Muslim and gave allegiance to the Messenger of Allah.

'Amira bint al-Harith

Her mother was Sawda bint Sawad. She is the full sister of Nasr ibn al-Harith who was present at Badr. She married 'Adi ibn Haram. 'Amira became Muslim and gave allegiance to the Messenger of Allah.

Bashira bint an-Nu'man ibn al-Harith

Her mother was Umm Sakhr bint Sharik. She married Sahl ibn al-Harith and bore him ar-Rabi' and Umm al-Harith. Bashira became Muslim and gave her allegiance to the Messenger of Allah.

Umayma bint an-Nu'man ibn al-Harith

Her mother was Umm Sakhr bint Sharik. She married 'Ubayd ibn Aws and bore him an-Nu'man. Umayma became Muslim and gave her allegiance to the Messenger of Allah.

Bashira bint Thabit ibn an-Nu'man

Her mother was Shumayla bint al-Harith. She married Abu Namla ibn Mu'adh. Bashira became Muslim and gave her allegiance to the Messenger of Allah.

'Amira bint Thabit ibn an-Nu'man

Her mother was Shumayla bint al-Harith. 'Amira became Muslim and gave her allegiance to the Messenger of Allah.

'A'isha bint Jaz' ibn 'Amr

She married Abu'l-Mundhir Yazid ibn 'Amir, the brother of Qutba ibn 'Amr, one of the people of Badr. She bore him al-Mundhir and 'Abdu'r-Rahman. 'A'isha bint Jaz' became Muslim and gave her allegiance to the Messenger of Allah.

Khulayda bint al-Hubab

Her mother was Bint Mudlij. She married 'Abdullah ibn Sa'd and did not bear him any children. Khulayda became Muslim and gave her allegiance to the Messenger of Allah.

Umm al-Harith bint al-Harith

Her mother was Sahla bint Imru'l-Qays. Umm al-Harith became Muslim and gave her allegiance to the Messenger of Allah.

'Aysa' bint al-Harith

Her mother was Qilaba bint Sayfi. She married Anas ibn Fadala. She bore him Muhammad ibn Anas, and Muhammad ibn Anas had twenty-two sons and five daughters. 'Aysa' became Muslim and gave allegiance to the Messenger of Allah.

Habiba

She is Umm Habib bint Mu'attab. She married Usayr ibn 'Urwa and bore him Abu Burda. Habiba became Muslim and gave allegiance to the Messenger of Allah.

Shumayla bint al-Harith

Her mother was Uthayla bint 'Abdu'l-Mundhir. She was the sister of Abu Lubaba ibn 'Abdu'l-Mundhir. Shumayla bint al-Harith married Thabit ibn an-Nu'man and bore him Khalid and Bashira. Shumayla became Muslim and gave allegiance to the Prophet.

Burayda bint Bishr ibn al-Harith

Her mother was Umayma bint 'Amr. She married 'Abbad ibn Nahik. Then she married to his brother, Ma'qil ibn Nahik. Then she married Abu Burda ibn Usayr and bore him Mu'attab. Burayda became Muslim and gave allegiance to the Messenger of Allah.

Umm Simak bint Fadala

She was the sister of Anas and Mu'nis, the sons of Fadala. Sawda bint Suwayd was the mother of all of them. Umm Simak became Muslim and gave her allegiance to the Messenger of Allah.

✳✳✳✳✳

The Women of the Banu 'Amr ibn 'Awf ibn Malik ibn Aws

Ash-Shamus bint Abi 'Amir ar-Rahib

Her mother was 'Amiq bint al-Harith. Ash-Shamus married Thabit ibn Abi'l-Aflah and bore him 'Asim ibn Thabit who was present at Badr and killed as a martyr at ar-Raji', and Jamila who gave allegiance to the Prophet and married 'Umar ibn al-Khattab and bore him 'Asim. Ash-Shamus became Muslim and gave allegiance to the Messenger of Allah.

Habiba bint Abi 'Amir ar-Rahib

Her mother was Salma bint 'Amir. She married Zayd ibn al-Khattab and bore him Asma,' and then she married Sa'd ibn Khaythama and bore him 'Abdullah. Habiba became Muslim and gave her allegiance to the Messenger of Allah.

'Usayma bint Abi'l-Aflah

Her mother was al-Fari'a bint Sayfi. She married 'Amir ibn Abi 'Amir ar-Rahib and he had no issue. 'Usayma became Muslim and gave her allegiance to the Messenger of Allah.

Jamila bint Thabit ibn Abi'l-Aflah

She married 'Umar ibn al-Khattab and bore him 'Asim. Then she was married to Yazid ibn Jariyya and bore him 'Abdu'r-Rahman. Jamila became Muslim and gave allegiance to the Messenger of Allah.

Ash-Shamus bint an-Nu'man ibn 'Amir

Her mother was Salima bint Mutarrif. She married Abu Sufyan ibn al-Harith and bore him children. Ash-Shamus bint an-Nu'man became Muslim and gave allegiance to the Messenger of Allah.

Tamima bint Abi Sufyan ibn al-Harith

Her mother was ash-Shamus bint an-Nu'man. She married 'Abdullah ibn Sahl. Tamima became Muslim and gave her allegiance to the Messenger of Allah.

Layla bint Abi Sufyan ibn al-Harith

Her mother was Salma bint 'Amr. She married Hudhayl ibn 'Amir, although it is also said that she married Bukayr ibn Jariyya. Layla became Muslim and gave allegiance to the Messenger of Allah.

'A'isha, or Maryam bint Abi Sufyan ibn al-Harith

Her mother was Salma bint 'Amr. She married Mu'adh ibn 'Amir. She became Muslim and gave her allegiance to the Messenger of Allah.

Lubaba bint Abi Lubaba

Her mother was Nusayba bint Faddala ibn an-Nu'man. She married Zayd ibn al-Khattab and bore him children. Then he was killed as a martyr in the Battle of Yamama. Then she married Abu Sa'id ibn Aws and bore him children. Lubaba became Muslim and gave her allegiance to the Messenger of Allah.

Nusayba bint Simak

Her mother was Bassama bint 'Abdullah. She married 'Uthman ibn Talha and bore him children. Then she married Bujad ibn 'Uthman. Nusayba became Muslim and gave allegiance to the Messenger of Allah.

Unaysa bint Sa'ida ibn A'ish

She was the sister of 'Uwaym ibn Sa'ida, one of the people of Badr. Her mother was 'Amira bint Salim. She married 'Amr ibn Suraqa. Unaysa became Muslim and gave allegiance to the Prophet.

'Umayra bint 'Umayr

Her mother was Umama bint Bukayr. She married Bujad ibn 'Uthman. 'Umayra became Muslim and gave allegiance to the Messenger of Allah.

Hafsa, who is Umm Zurara bint Hatib

She is the sister of al-Harith ibn Hatib and Tha'laba ibn Hatib, who were among the people of Badr. Their mother was Umama bint Samit. She became Muslim and gave allegiance to the Prophet.

Sa'ida bint Bashir ibn 'Ubayd

She became Muslim and gave allegiance to the Prophet.

'Amira bint Kulthum

She married 'Utba ibn 'Uwaym. 'Amira became Muslim and gave allegiance to the Messenger of Allah.

'Umayra

She is 'Amra bint 'Ubayd. She married Tha'laba ibn Sinan and bore him Labid and 'Amra. 'Umayra became Muslim and gave her allegiance to the Messenger of Allah.

The Women of the Banu 'Ubayd ibn Zayd ibn Malik ibn 'Awf

Thubayta bint Yi'ar

She is the wife of Abu Hudhayfa ibn 'Utba. She is one who freed Salim. Then Abu Hudhayfa adopted him. She became Muslim and gave her allegiance to the Messenger of Allah.

Salma bint Yi'ar

Her sister. She became Muslim and gave allegiance to the Prophet.

An-Nuwwar bint al-Harith ibn Qays

She married Qayzi ibn 'Amr and bore him children. An-Nuwwar became Muslim and gave allegiance to the Messenger of Allah.

Kabsha bint Hatib ibn Qays

She married Abu Namla ibn Mu'adh and bore him children. Then she married to Bashir ibn Umayya and bore him children. Kabsha became Muslim and gave allegiance to the Messenger of Allah.

Umm Thabit bint Jabr ibn 'Atik

Her mother was Hadba bint 'Amr. She married 'Atik ibn al-Harith. Umm Thabit became Muslim and gave allegiance to the Messenger of Allah.

'Amira bint Muhammad ibn 'Uqba

Her mother was from the family of Abu Farwa of Hudhayl. She was the sister of al-Mundhir ibn Muhammad who was martyred at Badr. 'Amira married 'Ubayd ibn Naqid and bore him Fadala. She became Muslim and gave her allegiance to the Messenger of Allah.

Nusayba bint Niyar

She married 'Uqba ibn 'Utuda. She became Muslim and gave her allegiance to the Messenger of Allah.

Sumayya bint Ma'bad

She married 'Abdullah ibn Abi Ahmad. She became Muslim and gave her allegiance to the Messenger of Allah.

Muti'a bint an-Nu'man ibn Malik

She married al-Jaz' ibn Malik and bore him children. She became Muslim and gave allegiance to the Messenger of Allah. Her name was 'Asiyya (rebel) and the Messenger of Allah renamed her Muti'a (obedient).

Al-Furay'a or Qurayba bint Qays

Her mother was Kabsha bint 'Amr. She married Abu Ahmad and bore him 'Abdullah. She became Muslim and gave allegiance to the Messenger of Allah.

Habta bint Jubayr ibn an-Nu'man

Her mother was from the Banu 'Abdullah ibn Ghatafan. She was the full sister of 'Abdullah and Khawwat Abu Jubayr who were present at Badr. She became Muslim and gave allegiance to the Prophet.

Umm Jamil bint al-Jullas

She married Salim ibn 'Utba. She became Muslim and gave her allegiance to the Messenger of Allah.

The Women of the Banu Khatma ibn Jusham

Hind bint Aws ibn 'Adi

Her mother was Layla bint 'Ubayd. She married 'Amr ibn Thabit of Aws and bore him Abu Hanna, one of the people of Badr. Then she married Khaythama ibn al-Harith and bore him Sa'd, who is the chief of the Banu 'Amr ibn 'Awf, who was present at Badr and killed as a martyr on that day.

Kabsha bint Aws ibn 'Adi

Her mother was Layla bint 'Ubayd. She married Thabit ibn al-Fakih and bore him Khuzayma and the rest of his children. Then she was married to Mas'ud ibn 'Amir and bore him al-Waqsa' who gave allegiance. She became Muslim and gave allegiance to the Prophet.

Layla bint Aws ibn 'Adi

Her mother was Layla bint 'Ubayd. She married al-Harith ibn Ghiyath al-Khatmi and bore him all his children. Layla became Muslim and gave allegiance to the Messenger of Allah.

Su'da bint Aws ibn 'Adi

Her mother was Layla bint 'Ubayd. She married Samit ibn 'Adi and bore him Suwayd and then she married Sahl ibn al-Harith and bore him children. Su'da became Muslim and gave allegiance to the Messenger of Allah.

Safiyya bint Thabit

Her mother was Kabsha bint Aws. Safiyya married 'Abdu'r-Rahman ibn Aws al-Khatbi. Safiyya became Muslim and gave allegiance to the Messenger of Allah.

Mulayka bint Thabit

Her mother was Kabsha bint Aws. She married Shutaym ibn Zayd. She became Muslim and gave allegiance to the Prophet.

Rifa'a, who is Umm al-Qasim bint Thabit

Her mother was Kabsha bint Aws. She married Mahmud ibn Wahwah. She became Muslim and gave allegiance to the Prophet.

Ar-Ra'i'a, who is Hasana bint Thabit

Her mother was Kabsha bint Aws. She became Muslim and gave allegiance to the Messenger of Allah. [*ra'i'a* means startling beauty]

'Umara bint Hubbasha ibn Juwaybir

Her mother was Layla bint Sahba. She became Muslim and gave allegiance to the Messenger of Allah.

'Amira, who is Umm al-Quhayd bint Hubbasha

Her mother was Layla bint Sahba. She married Aws ibn 'Amr and bore him children. She became Muslim and gave allegiance to the Messenger of Allah.

Unaysa bint Ruqaym ibn al-Harith

Her mother is Salma bint 'Amr. She married Wahwah ibn Thabit al-Khatmi. Unaysa became Muslim and gave allegiance to the Messenger of Allah.

Nusayba bint Abi Talha

Her mother was Umm Talha bint Mukhallad al-Khatmi. She married 'Umayr al-Qari' ibn 'Adi and bore him children. Unaysa became Muslim and gave allegiance to the Messenger of Allah.

✳✶✳✶✳

From al-Ja'adira, who are the Banu Sa'id ibn Murra, part of the Banu 'Abdu'l-Ashhal

Salma bint Zayd ibn Taym

Her mother was ar-Rahhala bint al-Mundhir of Khazraj. She married 'Amr ibn 'Abbad. Salma became Muslim and gave her allegiance to the Messenger of Allah.

✳✳✳✳✳

The Women of the Banu's-Salm ibn Imru'l-Qays

Khayra bint Abi Umayya ibn al-Harith

She married Miknaf ibn Muhayysa. She became Muslim and gave allegiance to the Messenger of Allah.

✳✳✳✳✳

Those are the women of Aws who gave their allegiance to the Messenger of Allah.

Chapter Thirteen:
The Names of the Women of Khazraj

Mahabba bint ar-Rabi' ibn 'Amr

Her mother was Huzayla bint 'Utba. She was the full sister of Sa'd ibn ar-Rabi', one of the people of Badr. She married Abu'd-Darda' and bore him Bilal. Mahabba became Muslim and gave allegiance to the Messenger of Allah.

Jamila bint Sa'd ibn ar-Rabi'

Her mother was 'Amra bint Hazm. She was the only child of Sa'd. She married Zayd ibn Thabit and bore him Sa'd, Kharija, Yahya, Isma'il, Sulayman, Umm 'Uthman, and Umm Zayd. Jamila was called Umm Sa'd.

Umm Sa'd bint Sa'd said, "On the Day of the Ditch I was two years old and my mother used to tell me about the Ditch after I came of age." Sa'd ibn ar-Rabi' was killed in the Battle of Uhud while her mother was pregnant with her. Muhammad ibn 'Umar includes her among those who gave allegiance in spite of her youth.

Habiba bint Kharija ibn Zayd

Her mother was Huzayla bint 'Utba. Her half-brother was Sa'd ibn ar-Rabi'. She married Abu Bakr as-Siddiq and bore him Umm Kulthum. Then she was married to Khubayb ibn Asaf. Habiba became Muslim and gave allegiance to the Messenger of Allah.

Zaynab bint Qays ibn Shammas

Her mother was Khawla bint 'Amr ibn Qays. She is the half-sister of Thabit ibn Qays, the *khatib* of the Messenger of Allah. Zaynab married Khubayb ibn Asaf and bore him Unaysa. Zaynab became Muslim and gave allegiance to the Messenger of Allah.

Umm Thabit bint Qays ibn Shammas

Her mother was Khawla bint 'Amr ibn Qays. She was the half-sister of Thabit ibn Qays. Umm Thabit married Thabit ibn Sufyan and bore him Simak. She became Muslim and gave allegiance to the Messenger of Allah.

'Amra bint Rawaha ibn Tha'laba

Her mother was Kabsha bint Waqid. She is the full sister of 'Abdullah ibn Rawaha, one of the people of Badr. 'Amra married Bashir ibn Sa'd and bore him an-Nu'man ibn Bashir. She became Muslim and gave her allegiance to the Messenger of Allah.

Layla bint Simak ibn Thabit

She became Muslim and gave allegiance to the Messenger of Allah. No one except Muhammad ibn 'Umar mentioned her.

Umm Ayyub bint Qays ibn Sa'd

No one except Muhammad ibn 'Umar mentioned her as becoming Muslim and giving allegiance.

Mandwas or Sadus bint Khallad

No one except Muhammad ibn 'Umar mentioned her as becoming Muslim and giving allegiance.

Umayya or Ubayya bint Bashir

Her mother was 'Amra bint Rawaha. She is the full sister of an-Nu'man ibn Bashir. She gave allegiance to the Messenger of Allah.

Huzayla bint Thabit ibn Tha'laba

She married al-Harith ibn Thabit, and then she was married to Abu Mas'ud 'Uqba ibn 'Amr, and then she was to married 'Abdu'r-Rahman ibn Sa'ida. She became Muslim and gave allegiance to the Prophet.

Unaysa or Nufaysa bint Tha'laba

Her mother was Unaysa bint Wafid. She married as-Sa'ib ibn Khallad. She became Muslim and gave allegiance to the Prophet.

Kabsha bint Waqid ibn 'Amr

Her mother was Hind bint Ruhm of Tayy'. She married Rawaha ibn Tha'laba and bore him 'Abdullah ibn Rawaha who was present at Badr, and 'Amra, who is Umm an-Nu'man ibn Bashir. Then she married Qays ibn Shammas and bore him Thabit ibn Qays. She became Muslim and gave allegiance to the Messenger of Allah.

Huzayla bint 'Utba ibn 'Amr

Huzayla bint 'Utba ibn 'Amr. Her mother was Umayma bint Suhaym. She married ar-Rabi' ibn 'Amr and bore him Sa'd Then she married Kharija ibn Zayd and bore him Zayd ibn Kharija who spoke after his death in the time of 'Uthman ibn 'Affan. Huzayla became Muslim and gave allegiance to the Messenger of Allah.

Unaysa bint Khubayb ibn Yasaf

Her mother was Zaynab bint Qays. She married Zayd ibn Kharija and bore him 'Abdullah, Muhammad, and Umm Kulthum. Unaysa became Muslim and gave allegiance to the Messenger of Allah.

It is reported from Unaysa's uncle, Khubayb ibn 'Abdu'r-Rahman, that she went on *hajj* with the Prophet ﷺ. She said, "Our men came in 'Umar's khalifate seeking the shade of the gardens, with their cloaks over their heads, and there they spent the midday after the *Jumu'a* prayer."

It is related from Unaysa's uncle, Khubayb ibn 'Abdu'r-Rahman, that she said, "The Messenger of Allah had two *mu'adhdhins*: Bilal and Ibn Umm Maktum. Between their *adhans* was only the amount of time that this would descend and that would go up. We used to keep him back and say, 'Stay where you are until we finish *sahur*.'"

It is reported from Unaysa's uncle, Khubayb ibn 'Abdu'r-Rahman, that she said, "We girls of the quarter used to take our sheep to Abu Bakr as-Siddiq."

Umm Zayd bint as-Sakan ibn 'Utba

She married Suraqa bint Ka'b and bore him Zayd. Umm Zayd became Muslim and gave allegiance to the Messenger of Allah.

Qurayba bint Zayd ibn 'Abd Rabbihi

She was the sister of 'Abdullah ibn Zayd, one of the people of Badr. He is one who saw the *adhan* in a dream. Muhammad ibn 'Umar says that she became Muslim and gave allegiance to the Prophet.

Kabsha bint Thabit ibn Haritha

Her mother was Salama bint Hasan. She became Muslim and gave allegiance to the Messenger of Allah.

Mu'adha bint 'Abdullah ibn 'Amr

Muhammad ibn 'Umar says that she became Muslim and gave allegiance to the Messenger of Allah.

Umm Hakam or Umm Hakim bint 'Abdu'r-Rahman ibn Mas'ud

She married Abu Mas'ud 'Uqba ibn 'Amr. Umm al-Hakam became Muslim and gave her allegiance to the Messenger of Allah.

Na'ila bint ar-Rabi' ibn Qays

Her mother was Fatima bint 'Amr. She was the full sister of 'Abdullah ibn ar-Rabi'. He was present at al-'Aqaba and Badr. Na'ila married Aws ibn Khalid. Na'ila became Muslim and gave allegiance to the Messenger of Allah.

Al-Furay'a bint Malik ibn Sinan

She was the full sister of Abu Sa'id al-Khudri. Their mother was Unaysa bint Abi Kharija. Their half-brother was Qatada ibn an-Nu'man. She married Sahl ibn Rafi' and then she later married Sahl ibn Bashir. Al-Furay'a became Muslim and gave allegiance to the Messenger of Allah.

It is related that al-Furay'a reported that her husband was killed at a place on the Madina road called Tarf al-Qadum. Al-Furay'a mentioned that to the Messenger of Allah. She wanted to move from her husband's house to her family. She said that the Messenger of Allah allowed her to do that. Then when she got up, he called her back and said, "Stay in your house until the book reaches its term."

Zaynab bint Ka'b, who was married to Abu Sa'id al-Khudri, said that Furay'a ibn Malik, Abu Sa'id's sister, informed her that she was married to a man of the Banu'l-Harith ibn al-Khazraj. Furay'a said, "He went out to look for some runaway non-Arab slaves and he caught up with them at Tarf al-Qadum and they attacked and killed him." She went to the Messenger of Allah ﷺ and told him that her husband had been killed and had not left her any maintenance nor lodging. She asked the Messenger of Allah for permission to join her brothers and their house. The Messenger of Allah ﷺ gave her permission. Furay'a said that when she had left the room, or was still in it, the Messenger of Allah called her back and told her to repeat her story to him. She did so. She said, "He told me not to leave my dwelling in which the news of my husband's death had reached me until the Book reached its term. I observed the waiting-period there for four months and ten days."

Furay'a said, "'Uthman was asked about that and I was mentioned to him. He sent for me and I went to him while he was with a group of people. He asked me about my situation and what the Messenger of Allah ﷺ had commanded me, and I informed him. He sent word to a woman whose husband had died to tell her not to leave her house until the book had reached its term.[i.e. the end of the *'idda*.]"

Ar-Rabab bint Harith ibn Sinan

She married Kulayb ibn Yasaf. She became Muslim and gave allegiance to the Messenger of Allah.

Ar-Rubbayi' bint Haritha ibn Sinan

Muhammad ibn 'Umar said that she became Muslim and gave allegiance to the Messenger of Allah.

Khulayda bint Thabit ibn Sinan

She married Ka'b ibn 'Amr and then after him 'Abdullah ibn Anas. She became Muslim and gave allegiance to the Prophet.

Umm Thabit bint Thabit ibn Sinan

Muhammad ibn 'Umar said that she became Muslim and gave allegiance to the Messenger of Allah.

Kabsha bint Rafi' ibn Mu'awiya

Her mother was Umm ar-Rabi' bint Malik. Kabsha married Mu'adh ibn an-Nu'man and bore him Sa'd ibn Mu'adh and 'Amr ibn Mu'adh, as well as Iyas, Aws, 'Iqrab, and Umm Hizam. Kabsha became Muslim and gave allegiance to the Messenger of Allah.

Su'ad bint Rafi' ibn Mu'awiya

Her mother was Umm ar-Rabi' bint Malik. She married Zurara ibn 'Adas and bore him Abu Umama As'ad, the chief of the Banu'n-Najjar, as well as Sa'd, Mas'ud, Ru'ayba and Furay'a. Su'ad became Muslim and gave her allegiance to the Messenger of Allah.

Umm al-Hubab

Her name is al-Furay'a bint al-Hubab ibn Rafi'. She married Mas'ud ibn Khalda and bore him children. Then she was married to Miri' ibn Simak. She became Muslim and gave allegiance to the Messenger of Allah.

'Iqrab bint as-Sakan ibn Rafi'

She married Thabit ibn Suhayb. She became Muslim and gave allegiance to the Messenger of Allah.

*****

The Women of the Banu Sa'ida ibn Ka'b

Mandwas bint 'Amr

Her mother was Hind bint al-Mundhir. She was the full sister of al-Mundhir ibn 'Amr who was at al-'Aqaba and Badr. He was a chief. He was killed at the Day of Bi'r Ma'una as a martyr. She married Mukhallad ibn Samit and bore him Maslama. She became Muslim and gave allegiance to the Messenger of Allah.

Salma bint 'Amr

Her mother was Hind bint al-Mundhir. She was the full sister of al-Mundhir ibn 'Amir who was at al-'Aqaba and Badr. Salma married 'Uqba ibn Rafi'. She became Muslim and gave allegiance to the Messenger of Allah.

Al-Furay'a bint Khalid ibn Khunays

Her mother was Hind bint al-Abarr. She married Thabit ibn al-Mundhir and bore him Hassan ibn Thabit ash-Sha'ir. She is called Umm Hassan ibn Thabit. Al-Furay'a became Muslim and gave allegiance to the Messenger of Allah.

Umm Sharik bint Khalid

Her mother was Hind bint al-Abarr. She married Anas ibn Rafi'. Umm Sharik became Muslim and gave allegiance to the Prophet.

Mandwas bint 'Ubada ibn Dulaym

She is the sister of Sa'd ibn 'Ubada. Her mother was 'Amra ath-Thalitha bint Mas'ud. Mandwas married Simak ibn Thabit and bore him Thabit. Mandwas became Muslim and gave allegiance to the Messenger of Allah.

Layla bint 'Ubada ibn Dulaym

She is the sister of Sa'd ibn 'Ubada. Her mother was 'Amra ath-Thalitha bint Mas'ud. Layla married Khallad ibn Suwayd and bore him as-Sa'ib. Layla became Muslim and gave allegiance to the Messenger of Allah.

Fukayha bint 'Ubayd ibn Dulaym

She married Sa'd ibn 'Ubada and bore him Qays and Umama. Fukayha became Muslim and gave allegiance to the Prophet.

Ghaziyya bint Sa'd ibn Khalifa

Her mother was Salma bint 'Azib. She married Sa'd ibn 'Ubada and bore him Sa'id. Ghaziyya became Muslim and gave allegiance to the Messenger of Allah.

Kabsha, who is Kubaysha bint 'Abdu 'Amr

She married Abu Hamid 'Abdu'r-Rahman She became Muslim and gave allegiance to the Messenger of Allah.

'Amra bint Sa'd ibn Sa'd

Her mother was Hind bint 'Amr. She married Mubashshir ibn al-Harith and bore him Rifa'a. She became Muslim and gave allegiance to the Messenger of Allah.

Na'ila bint Sa'd ibn Sa'id

She is the sister of Sahl ibn Sa'd as-Sa'idi. Muhammad ibn 'Umar mentions that she became Muslim and gave allegiance to the Prophet.

*****

The Women of the Qawaqila, the Banu 'Awf ibn al-Khazraj

Qurratu'l-'Ayn bint 'Ubada ibn Nadla

Her mother was 'Amira bint Tha'laba. She married as-Samit ibn Qays and bore him 'Ubada ibn as-Samit. He was present at 'Aqaba and Badr and was a chief. She also bore Aws and Khawla. She became Muslim and gave allegiance to the Messenger of Allah.

Habiba bint Mulayl ibn Wabra

Her mother was Umm Zayd bint Nadla. She married Farwa ibn 'Amr and bore him 'Abdu'r-Rahman. She became Muslim and gave allegiance to the Messenger of Allah.

Bushra bint Mulayl ibn Wabra

Her mother was Umm Zayd bint Nadla. She married Hamza ibn al-'Abbas and bore him Muhammad, Hamid, Khadija and Kulthum. She became Muslim and gave allegiance to the Messenger of Allah.

'Amra bint Hazzal ibn 'Amr

Muhammad ibn 'Umar mentions that she became Muslim and gave allegiance to the Messenger of Allah.

Layla bint Rithab ibn Hunayf

Her mother was Amatu'llah bint Ghanima. She married 'Itban ibn Malik and bore him 'Abdu'r-Rahman. Then she was married to 'Abdu'r-Rahman ibn 'Amir and bore him an-Nu'man, Umama, and Umm Husayn. Then she was married to 'Abdullah ibn 'Amr and bore him Sa'da. She became Muslim and gave allegiance to the Prophet.

Khawla bint Samit ibn Qays

She was the full sister of 'Ubada and Aws, the people of Badr. Their mother was Qurratu'l-'Ayn bint 'Ubada. She married Abu 'Abdu'r-Rahman Yazid ibn Tha'laba, their ally, and bore him 'Amir and Umm 'Uthman. Khawla became Muslim and gave allegiance to the Messenger of Allah. Some of them report that she is the one who argued about her husband and then Allah revealed: *"Allah has heard the words of her who disputes with you about her husband."* (58:1)

It is related that this is a mistake and that it is about Khawla bint Tha'laba.

Umama bint Samit ibn Qays

Her mother was ar-Rabab bint Malik. She was the half sister of 'Ubada ibn as-Samit. She married Jumay' ibn Mas'ud. Umama became Muslim and gave allegiance to the Messenger of Allah.

Khawla bint Tha'laba

She married Aws ibn as-Samit, the brother of 'Ubada ibn as-Samit. She is one who argued. She became Muslim and gave allegiance to the Messenger of Allah.

Salih ibn Kaysan said, "The first Muslim that we heard about pronouncing the *dhihar*-divorce from his wife was Aws ibn Samit al-Waqifi. He was married to his cousin, Khawla bint Tha'laba. They say that he was a man who was somewhat crazy. He said to his cousin, 'You are to me like my mother's back.' She said, 'By Allah, you have uttered something terrible. I do not know how far it reaches.'

Then she went to the Messenger of Allah ﷺ and told him her situation and what her husband had done. So the Messenger of Allah sent for Aws ibn Samit and he came. The Messenger of Allah said, 'What about what your cousin says?' He said, 'She spoke the truth. I pronounced a *dhihar* of her and made her like my mother's back. What do you command about that, Messenger of Allah?' The Messenger of Allah said, 'Do not go near her and do not go in to her until I give you permission.' Khawla said, 'Messenger of Allah, he is penniless and no one spends on him but me.' There was some discussion between them about that for a time and then Allah revealed this in the Qur'an: *'Allah has heard the words of her who disputes with you about her husband and lays her complaint before Allah. Allah hears the two of you talking together...'* (58:1) So the Messenger of Allah commanded him to expiate the *dhihar*. Aws said, 'If it had not been for Khawla, I would have been destroyed.'"

'Imran ibn Abi Anas said, "In the Jahiliyya there were those who made their wives unlawful to them for all time by the *dhihar*. The first to pronounce the *dhihar* in Islam was Aws ibn Samit. He was somewhat crazy. He had somewhat recovered and partially regained his senses and then had courted his wife, Khawla bint Tha'laba, the sister of Abu 'Abdu'r-Rahman Yazid ibn Tha'laba, in one of his saner periods. He said, 'You are like my mother's back to me.' Then he regretted what he had said and said to his wife, 'I only think that you are now unlawful for me.' She said, 'You did not mention divorce. This is something from the time before Allah sent His Messenger. Go to the Messenger of Allah and ask him about what you should do.' He said, 'I am ashamed to go and ask him about this. You go to the Messenger of Allah. Perhaps you will obtain some good for us by which you will relieve our situation.' So she got dressed and went to him in 'A'isha's house. She said, 'Messenger of Allah, you know who Aws is, the father of my children and my cousin, and the most beloved of people to me. You know about the slight derangement which afflicts him and his lack of ability, his weakness, and his lack of ability to express himself. He has said something, and by the One who sent down the Qur'an on you, he did not mention divorce. He said, "You are like my mother's back to me."' The Messenger of Allah said, 'I only think that you are unlawful to him.' She argued with the Messenger of Allah for a time and then she said, 'O Allah! I complain to You of the intensity of my feeling and how it is hard on me to part from him! O Allah! Send down on the tongue of your Prophet that which contains relief for us!' 'A'isha said, 'I wept and those of the people of the house with us wept out of mercy for her and compassion for her.'

"While she was talking to the Messenger of Allah, the revelation descended on the Messenger of Allah and he snored and his face trembled and he perspired until it fell from him like drops. 'A'isha said, 'Khawla, what is being sent down on him can only be about you!' She said, 'O Allah, good! I only desire good from your Prophet!' 'A'isha said, 'When it left the Messenger of Allah, I thought that her soul would depart out of fear of separation being revealed.' It left the Messenger of Allah smiling. He said, 'Khawla.' She said, 'At your service!' and she leapt to her feet out of joy at the smile of the Messenger of Allah. Then he said, 'Allah has given revelation about you and him.' Then he recited to her: *'Allah has heard the words of her who disputes with you about her husband ...'* (58:1) Then he said, 'Command him to free a slave.' She said, 'What slave! By Allah, he does not have a slave and has no servant except me!' Then he said, 'Command him to fast for two consecutive months.' She said, 'By Allah, Messenger of Allah, he will not be able to do that. He drinks often in the day. His sight has gone and his body is weak.' He said, 'Then command him to feed sixty poor people.' She said, 'How will he get that? It is one meal a day.' He said, 'Tell him to go to Umm al-Mundhir bint Qays and take half a *wasq* of dates from her and give it as *sadaqa* to sixty poor people.' She got up and went back to him and found him sitting at the door waiting for her. He said to her, 'Khawla, what has happened?' She said, 'Good, and you are ugly! The Messenger of Allah has commanded you to go to Umm al-Mundhir bint Qays and take from her half a *wasq* of dates and give it as *sadaqa* to sixty poor people.'"

Khawla said, "He left me and brought it on his back and my custom with him was that I would not let him carry five *sa's*. He began to feed two *mudds* of dates to every poor person. "

Al-Furay'a bint Malik ibn ad-Dukhsham

Her mother was Jamila bint 'Abdullah ibn Ubayy. She married Hilal ibn Umayya of Aws. She became Muslim and gave allegiance to the Messenger of Allah.

Jamila bint Khuzayma ibn Hazma

It is also said that her name was Habiba. Her mother was 'Amira bint 'Adi. She married 'Abdullah ibn Sa'd. Jamila became Muslim and gave allegiance to the Messenger of Allah.

Umm Anas bint Waqid ibn 'Amr

She married 'Amr ibn 'Utba. She became Muslim and gave allegiance to the Messenger of Allah.

Buzay'a bint Abi Kharija ibn Aws

Her mother was Maryam bint 'Isma. She married al-Walid ibn 'Ubada. She became Muslim and gave allegiance to the Prophet.

❄✦❄✦❄

The Women of Balhabla
'al-Habla' is Salim ibn Ghanm ibn 'Awf

Umm Malik bint Ubayy ibn Malik

Her mother was Salma bint Matruf. Umm Malik became Muslim and gave allegiance to the Messenger of Allah. Umm Malik married Rafi' ibn Malik and bore him Rifa'a and Khallad who were present at Badr. Her grandfather was 'Ubayd ibn Malik, who is al-Murammaq the poet.

Jamila bint 'Abdullah ibn Ubayy

Her mother was Khawla bint al-Mundhir. She married Hanzala ibn Abi 'Amir ar-Rahib who was killed as a martyr at Uhud. She bore him 'Abdullah ibn Hanzala after his death. Then she married Thabit ibn Qays and bore him Muhammad. Then she married Malik ibn ad-Dukhshum. Then she married Khubayb ibn Yasaf. Jamila became Muslim and gave allegiance to the Messenger of Allah. Jamila's full brother was 'Abdullah ibn Ubayy who was present at Badr. Both her sons were killed at the Battle of al-Harra. Hanzala ibn Abi 'Amir was the one who was washed by the angels.

Mulayka bint 'Abdullah ibn Ubayy

Her mother was Khalid ibn Sinan. She married Hilal ibn Umayya of Aws. She became Muslim and gave allegiance to the Prophet.

Ramla bint 'Abdullah ibn Ubayy

Her mother was Lubna bint 'Ubada. She married 'Isma ibn Zayd. Ramla became Muslim and gave allegiance to the Prophet.

Umm Sa'd or Umm Sa'id bint 'Abdullah ibn Ubayy

Her mother was Lubna bint 'Ubada. She married Jubayr ibn Thabit. She became Muslim and gave allegiance to the Prophet.

Khawla bint Khawli ibn 'Abdullah

She is the full sister of Aws ibn Khawli who was present at Badr and present at the washing of the Prophet. Her mother was Jamila bint Ubayy. Khawla became Muslim and gave allegiance to the Messenger of Allah.

Fushum bint Aws ibn Khawli

She married 'Itban ibn Murra. She became Muslim and gave allegiance to the Messenger of Allah.

Zaynab bint Sahl ibn as-Sa'b

She married Wadi'a ibn 'Amr. She became Muslim and gave allegiance to the Messenger of Allah.

Layla bint Tiba'

She married Wahb ibn Kalda. She became Muslim and gave allegiance to the Messenger of Allah.

✳✳✳✳✳

The Women of the Banu Bayada ibn 'Amr

Unaysa bint 'Urwa ibn Mas'ud

Her mother was Rughayba bint Tha'laba. She married Hanzala ibn Malik. She became Muslim and gave allegiance to the Prophet.

Halima or Jamila bint 'Urwa

Her mother was Rughayba bint Tha'laba. She married Khadij ibn Rafi' and bore him Rifa'a. She became Muslim and gave allegiance to the Messenger of Allah.

Khalida bint 'Amr ibn Wadhafa

Her mother was Hind bint Khalid. She married Abu 'Ubada Sa'd ibn 'Uthman. She became Muslim and gave allegiance to the Messenger of Allah. She is the half-sister of Farwa ibn 'Amr who was present at al-'Aqaba and Badr.

Kabsha or Kubaysha bint Farwa

Her mother was an *umm walad*. She married 'Abdu'r-Rahman ibn Sa'd. She became Muslim and gave allegiance to the Messenger of Allah.

Umm Sharahbil bint Farwa ibn 'Amr

Her mother was an *umm walad*. She married al-Yaqazan ibn 'Ubayd. She became Muslim and gave allegiance to the Prophet.

Buthayna bint an-Nu'man ibn 'Amr

Her mother was Habiba ibn Qays. She married Muhammad ibn 'Amr. She became Muslim and gave allegiance to the Prophet.

Al-Fari'a bint 'Isam ibn 'Amir

She married 'Amr ibn an-Nu'man. She became Muslim and gave allegiance to the Messenger of Allah.

Umama bint 'Isam

She married Kabsha ibn Mabdhul. She became Muslim and gave allegiance to the Messenger of Allah.

Umayya bint Khalifa ibn 'Adi

She married Farwa ibn 'Amr and bore him Umm Sa'd. She became Muslim and gave allegiance to the Messenger of Allah.

Unaysa bint 'Abdullah ibn 'Amr

She married 'Abbas ibn 'Ubada. Then she was married to 'Amr ibn Aws. She became Muslim and gave allegiance to the Prophet.

✵✶✵✶

The Women of the Banu Zurayq ibn 'Amir

Umama bint 'Uthman ibn Khalida

She is the full sister of Abu 'Ubada ibn Sa'd, who was present at Badr. Their mother was Umm Jamil bint Qutba. Umama married Thabit ibn al-Jadha'. She became Muslim and gave allegiance to the Messenger of Allah.

Umm Rafi' bint 'Uthman ibn Khalida

She was the sister of Abu 'Ubada Sa'd who was present at Badr and the mother of Umm Rafi' was Umm Jamil bint Qutba. She married Khallad ibn Rafi'. She became Muslim and gave allegiance to the Messenger of Allah.

Fukayha who is Umm al-Hakam bint al-Muttalib

Her mother was Hind bint al-'Ajlan. She married ar-Rabi' ibn 'Amir. Then she was married to 'Amr ibn Khalida. She became Muslim and gave allegiance to the Messenger of Allah.

Habiba bint Mas'ud ibn Khalida

Her mother was al-Fari'a bint al-Hubbab. She married 'Abdu'r-Rahman ibn 'Amr. She became Muslim and gave allegiance to the Messenger of Allah.

Buhaysa bint 'Amr ibn Khalida

Her mother Umm al-Hakam, who is Fukayha bint al-Muttalib. She married an-Nu'man ibn 'Ajlan. She became Muslim and gave allegiance to the Messenger of Allah.

Umm Qays bint Hisn ibn Khalida

She was the sister of Qays ibn Hisn who was present at Badr. Muhammad ibn 'Umar mentioned that she became Muslim and gave allegiance to the Messenger of Allah.

Umm Sa'd bint Qays ibn Hisn

Her mother was Khawla bint al-Fakih. She married Qays ibn 'Amr and then married the older Mas'ud ibn 'Ubada. She became Muslim and gave allegiance to the Messenger of Allah.

Hubba bint 'Amr

Her mother was Habiba bint Qays. She married Sayfi ibn Aswad. She became Muslim and gave allegiance to the Messenger of Allah.

Kabsha bint al-Fakih ibn Qays

Her mother was Salma bint Umayya. She married Mas'ud ibn Sa'd and then she was married to al-'Ajlan ibn an-Nu'man. Kabsha became Muslim and gave allegiance to the Messenger of Allah.

Layla bint Rib'i ibn 'Amir

She married at-Tufayl ibn Malik. Then she married Sayfi ibn Rafi', the ally of the Banu 'Amr ibn 'Awf. Layla became Muslim and gave allegiance to the Messenger of Allah.

Sunbula bint Ma'is ibn Qays

Her mother was Sukhta bint Aws. She married Abu 'Ubada Sa'd ibn 'Uthman. She became Muslim and gave allegiance to the Messenger of Allah. She was the half-sister of Mu'adh and 'A'idh, the sons of Ma'is, who was present at Badr.

Unaysa bint Mu'adh ibn Ma'is

Her mother was Umm Thabit bint 'Ubayd. She married 'Amir ibn 'Amr. She became Muslim and gave allegiance to the Prophet.

Umm Sa'd bint Mas'ud

Her mother was Kabsha bint al-Fakih. She became Muslim and gave allegiance to the Messenger of Allah.

Umm Thabit bint Mas'ud

Her mother was Kabsha bint al-Fakih. She became Muslim and gave allegiance to the Messenger of Allah.

Umm Sahl bint Mas'ud

Her mother was Kabsha bint al-Fakih. She became Muslim and gave allegiance to the Messenger of Allah.

Khawla bint Malik ibn Bishr

She married Ziyad ibn Zayd. She became Muslim and gave allegiance to the Messenger of Allah.

*****

The Women of the Banu Habib ibn 'Abd Haritha

Unaysa bint Hilal

Her mother was Salma bint Taliq. She married al-'Ajlan ibn an-Nu'man. She became Muslim and gave allegiance to the Prophet.

Nusayba bint Rafi'

Her mother was from the Banu 'Abdullah ibn Ghatafan. She married Abu Sa'id ibn Aws. Nusayba became Muslim and gave allegiance to the Messenger of Allah.

*****

The Women of the Banu Salama ibn Sa'd

Ash-Shamus bint 'Amr ibn Haram

Her mother was Hind bint Qays. She married Mahmud ibn Maslama and bore him children. Ash-Shamus became Muslim and gave allegiance to the Messenger of Allah.

Hind bint 'Amr ibn Haram

Her mother was Hind bint Qays. She married 'Amr ibn al-Jamuh and bore him children. Hind became Muslim and gave allegiance to the Messenger of Allah.

Lumays bint 'Amr

Her mother was Hind bint Qays. She married Zayd ibn Yazid. She became Muslim and gave allegiance to the Messenger of Allah.

Umm 'Amr bint 'Amr

Her mother was Hind bint Qays. She married Abu'l-Yasr ibn 'Amr. She became Muslim and gave allegiance to the Prophet.

Umm Mu'adh bint 'Abdullah

Muhammad ibn 'Umar mentioned that she became Muslim and gave allegiance to the Messenger of Allah.

Umm Hibban bint 'Amir

Her mother was Fukayha bint Sakan. She was the full sister of 'Uqba ibn 'Amir who was present at Badr. She married Haram ibn Muhayyisa. Umm Hibban became Muslim and gave allegiance to the Messenger of Allah.

Adam bint al-Jamuh ibn Zayd

Her mother was Ruhm bint al-Qayn. She was the full sister of 'Amr ibn al-Jamuh who was martyred at Uhud. She became Muslim and gave allegiance to the Messenger of Allah.

Hind bint 'Amr ibn al-Jamuh

Her mother was Hind bint 'Amr. She married Muhayyisa ibn Mas'ud. She became Muslim and gave allegiance to the Prophet.

Humayma bint al-Humam ibn al-Jamuh

She was the sister of 'Umayr ibn al-Humam who was present at Badr and martyred there. Her mother was an-Nuwwar bint 'Amir.

Humayma married Sinan ibn Qays and bore him Mas'ud. She became Muslim and gave allegiance to the Messenger of Allah.

Hind bint al-Mundhir ibn al-Jamuh

She was the full sister of al-Hubab ibn al-Mundhir who was present at Badr. Their mother was ash-Shamus bint Haqq. She married 'Amr ibn Khunays and bore him al-Mundhir ibn 'Amr who was martyred at Bi'r Ma'una. Hind became Muslim and gave allegiance to the Messenger of Allah.

Umm Jamil bint al-Hubbab ibn al-Mundhir

Her mother was Zaynab bint Sayfi. She married al-Mundhir ibn 'Amr. She became Muslim and gave allegiance to the Prophet.

Umm Tha'laba bint Zayd ibn al-Harith

She is the full sister of Tha'laba ibn Zayd. Their mother was Umama bint Khalid. She married 'Amr ibn Aws. She became Muslim and gave allegiance to the Messenger of Allah.

Umm al-Harith or Umm Iyas bint Thabit

Her mother was Umama bint 'Uthman. She married Mirdas ibn Marwan. She became Muslim and gave allegiance to the Prophet.

'A'isha bint 'Umayr ibn al-Harith

Muhammad ibn 'Umar mentioned that she became Muslim and gave allegiance to the Messenger of Allah.

Fukayha bint as-Sakan ibn Zayd

Her mother was az-Zahra bint Aws. She married 'Amir ibn Nabi'. She became Muslim and gave allegiance to the Messenger of Allah.

Qubaysa bint Sayfi ibn Sakhr

Her mother was Na'ila bint Qays. She married Jabir ibn Sakhr and bore him 'A'isha. Then she married Bishr ibn al-Bara' and bore him al-'Aliyya. She became Muslim and gave allegiance to the Prophet.

Zaynab bint Sayfi ibn Sakhr

Her mother was Na'ila bint Qays. She married al-Hubab ibn al-Mundhir and bore him Khishrim and al-Mundhir. She became Muslim and gave allegiance to the Messenger of Allah.

Humayma bint Sayfi ibn Sakhr

Her mother was Na'ila bint Qays. She married al-Bara' ibn Ma'rur and then she was married to Zayd ibn Haritha al-Kalbi, the beloved of the Prophet. She became Muslim and gave allegiance to the Messenger of Allah.

Mulayka bint 'Abdullah ibn Sakhr

Her mother was Busra bint Zayd. She married Mas'ud ibn Zayd and bore him Abu Jihad, 'Abdu'r-Rahman, and Huzayla. Mulayka became Muslim and gave allegiance to the Messenger of Allah.

Hind bint al-Bara' ibn Ma'rur

Her mother was Humayma bint Sayfi. She married Jabir ibn 'Atik. She became Muslim and gave allegiance to the Prophet.

Sulafa bint al-Bara' ibn Ma'rur

Her mother was Humayma bint Sayfi. She married Abu Qatada ibn Rib'i and bore him 'Abdullah and 'Abdu'r-Rahman. Sulafa became Muslim and gave allegiance to the Messenger of Allah.

Ar-Rabab bint al-Bara' ibn Ma'rur

Her mother was Humayma bint Sayfi. She married Mu'adh ibn al-Harith and bore him Sa'd. She became Muslim and gave allegiance to the Messenger of Allah.

Umm al-Harith bint Malik ibn Khansa'

She was the full sister of at-Tufayl ibn Malik who was present at Badr. Their mother was Asma' bint al-Qayn. She married Thabit ibn Sakhr. Umm al-Harith became Muslim and gave allegiance to the Messenger of Allah.

Arwa bint Malik ibn Khansa'

She is the full sister of at-Tufayl ibn Malik who was present at Badr. Their mother was Asma' bint al-Qayn. She married 'Amr ibn 'Adi and bore him Khalid and Umm Mani'. She became Muslim and gave allegiance to the Messenger of Allah.

Umm al-Harith ibn an-Nu'man ibn Khansa'

Her mother was Khansa' bint Rabab. She married Sawad ibn Razn. She became Muslim and gave allegiance to the Prophet.

Ar-Rubayyi' bint at-Tufayl ibn an-Nu'man

Her mother was Asma' bint Qurat. She married Abu Yahya 'Abdullah ibn 'Abdu Manaf. She became Muslim and gave allegiance to the Messenger of Allah.

'Umayra bint Qurat ibn Khansa'

Her mother was Mawiya bint al-Qayn. She married Qutba ibn 'Abdu 'Amr and bore him Mandwas. She became Muslim and gave allegiance to the Messenger of Allah.

Asma' bint Qurat ibn Khansa'

Her mother was Mawiya bint al-Qayn. She married at-Tufayl ibn an-Nu'man and bore him ar-Rubayya'. Asma' became Muslim and gave allegiance to the Messenger of Allah.

Adam bint Qurat ibn Khansa'

Her mother was Mawiya bint al-Qayn. She married at-Tufayl ibn

Malik and bore him 'Abdullah and an-Nu'man She became Muslim and gave allegiance to the Messenger of Allah.

Umama bint Qurat ibn Khansa'

Her mother was Mawiya bint al-Qayn. She married Yazid ibn Qayzi. She became Muslim and gave allegiance to the Prophet.

Amina bint Qurat ibn Khansa'

Her mother was Mawiya bint al-Qayn. She married Aws ibn al-Mu'alla and bore him Abu Sa'id. She became Muslim and gave allegiance to the Messenger of Allah.

Khansa' bint Rabab ibn an-Nu'man

Her mother was Adam bint Haram. She is the paternal aunt of Jabir ibn 'Abdullah who was present at Badr. She married 'Amir ibn 'Adi and then married an-Nu'man ibn Khansa'. She became Muslim and gave allegiance to the Messenger of Allah.

Umm Zayd bint Qays ibn an-Nu'man

Her mother was Adam bint Haram. She married Khalid ibn 'Adi. She became Muslim and gave allegiance to the Messenger of Allah.

Umm Thabit bint Haritha ibn Zayd

Her mother was Hind ibn Malik. She married 'Abdullah ibn al-Himyar, the ally of the Banu 'Ubayd. Umm Thabit became Muslim and gave allegiance to the Messenger of Allah.

Umama bint Muharrith ibn Zayd

Her mother was Salma bint Abi ad-Dahdaha, the one with the grapes brought near in the Garden. He is Abu ad-Dahdada ibn Tamim. She married ar-Rabi' ibn at-Tufayl. Then she married ad-Dahhak ibn Haritha. She became Muslim and gave allegiance to the Prophet.

Umm 'Abdullah bint Sawad ibn Razn

Her mother was Umm al-Harith bint an-Nu'man. She married Abu Muhammad ibn Mu'adh. She became Muslim and gave allegiance to the Messenger of Allah.

Umm Razn bint Sawad ibn Razn

Her mother was Umm al-Harith bint an-Nu'man. She married Yazid ibn ad-Dahhak. She became Muslim and gave allegiance to the Messenger of Allah.

Su'ad bint Salama ibn Zuhayr

Her mother was Umm Qays bint Haram. She married Jubayr ibn Sakhr, Su'ad became Muslim and gave allegiance to the Messenger of Allah. She is the one who asked the Messenger of Allah ﷺ to take her allegiance on behalf of what was in her womb when she was pregnant. The Prophet said to her, "You are the free of the free."

'Umayra bint Jubayr ibn Sakhr

Her mother was Su'ad bint Salama. She married Ka'b ibn Malik and bore him 'Abdullah, 'Ubaydullah, Faddala, Qahb, Ma'bad, Khawla, and Su'ad. She became Muslim, and gave allegiance to the Messenger of Allah. She prayed towards both *qiblas* with him and related from him. She said, "I heard the Messenger of Allah say, 'Do not make *nabidh* from dates and raisins mixed. Make it from each of them alone.'"

Sumayka bint Jabbar ibn Sakhr

Her mother was Umm al-Harith bint Malik. She married an-Nu'man ibn Jubayr. She became Muslim and gave allegiance to the Messenger of Allah.

'Usayma bint Jabbar ibn Sakhr

Muhammad ibn 'Umar al-Waqidi mentioned that she became Muslim and gave allegiance to the Messenger of Allah.

Huzayla bint Mas'ud ibn Zayd

Her mother was Mulayka bint 'Abdullah. She married 'Abdullah ibn Unays, the ally of the Banu Sawad. Huzayla became Muslim and gave allegiance to the Messenger of Allah.

Umm Sulaym bint 'Amr ibn 'Ubbad

She is the full sister of Abu'l-Yasar Ka'b ibn 'Amr who was present at 'Aqaba and Badr. She married Nabi' ibn Zayd. She became Muslim and gave allegiance to the Messenger of Allah.

Umm Mani' bint 'Amr ibn 'Adi

She is Umm Shibath. Her mother was Arwa bint Malik. She married Abu Shibath Khadij ibn Salama, the ally of Banu Haram and bore him Shibath on the night of al-'Aqaba. Khadij was present at al-'Aqaba along with his wife. She became Muslim and gave allegiance to the Messenger of Allah. Umm Shibath was also present at Khaybar with the Messenger of Allah.

Unaysa bint 'Anma ibn 'Adi

Her mother was Jahiza bint al-Qayn. She was the full sister of Tha'laba ibn 'Anma who was present at 'Aqaba and Badr. She married 'Abdullah ibn 'Amr. She became Muslim and gave allegiance to the Messenger of Allah.

Umm Bishr bint 'Amr ibn 'Anma

Her mother was Umm Zayd bint 'Amir. She married 'Abdu'r-Rahman ibn Khirash and bore him children. Then she was married to 'Abdullah ibn Bashir. She became Muslim and gave allegiance to the Messenger of Allah.

Sukhta bint Aswad ibn 'Abbad

Her mother was Humayma bint 'Ubayd. She married Ma'is ibn Qays and then she was married to 'Ubayd ibn al-Mu'alla. She became Muslim and gave allegiance to the Messenger of Allah.

Umm 'Amr bint 'Amr ibn Hadida

Her mother was Umm Sulaym bint 'Amr. She married Qutba ibn Amir. She became Muslim and gave allegiance to the Messenger of Allah. She was the full sister of Sulaym ibn 'Amr who was present at ıl-'Aqaba and Badr.

Umm Jamil bint Qutba ibn 'Amir

Her mother was Umm 'Amr ibn 'Amr. She married 'Uthman ibn Khalda and bore him Umama. Then she was married by Zayd ibn Thabit. Then she was married to Anas ibn Malik. Umm Jamil became Muslim and gave allegiance to the Messenger of Allah. Her mother's mother also gave allegiance.

Sukhta bint Qays ibn Abi Ka'b

Her mother was Na'ila bint Salama. She married al-Harith ibn Suraqa. She was the full sister of Sahl ibn Qays who was present at Badr and martyred at Uhud. She became Muslim and gave allegiance to the Messenger of Allah.

'Amra bint Qays

Her mother was Na'ila bint Salama. She married Zayd ibn Tha'laba. 'Amra became Muslim and gave allegiance to the Prophet

Fukayha bint as-Sakan

Muhammad ibn 'Umar mentioned that she became Muslim and gave allegiance to the Messenger of Allah.

❋❋❋❋❋

The Women of the Banu Udi ibn Sa'd

As-Sa'ba bint Jabal ibn 'Amr

Her mother was Hind bint Sahl of Juhayna. She was the full sister of Mu'adh ibn Jabal. She married Tha'laba ibn 'Ubayd and bore him 'Ubayd. She became Muslim and gave allegiance to the Prophet.

Umm 'Abdullah bint Mu'adh ibn Jabal

Her mother was Umm 'Amr ibn Khallad. She married 'Abdullah ibn 'Amir and bore him Amina. She became Muslim and gave allegiance to the Messenger of Allah.

✷✷✷✷✷

The Women of the Banu'n-Najjar

Umm 'Umara

She is Nusayba bint Ka'b ibn 'Amr. Her mother was ar-Rabab bint 'Abdullah ibn Habib. She was the full sister of 'Abdullah ibn Ka'b who was present at Badr, and the sister of Abu Layla 'Abdu'r-Rahman ibn Ka'b, one of the weepers. Umm 'Umara married Zayd ibn 'Asim and bore him 'Abdullah and Habib who were both Companions of the Prophet ﷺ. Then she was married to Ghaziya ibn 'Amr and bore him Tamim and Khawla. She became Muslim and was present at the Pledge of 'Aqaba and gave allegiance to the Messenger of Allah. She was present at Uhud, al-Hudaybiyya, Khaybar, the Fulfilled *'Umra*, Hunayn and the Battle of Yamama in which her hand was cut off. She heard *hadiths* from the Prophet.

It is related that Nusayba bint Ka'b said, "I was present at the pledge with the Prophet ﷺ when allegiance was given to him on the Night of 'Aqaba. At that time, I gave allegiance with the people."

Muhammad ibn 'Umar said, "Umm 'Umara bint Ka'b was present at Uhud with her husband, Ghaziya ibn 'Amr, and her two sons. She set out with them at the beginning of the day with a waterskin with the intention of giving water to the wounded. On that day she fought and proved herself courageous. She received twelve wounds, either from a spear or a sword. Umm Sa'd bint Sa'd ibn Rabi' said, 'I went to visit her and said, "Tell me your story about the Battle of Uhud."

She replied, "I went out at the beginning of the day to Uhud to see what the people were doing. I took a skin with some water in it. I went to the Messenger of Allah who was with his Companions when things were going the way of the Muslims. When the Muslims were routed, I joined the Messenger of Allah and began to take part in the fighting. I defended the Messenger of Allah with the sword and I shot with the bow until I was wounded." I saw the scar of a deep wound on her neck. I said, "Umm 'Umara, who gave you this?" She said, "Ibn Qumay'a advanced when the people left the Messenger of Allah. He was shouting, 'Show me Muhammad! I will not be saved if he is saved!' So Mus'ab ibn 'Umayr and some people confronted him. I was among them. He dealt me this blow, and I dealt him several blows in exchange, but the enemy of Allah was wearing double armour.""

Damra ibn Sa'id al-Mazini reported that his grandmother, who was present at Uhud giving water, said, "I heard the Messenger of Allah ﷺ say, 'The stand of Nusayba bint Ka'b today is better than the stand of so-and-so.' On that day, he saw her fighting fiercely. She kept at it until she had received thirteen wounds. I saw Ibn Qumay'a strike her neck, and that was the worst of her wounds. She was treated for it for a year. Then the caller of the Messenger of Allah called out, 'To Hamra' al-Asad,' and she tried to go, but was unable to move because of loss of blood. We put compresses on the wound through the night until morning. When the Messenger of Allah returned from Hamra', he did not go to his house before sending 'Abdullah ibn Ka'b al-Mazini to ask about her. He returned with the news that she was safe. The Prophet was happy about that."

Umm 'Umara said, "When the people left the Messenger of Allah exposed, only a group of not more than ten remained. I, my two sons and my husband were in front of him, defending him. The people were passing by him in their flight. He saw that I did not have a shield and he saw a man retreating with a shield. He said to the man with the shield, 'Give your shield to the one who is fighting.' So he handed over his shield and I took it and used it to shield the Messenger of Allah. The horsemen did to us as horsemen do. If they had been on foot as we were, we would have trounced them, Allah willing. A man would come on his horse and strike at me and I would use the shield against him and his sword. Then I would strike the hocks of his horse and he would fall off its back. The Messenger of Allah ﷺ began to shout, 'Umm 'Umara! Your mother! Your mother!'" She said, "He helped me against him until I finished him off."

'Abdullah ibn Zayd said, "I was wounded in my left arm that day. A man like a great tree struck me, but did not stay and went on. The blood would not stop. The Messenger of Allah said, 'Bind your wound.' My mother came with some bandages in her bag which she had prepared for wounds. The Prophet was standing looking at me. Then she said, 'Go and fight the people, my son!' The Prophet ﷺ was saying, 'Who can endure what you can endure, Umm 'Umara!'"

She said, "The man who had struck my son advanced and the Messenger of Allah said, 'That is the one who struck your son.' I confronted him and struck his leg and he went down on his knees. I saw the Messenger of Allah smiling so that I could see his teeth. He said, 'You have retaliated, Umm 'Umara!' Then we advanced on him with weapons until we finished him off. The Prophet ﷺ said, 'Praise be to Allah who has given you victory and delighted you over your enemy and let you enjoy your revenge directly.'"

'Abdullah ibn Zayd said, "I was present at Uhud with the Messenger of Allah. When the people dispersed from around him, I and my mother went close to him to defend him. He said, 'Is it the son of Umm 'Umara?' I said, 'Yes.' He said, 'Throw!' So, standing in front of him, I threw a stone at one of the idolworshippers who was on horseback. I hit his horse's eye and the horse bolted so that both it and its rider fell. I began to overwhelm him with stones until I had made a pile. The Prophet ﷺ was looking and smiling. He saw that my mother was wounded on her neck and said, 'Your mother! Your mother! Bind her wound! May Allah bless you, the people of a house! The stand of your mother is better than the stand of so-and-so. May Allah have mercy on you, the people of a house! The stand of your foster father (meaning his mother's husband) is better than the stand of so-and-so. May Allah have mercy on you, the people of a house!' She said, 'Ask Allah to make us your companions in the Garden!' He said, 'O Allah, make them my companions in the Garden!' She said, 'I do not care about what afflicts me in this world!'"

It is related that Damra ibn Sa'id said, "'Umar ibn al-Khattab was brought some silk garments which contained an excellent ample garment. One of them said, 'This garment is worth such-and-such. You should send it to the wife of 'Abdullah ibn 'Umar, Safiyya bint Abi 'Ubayd.' He said, 'That is something which I will not give to Ibn 'Umar.' He said, 'I will send it to someone who is more entitled to it than her - Umm 'Umara Nusayba bint Ka'b. On the day of Uhud, I heard the Messenger of Allah ﷺ say, 'Whenever I looked to the right or the left I saw her fighting in front of me.'"

Nusayba bint Ka'b said, "The Messenger of Allah came to visit me and I offered him a vegetable dish and barley bread. He took some of it. He said, 'Come and eat.' I said, 'Messenger of Allah, I am fasting.' He said, 'When someone eats in the presence of someone who is fasting, the angels continue to bless him until he finishes his food.'"

Umm 'Umara said, "The Messenger of Allah ﷺ came to us and we brought him some food. Some of those present were fasting. The Prophet said, 'When food is eaten in the presence of the faster, the angels bless him.'"

Muhammad ibn Yahya ibn Hibban said, "Umm 'Umara received twelve wounds at Uhud and her hand was cut off at Yamama. In addition to the loss of her hand, in the Battle of Yamama she received eleven wounds. She came to Madina where they were treated. Abu Bakr thought he should go to her to inquire after her. He was the khalif at that time." He said, "She married three men and had children from all of them. From Ghaziya ibn 'Amr al-Mazini she had Tamim. She married Zayd ibn 'Asim and from him had Habib who was cut up by Musaylima, and 'Abdullah who was killed at al-Harra. The child of the third man died without issue.

Fatima bint Munqidh ibn 'Amr

Her mother was an *umm walad*. She married Dawud ibn Abi Dawud and bore him children. Fatima became Muslim and gave allegiance to the Messenger of Allah.

Zaynab bint al-Hubab ibn al-Harith

She married Qays ibn 'Amr and bore him Sa'id. She became Muslim and gave allegiance to the Messenger of Allah.

Jamila bint Abi Sa'sa'a

Her mother was Unaysa bint 'Asim. She married 'Ubada ibn as-Samit and bore him al-Walid. Then she was married to ar-Rabi' ibn Suraqa and bore him 'Abdullah, Muhammad, and Buthayna. Then she was married to Khalda ibn Abi Khalid. Jamila became Muslim and gave allegiance to the Messenger of Allah.

Na'ila bint 'Ubayd ibn al-Hurr

Her mother was Rughayba bint Aws. She married Ma'mar ibn Hazm and bore him 'Abdu'r-Rahman. She became Muslim and gave allegiance to the Messenger of Allah.

Uthayla bint al-Harith ibn Tha'laba

Her mother was Fatima bint Zayd Manat. She became Muslim and gave allegiance to the Messenger of Allah.

Shaqiqa bint Malik ibn Qays

Her mother was Suhayma bint 'Umaymir. She married al-Harith ibn Suraqa and bore him 'Abdullah and Umm 'Ubayd. Shaqiqa became Muslim and gave allegiance to the Messenger of Allah.

Kabsha bint Malik ibn Qays

Her mother was Suhayma bint 'Umaymir. She married Tha'laba ibn Mihsan. Then she married al-Hubab ibn al-Harith and bore him Zaynab. She became Muslim and gave allegiance to the Messenger of Allah.

Ash-Shamus bint Malik ibn Qays

Her mother was Suhayma bint 'Umaymir. She became Muslim and gave allegiance to the Messenger of Allah.

Umm Salit an-Najjariyya

She is Umm Qays bint 'Ubayd. Her mother was Umm 'Abdullah bint Shibl. She married Abu Salit ibn Abi Haritha and bore him Salit and Fatima. She became Muslim and gave allegiance to the Prophet.

❋❋❋❋❋

The Women of the Banu 'Adi ibn an-Najjar

An-Nuwwar bint Malik ibn Sirma

Her mother was Salma bint 'Amir. She married Thabit ibn ad-Dahhak and bore him Zayd and Yazid. Then she was married to 'Umara ibn Hazm and bore him Malik. She became Muslim and gave allegiance to the Messenger of Allah.

An-Nuwwar bint Malik said, "When I was pregnant with Zayd ibn Thabit, I saw on the Ka'ba green and yellow silk shawls, and carpets and cloths from the weaving of the desert Arabs and squares of hair."

Umm Zayd ibn Thabit an-Nuwwar said, "My house was the tallest house around the mosque and Bilal used to give the *adhan* on top of it from when the *adhan* was first given until the Messenger of Allah built his mosque. Then he gave the *adhan* on top of the mosque and something was raised up for him on top of it."

Thabit ibn 'Ubayd states that Zayd ibn Thabit said the four *takbirs* over his mother.

Umm 'Ubayd bint Suraqa ibn al-Harith

She is the full sister of Haritha ibn Suraqa who was present at Badr and was martyred on that day. Their mother was Umm Harith ar-Rubayyi'. She married Rafi' ibn Zayd. Then she married Tamim ibn Ghaziya. She became Muslim and gave allegiance to the Prophet.

Unaysa bint 'Amr ibn Qays

She was the full sister of Abu Salit, Usayra ibn 'Amr who was present at Badr. Their mother was Amina bint Aws. She married an-Nu'man ibn 'Amir and bore him Qatada who was present at Badr, and Umm Sahl. Then she was married to Malik ibn Sinan and bore him Abu Sa'id al-Khudri and al-Furay'a. She became Muslim and gave allegiance to the Messenger of Allah.

Umm Sahl bint 'Amr

Her mother was Amina bint Aws. She married Mihraz ibn 'Amir. She became Muslim and gave allegiance to the Messenger of Allah.

Umm al-Mundhir bint Qays ibn 'Amr

She was the sister of Salit ibn Qays who was present at Badr and killed at the Battle of the Bridge of Abu 'Ubayd as a martyr. Their mother was Rughayba bint Zurara. She married Qays ibn Sa'sa'a and bore him al-Mundhir. She became Muslim and gave allegiance to the Messenger of Allah.

Umm al-Mundhir bint Qays al-'Adawiyya, who was one of the maternal aunts of the Messenger of Allah, said, "The Messenger of Allah visited me with 'Ali when 'Ali was recovering from an illness. We had some grapes. The Messenger of Allah began to eat from them and 'Ali ate with him. The Messenger of Allah said to him, 'Go easy. You are convalescing.' 'Ali sat down, and the Messenger of Allah ate some of them. I made some chard and barley and when I went to the Messenger of Allah, he said to 'Ali, 'Take some of this. It is better for you.'"

Umm Sulaym bint Qays ibn 'Amr

Muhammad ibn 'Umar mentioned that she became Muslim and gave allegiance to the Messenger of Allah.

'Amira bint Qays

Muhammad ibn 'Umar mentioned that she became Muslim and gave allegiance to the Messenger of Allah.

Thubayta bint Salit ibn Qays

Her mother was Sukhayla bint as-Simma. She married 'Abdullah ibn Sa'sa'a and bore him 'Abdu'r-Rahman, Salima and Maymuna. She became Muslim and gave allegiance to the Messenger of Allah.

Asma' bint Mihraz ibn 'Amir

Her mother was Umm Sahl bint Abi Kharija. She married Abu Bashir Qays ibn 'Ubayd and bore him Bashir and al-Ja'd. She became Muslim and gave allegiance to the Messenger of Allah.

Kulthum bint Mihraz ibn 'Amir

Her mother was Umm Sahl bint Abi Kharija. She became Muslim and gave allegiance to the Messenger of Allah.

Umm Haritha ar-Rubbayi' bint an-Nadr

Her mother was Hind bint Zayd. She married Suraqa ibn al-Harith and bore him Haritha who was martyred at Badr and Umm 'Umayr. She became Muslim and gave allegiance to the Messenger of Allah.

Umm Hakim bint an-Nadr

Her mother was Hind bint Zayd. She married 'Amr ibn Tha'laba and bore him Abu Hakim, 'Abdu'r-Rahman, and Umm Hakim, whose name is Sahla. She became Muslim and gave allegiance to the Messenger of Allah.

Umm Sulaym bint Milhan ibn Khalid

She is al-Ghumaysa' or ar-Rumaysa'. It is said that her name was Sahla or Rumayla or Unayfa or even Rumaytha. Her mother was

Mulayka bint Malik. She married Malik ibn an-Nadr and bore h
Anas ibn Malik. Then she was married to Abu Talha and bore h
'Abdullah and Abu 'Umayr. She became Muslim and gave allegiaı
to the Messenger of Allah. She was present at the Battle of Hun;
while she was pregnant with 'Abdullah ibn Abi Talha. Before that
she had been present at the Battle of Uhud giving water to the thirsty
and treating the wounded.

It is related that Umm Sulaym was with the Prophet ﷺ on the
Day of Uhud carrying a dagger.

'Umara ibn Ghaziya said, "Umm Sulaym was present with the
Messenger of Allah while she was pregnant with 'Abdullah, and she
had a dagger which she had strapped to her waist."

It is related from Anas that Umm Sulaym took a dagger on the
Day of Hunayn. Abu Talha said, "Messenger of Allah, here is Umm
Sulaym with a dagger." She said, "Messenger of Allah, I have it. If
one of the idolworshippers comes near me, I will slit open his stom-
ach. Kill those brought into Islam by power and strike off their heads
if they retreat from you." The Messenger of Allah smiled and said,
"Umm Sulaym, Allah is enough and better."

It is related that Umm Sulaym believed in the Messenger of Allah,
and Abu Anas came. He had been absent and he said, "Have you
become a heretic?" She said, "I have not become a heretic. I have
believed in this man." I have begun to teach Anas. I told him to say:
"There is no god but Allah," and to say: "I testify that Muhammad is
the Messenger of Allah." He did that. His father said to her, "Do not
corrupt my son for me." She said, "I am not corrupting him." Then
her husband went out and encountered an enemy who killed him.
When she heard that he had been killed, she said, "I must wean Anas,
and I will not marry until Anas tells me to and he says that I have
done my duty." So he was weaned. Abu Talha, who was an idolworshipper, proposed to her and she refused. One day she said to him,
"Do you think that a stone should be worshipped when it can neither
harm nor benefit you? Or what about a piece of wood which you take
to a carpenter who carved it for you? Does it help or harm you?"
What she said had a profound effect on him and he went to her and
said, "What you said has had a profound effect on me." He believed.

She said, "I will marry you and will not take any dower from you except that."

Anas ibn Malik said, "Abu Talha proposed to Umm Sulaym and she said, 'I have believed in this man and I testify that he is the Messenger of Allah. If you follow me, I will marry you.' He said, 'I am in accord with the like of what you have.' So Umm Sulaym married him, and her dower was his Islam."

'Abdullah ibn 'Abdullah ibn Abi Talha said, "Abu Talha proposed to Umm Sulaym bint Milhan. Umm Sulaym had said, 'I will not marry until Anas comes of age and sits in the assemblies and says, "May Allah repay my mother well. She was an excellent guardian."' Abu Talha said, 'Anas has sat and has spoken in the assemblies.' Umm Sulaym said, 'What will you give me to marry you? Either you follow me in what I believe or you keep quiet about me. I have believed in this man as the Messenger of Allah.' Abu Talha said, 'I am in accord with the like of what you have.' So the dower between them was his Islam."

Anas ibn Malik said, "The Messenger of Allah ﷺ visited Umm Sulaym and prayed a voluntary prayer in her house. He said, 'Umm Sulaym, when you pray the obligatory prayer, say, "Glory be to Allah," ten times, "Praise be to Allah" ten times, and "Allah is greater" ten times, and then ask whatever you wish of Allah. He will say to you, "Yes, yes, yes."'"

Anas said, "Abu Talha came to propose to Umm Sulaym. She said, 'I must not marry an idolworshipper. Abu Talha, do you not know that your god whom you worship was carved by the carpenter slave of such-and-such a family? If you were to kindle a fire under it, it would burn up.' He went away and that had a profound effect on his heart. Every day he came she said that to him. One day he came and said, 'I have accepted what you have offered me.' Her dower was the Islam of Abu Talha."

Thabit reported that Umm Sulaym said, "Abu Talha! Do you not know that your god which you worship is only a tree which grows from the earth which was carved by an Abyssinian of a certain tribe?" He said that he did. She said, "Are you not ashamed to prostrate yourself to a piece of wood which grows from the earth which was carved by an Abyssinian of a certain tribe? If you testify that there is no god but Allah and that Muhammad is the Messenger of Allah, I will marry you without desiring any other dower from you." He said to her, "Let me think." So he went away and thought and then came back and said, "I testify that there is no god but Allah and that Muhammad is the Messenger of Allah." She said, "Anas! Get up and marry me to Abu Talha."

Anas ibn Malik said, "The Prophet ﷺ sometimes used to visit Umm Sulaym, and when the prayer came, he would pray on a carpet of ours. It was a mat moistened with water."

Anas ibn Malik reported that the Prophet ﷺ used to visit his mother, Umm Sulaym, and give her something to prepare for him. Anas said, "I had a younger brother called Abu 'Umayr. One day the Prophet visited us and said, 'Umm Sulaym, why do I see your son, Abu 'Umayr, depressed?' She said, 'O Prophet of Allah, a bird of his that he used to play with has died.' The Prophet began to stroke his head, saying, 'Abu 'Umayr, what did the little songbird do?'"

Anas ibn Malik said, "The Prophet ﷺ did not enter a house without the husband being present except for that of Umm Sulaym. He was asked about that. He said, 'I have compassion for her. Her brother was killed with me.'"

Umm Sulaym said, "The Messenger of Allah ﷺ used to spend midday in my house. I would spread out a leather mat and he would spend midday on it and perspire. I used to mix some perfume with his sweat."

It is related from Anas ibn Malik that the Prophet ﷺ visited Umm Sulaym in her house and there was a waterskin hanging in the house which contained water. He took it and drank from it while standing. Umm Sulaym took it and cut off its mouth and kept it.

It is related from Anas that the Prophet ﷺ visited Umm Sulaym and she brought him some dates and ghee. He said, "Put your ghee back in your skin and your dates back in your vessel. I am fasting."

Then he stood in a corner of the house and prayed a non-obligatory prayer. He made supplication for Umm Sulaym and the people of her house. Umm Sulaym said, "Messenger of Allah, I have a private request to ask of you." He said, "What is it?" She said, "Your servant Anas." He did not omit any of the good of either of the Next World or of this world without praying for it for him. Then he said, "O Allah, provide him with wealth and children and bless him." Anas said, "I was the Ansar with the greatest wealth. My daughter Umayna told me that some one hundred and twenty of my offspring had been buried before al-Hajjaj came to Basra."

Anas said, "Umm Sulaym sent me to the Messenger of Allah with a basket of dates, but I did not find him at home. There was a tailor who was doing something for him. He had made some stew for him of meat and pumpkins. He invited me. When I saw that he liked pumpkin, I began to put it near him. When he returned to his house, I placed the basket before him and he begin to eat from it and divide it up until he finished it."

Anas said that the Prophet said, "I entered the Garden and heard a rustle before me and there was al-Ghumaysa' bint Milhan."

The Prophet ﷺ said to Umm Sulaym, "Why doesn't Umm Sulaym go on *hajj* with us this year?" She said, "Prophet of Allah, my husband has only two camels. He will make *hajj* on one of them, and the other is being left to irrigate his palm trees." He said, "Go on *'umra* in Ramadan. *'Umra* in it is like *hajj* - or takes the place of *hajj*."

It is related from Ibn 'Abbas that Umm Sulaym said, "Messenger of Allah, Abu Talha and his son are going on *hajj* on their camel, leaving me behind." The Messenger of Allah ﷺ said, "'*Umra* in Ramadan will compensate for the *hajj* with me."

Anas said, "Umm Sulaym was with the wives of the Prophet and they were being driven on by a camel-driver. The Prophet came to them and said, 'Anjasha! Take it easy when driving the glass vessels!'"

It is related from Anas that Abu Talha had a son called Abu

'Umayr. The Prophet used to meet him and say, "Abu 'Umayr, what did the bird do?" Anas said, "He became ill while Abu Talha was away in one of his gardens and the child died. Umm Sulaym washed him, shrouded him, perfumed him, and covered him with a cloth and then she said, 'No one should tell Abu Talha before I tell him.' Abu Talha came and she had perfumed herself for him and prepared herself for him. She brought the supper and he asked, 'How is Abu 'Umayr?' She said, 'He has had supper and is finished.' Abu Talha had supper and had relations with her as a man does with his wife. Then Umm Sulaym said, 'Abu Talha, what do you think about the people of a house who make a loan to the people of a house and then its owner asks for it back? Should they return it or keep it?' He said, 'They should return it to them.' She said, 'Expect the reward for the loss of Abu 'Umayr.' He went straightaway to the Prophet ﷺ and told him what Umm Sulaym had said. He said, 'May Allah bless you in the result of your night!' She became pregnant and gave birth to 'Abdullah ibn Abi Talha. On the seventh day, Umm Sulaym said, 'Take this child and this basket which contains some dates to the Messenger of Allah so that he can be the one to put the dates in the child's mouth and name him.' I took him to the Prophet ﷺ and he stretched out his feet and laid him down. He took a date and chewed it and then put it in the child's mouth. The child began to suck it. The Prophet said, 'The Ansar have a deep love for dates.'"

It is related from Anas that Abu Talha's son died and Umm Sulaym said, "Do not tell Abu Talha until I have told him." She wrapped him in a cloth. When Abu Talha came, she put food before him and he ate. Then she perfumed herself for him and he had sex with her and she became pregnant with a boy. She said to him, "Abu Talha, what if a family borrows something from another family, and then they send to ask for the return of their loan, and they refuse to return it?" Abu Talha said, "They cannot do that. The loan must be returned to its people." She said, "Your son was a loan from Allah, and Allah has taken it back." He said, *"We belong to Allah and to Him we return!"* The Prophet ﷺ was informed and he said, "May Allah bless them in their night!" Anas said, "Umm Sulaym had a boy and sent him with me to the Prophet. I took some dates with me and went to the Prophet. He was wearing a cloak, and was tending to some camels of his. The Messenger of Allah said, 'Do you have some dates with you?' I said, 'Yes.' He took the dates and put them in his mouth and chewed them and then gathered his spittle and then opened his mouth and put it in it. The child began to suck. The Messenger of Allah said, 'The Ansar love dates.' He put the date in his mouth and named him 'Abdullah. None grew up among the Ansar better than him."

Umm Haram bint Milhan

Her mother was Mulayka bint Malik. She married 'Ubada ibn as-Samit and bore him Muhammad. Then she was married to 'Amr ibn Qays and bore him Qays and 'Abdullah. Umm Haram became Muslim and gave allegiance to the Messenger of Allah.

It is related from Anas that Umm Haram bint Milham said, "The Messenger of Allah ﷺ napped in my house and then woke up smiling. I said, 'O Prophet of Allah, may my father and mother be your ransom, what makes you smile?' He said, 'I dreamt that some people among my community were sailing on this sea like kings on thrones.' I said, 'Messenger of Allah, ask Allah to put me among them!' He said, 'You are among them.' Then he napped again and woke up smiling. I said, 'Messenger of Allah, what makes you smile?' He said, 'I dreamt that some people among my community were sailing on this sea like kings on thrones.' I said, 'Messenger of Allah, ask Allah to put me among them!' He said, 'You are among the first.'" He said, "She went on an expedition with her husband, 'Ubada ibn as-Samit, and her mount threw her and she died."

Anas said that a mule was brought up for her to mount, and it threw her and broke her neck and she died.

Umm 'Abdullah bint Milhan

Muhammad ibn 'Umar said that she became Muslim and gave allegiance to the Messenger of Allah.

Umm Burda

She is Khawla bint al-Mundhir ibn Zayd. Her mother was Zaynab bint Sufyan. She married al-Bara' ibn Aws. She became Muslim and gave allegiance to the Messenger of Allah. She is the one who was the nurse of Ibrahim, the son of the Messenger of Allah.

Khawla bint Qays ibn as-Sakan

Her mother was Umm Khawla bint Sufyan. She married Hisham ibn 'Amir. She became Muslim and gave allegiance to the Prophet.

✳✶✳✶✳

The Women of the Banu'd-Dar ibn an-Najjar

Su'ayda bint 'Abdu 'Amr ibn Mas'ud

She is Umm ar-Riya'. Her mother was as-Sumayra' bint Qays. She married Abu'l-Yasar Ka'b ibn 'Amr of the Banu Salama of Khazraj. Then she married Ka'b ibn Zayd and bore him 'Abdullah and Jamila. She became Muslim and gave allegiance to the Messenger of Allah. She is the full sister of an-Nu'man and ad-Dahhak, the sons of 'Abu 'Amr who were both present at Badr.

Mandwas bint Qubta

Her mother was 'Umayra bint Qurat. She married al-Hubab ibn Sa'd and bore him Abu 'Amr. Then she married 'Abdullah ibn Ka'b and bore him 'Utba and Umm Sa'd. Then she married 'Abdullah ibn Abi Salit and bore him Marwan. She became Muslim and gave allegiance to the Messenger of Allah.

Huzayla bint Sa'id ibn Suhayl

She married Shabbath ibn Khadij, the ally of the Banu Haram. Huzayla became Muslim and gave allegiance to the Prophet.

As-Sumayra' bint Qays ibn Malik

Her mother was Salma bint al-Aswad. She married 'Abd 'Amr ibn Mas'ud and bore him an-Nu'man and ad-Dahhak who were present at Badr, Qutba, who was killed at Bi'r Ma'una; and Umm ar-Riya'. Then she married al-Harith ibn Tha'laba and bore him Salm who was present at Badr and martyred at Uhud, and Umm al-Harith. She became Muslim and gave allegiance to the Messenger of Allah.

Umm al-Harith bint al-Harith ibn Tha'laba

Her mother was as-Sumayra' bint Qays. She married 'Amr ibn Ghaziya and bore him al-Harith and 'Abdu'r-Rahman. Then she was married to al-Harith ibn Khazama and bore him Suhayma. She became Muslim and gave allegiance to the Messenger of Allah.

✳✱✳✱✳

The Women of the Banu Malik ibn an-Najjar

Al-Fari'a bint Zurara

She is al-Furay'a bint Zurara. Her mother was Su'ad bint Rafi'. She was the full sister of Abu Umama As'ad ibn Zurara who was a chief. She married Qays ibn Qahd، She became Muslim and gave allegiance to the Messenger of Allah.

Ru'ayba bint Zurara

Her mother was Su'ad bint Rafi'. She married al-Ghard, who is Khalid ibn al-Hashas. She became Muslim and gave allegiance to the Messenger of Allah.

Habiba bint As'ad ibn Zurara

Her mother was 'Amira bint Sahl. She married Sahl ibn Hunayf and bore him Abu Umama. Sahl took him to the Messenger of Allah and said, "Give him a name." So the Messenger of Allah named him Sahl and gave him the *kunya* of Abu Umama. She became Muslim and gave allegiance to the Messenger of Allah.

Kabsha bint As'ad ibn Zurara

Her mother was 'Amira bint Sahl. She married 'Abdullah ibn Abi Habiba ibn al-Az'ar, and the Messenger of Allah gave her in marriage to him. She was the youngest of the daughters of As'ad ibn Zurara. Kabsha became Muslim and gave allegiance to the Prophet.

Al-Fari'a

She is al-Furay'a bint As'ad ibn Zurara. Her mother was 'Amira bint Sahl. She was the oldest of the daughters of As'ad ibn Zurara. When she came of age, Nubayt ibn Jabir proposed to her and the Messenger of Allah gave her in marriage to him. On the wedding night, he told them to say :

> We have come to you. We have come to you.
> Greet us, we greet you.
> If it were not for golden wheat,
> we would not have alighted in your valley.
> If it were not for red gold, we would not have come to you.

She married Nubayt and became pregnant with 'Abdu'l-Malik. When she gave birth, his father took him to the Messenger of Allah and said, "Messenger of Allah, give him a name!" The Messenger of Allah named him 'Abdu'l-Malik and blessed him. She became Muslim and gave allegiance to the Messenger of Allah.

'Amira bint Mas'ud ibn Zurara

Her mother was a woman of Makhzum of Quraysh. 'Amira married 'Alqama ibn 'Amr. She became Muslim and gave allegiance to the Messenger of Allah.

Sawda bint Haritha ibn an-Nu'man

Her mother was Umm Khalid bint Khalid. She married 'Abdullah ibn Abi Haram. She became Muslim and gave allegiance to the Messenger of Allah.

'Amra bint Haritha ibn an-Nu'man

Her mother was Umm Khalid bint Khalid. She married Qays ibn 'Amr. Then she married 'Uthman ibn Sahl. She became Muslim and gave allegiance to the Messenger of Allah.

Umm Hisham bint Haritha ibn an-Nu'man

Her mother was Umm Khalid bint Khalid. She married 'Umara ibn al-Jahhab. She became Muslim and gave allegiance to the Prophet.

Umm Hisham bint Haritha ibn an-Nu'man said, "The Messenger of Allah ﷺ stayed with us for a year or part of a year. He illuminated our dwelling and the Messenger of Allah illuminated it for one year. I learned, *"Qaf, by the Noble Qur'an"* directly from the tongue of the Messenger of Allah who recited it to the people every *Jumu'a* when he addressed them in the *khutba*."

Ja'da bint 'Ubayd ibn Tha'laba

Her mother was ar-Ru'a bint 'Adi. She married an-Nu'man ibn Nafi' and bore him Haritha who was present at Badr. Then she married al-Hubab ibn al-Arqam and bore him al-Harith. Ja'da became Muslim and gave allegiance to the Messenger of Allah.

'Afra' bint 'Ubayd ibn Tha'laba

Her mother was ar-Ru'a bint 'Adi. She married al-Harith ibn Rifa'a and bore him Mu'adh, Mu'awwidh, and 'Awf who were present at Badr. She became Muslim and gave allegiance to the Messenger of Allah.

Khawla bint 'Ubayd ibn Tha'laba

Her mother was ar-Ru'a bint 'Adi. She married Samit ibn Zayd and bore him Mu'awiya. She became Muslim and gave allegiance to the Messenger of Allah.

Khawla bint Qays ibn Qahd

She is Khuwayla and Umm Muhammad. Her mother was al-Furay'a bint Zurara. She married Hamza ibn 'Abdu'l-Muttalib and bore him Ya'la, 'Umara, and two daughters who did not reach adulthood. Then she married Hanzala ibn an-Nu'man and bore him Muhammad. Khawla became Muslim and gave allegiance to the Messenger of Allah.

Rughayba bint Sahl ibn Tha'laba

Her mother was 'Amra bint Mas'ud. She married Rafi' ibn Abi 'Amr. She became Muslim and gave allegiance to the Prophet.

Umm ar-Rabi' bint 'Abd ibn an-Nu'man

She married Kudaym ibn 'Adi. She became Muslim and gave allegiance to the Messenger of Allah.

Habiba bint Sahl ibn Tha'laba

Yahya ibn Sa'd said, "The Prophet ﷺ wanted to marry Habiba bint Sahl. Then he remembered the jealousy of the Ansar and disliked to harm their women. So she married Thabit ibn Qays. She became Muslim and gave allegiance to the Messenger of Allah.

It is related from 'Amra bint 'Abdu'r-Rahman that Habiba bint Sahl married Thabit ibn Qays. The Messenger of Allah ﷺ had wanted to marry her when she was a girl. Thabit beat her and she went to the door of the Messenger of Allah in the morning in the darkness to complain about him. She said, "I will not remain with Thabit." The Messenger of Allah said, "Take back from her what you gave her." She had a *khul'* divorce from him for what he had given her, and she remained with her family.

It is related that Habiba bint Sahl was married to Thabit ibn Qays who had some severity in his character. She went to the Prophet in the darkness. When the Prophet went out, he saw her and said, "Who is this?" She said, "I am Habiba." He said, "What is wrong?" She said, "I will not remain with Thabit." At that point Thabit arrived and the Prophet said, "Take from her." She said, "Messenger of Allah, all that he has given me is with me." She sent it to him and remained with her family. Then she married Ubayy ibn Ka'b. The Prophet had wanted to marry her, but thought better of it because of the jealousy of the Ansar and because he disliked to harm their women.

It is related that Habiba was in the house of the Messenger of Allah when the Prophet ﷺ entered and sat down. He said, "There is no Muslim who has three of his children who have not reached puberty die but that they will be brought on the Day of Rising to the gate of the Garden and be told, 'Enter.' They will say. 'Not until our parents enter.' After the second or third time, it will be said, 'Enter, both you and your parents.'" 'A'isha said to the woman, "Did you hear?" She said, "Yes." Muhammad ibn 'Umar reports that Muhammad ibn Sirin relates this from Habiba without her lineage, and so we do not know whether it is bint Sahl or someone else."

'Amira bint Sahl ibn Tha'laba

Her mother was Umayma bint 'Amr. She married Abu Umama As'ad ibn Zurara and bore him his daughters, al-Furay'a, Kabsha and Habiba. They became Muslim and gave allegiance to the Messenger of Allah as did their mother, 'Amira.

Ramla bint al-Harith ibn Tha'laba

She is Umm Thabit. Her mother was Kabsha bint Thabit. She married Mu'adh ibn al-Harith. She became Muslim and gave allegiance to the Messenger of Allah.

Ar-Rubbayi' bint Mu'awwidh ibn 'Afra'

Her mother was Umm Yazid bint Qays. She married Iyas ibn al-Bukayr of the Banu Layth and bore him Muhammad. She became Muslim and gave allegiance to the Messenger of Allah.

Abu Husayn Khalid ibn Dhakwan said, "We visited ar-Rubayyi' bint Mu'awwidh ibn 'Afra'. She said, 'The Messenger of Allah visited me on the day of my wedding and he sat where this bed of mine is. We had two slavegirls who were beating a drum and chanting about my fathers who were killed at Badr. Part of what they said was, "Among us is a Prophet who knows what will happen tomorrow." The Prophet of Allah said, "Stop this. Do not say it.""'

Ar-Rubayyi' bint Mu'awwidh ibn 'Afra' al-Ansari said, "I said to my husband, 'Will you give me a *khul'* divorce in return for all I possess?' He said 'Yes.' I gave him everything except my wrap and he litigated with me before 'Uthman. He said, 'It is his precondition.' So I give it to him."

It is related that ar-Rubayyi' bint Mu'awwidh said, "Some words or discussion passed between me and my cousin, who was my husband. I said to him, 'You can have all that I own if you divorce me.' He said, 'I have done it.' By Allah, he took everything of mine, even my bed. I went to 'Uthman ibn 'Affan and mentioned that to him while he was under siege. He said, 'The condition stipulated was your property. Take everything that is hers, even the locks of her hair if you like.'"

'Amira bint Mu'awwidh ibn al-Harith

Her mother was Umm Yazid bint Qays. She married Abu Hasan ibn 'Abd 'Amr and bore him 'Umara, 'Amr and Sariyya. She became Muslim and gave allegiance to the Messenger of Allah.

'Amra bint Hazm ibn Zayd

She is the full sister of 'Umara, 'Amr and Ma'mar, the sons of Hazm. Their mother was Khalida bint Anas. She married Sa'd ibn ar-Rabi' of Khazraj. She became Muslim and gave allegiance to the Messenger of Allah.

'Amira bint ar-Rubayya' ibn an-Nu'man

Her mother was an *umm walad*. She became Muslim and gave allegiance to the Messenger of Allah.

'Amra bint Abi Ayyub ibn Zayd

Her mother was Umm Ayyub bint Qays. She married Safwan ibn Aws and bore him Khalid. She became Muslim and gave allegiance to the Messenger of Allah.

Kabsha bint Thabit ibn al-Mundhir

Her mother was Sukhta bint Haritha. She married 'Amr ibn Mihsan and bore him Tha'laba, Abu 'Amra and Abu Habiba. Then she was married to al-Harith ibn Tha'laba and bore him Ramla, who is called Umm Thabit. Then she married Haritha ibn an-Nu'man. Kabsha bint Thabit became Muslim and gave allegiance to the Messenger of Allah. She is the half-sister of Hassan ibn Thabit.

Lubna bint Thabit ibn al-Mundhir

Her mother was Sukhta bint Haritha. She became Muslim and gave allegiance to the Messenger of Allah.

'Amra al-Ula bint Mas'ud ibn Qays

Her mother was 'Amira bint 'Amr. She married Zayd ibn Malik and bore him Sa'd who was present at Badr, and Thabit. She became Muslim and gave allegiance to the Messenger of Allah.

'Amra ath-Thaniyya bint Mas'ud ibn Qays

Her mother was 'Amira bint 'Amr. She married Aws ibn Zayd and bore him Abu Muhammad whose name is Mas'ud. Then she married Sahl ibn Tha'laba and bore him 'Amra and Rughayba. She became Muslim and gave allegiance to the Messenger of Allah.

'Amra ath-Thalitha bint Mas'ud ibn Qays

Her mother was 'Amira bint 'Amr. She married Thabit ibn al-Mundhir and bore him Abu Shaykh Ubayy who was present at Badr. He is the half-brother of Hassan ibn Thabit by the same father.

'Amra ar-Rabi'a bint Mas'ud ibn Qays

Her mother was 'Amira bint 'Amr. She married 'Ubada ibn Dulaym and bore him Sa'd ibn 'Ubada. She became Muslim and gave allegiance to the Messenger of Allah. She died while the Prophet ﷺ was on the expedition of Dumat al-Jandal in Rabi' al-Awwal, 5 AH. Sa'd ibn 'Ubada was with him and the Messenger of Allah arrived and went to her grave and prayed over her.

'Amra al-Khamisa bint Mas'ud ibn Qays

Her mother was 'Amira bint 'Amr. She is the mother of Qays ibn 'Amr an-Najjari. 'Amra became Muslim and gave allegiance to the Messenger of Allah.

Duba'a bint 'Amr ibn Mihsan

She is the sister of Tha'laba ibn 'Amr who was present at Badr, and the half-sister of Abu 'Amr Bashir. Her mother was 'Amra bint Hazzal. She married 'Ubayd ibn 'Umayr. Duba'a became Muslim and gave allegiance to the Messenger of Allah.

Umm Thabit bint Tha'laba ibn 'Amr

Her mother was Kabsha bint Malik. She married al-'Ala' ibn 'Amr. She became Muslim and gave allegiance to the Prophet.

Umm Sahl or Umm Thabit bint Sahl

Her mother was Umayma bint 'Uqba. She married Sinan ibn al-Harith and bore him children. Then she was married to 'Abdullah ibn Zayd. She became Muslim and gave allegiance to the Prophet.

Umm Sa'd bint Thabit

She is Kabsha bint Thabit ibn 'Atik. Her mother was Mu'adha bint Anas. She married Yazid ibn Abi'-Yusr of the Banu Salama and bore him Sa'id, 'Abdu'r-Rahman, and Umm Kathir. She became Muslim and gave allegiance to the Messenger of Allah.

Umm Jamil bint Abi Akhzam ibn 'Atik

Her mother was the daughter of Khabbab ibn al-Aratt. She married Sa'id ibn 'Ubayd and bore him 'Abdullah, Khalid, Jamil, and 'Ubayda. She became Muslim and gave allegiance to the Prophet.

Umm Simak bint Thabit

She is Dubayya bint Thabit. Her mother was Adam bint 'Amr of the Banu Murra. She married Yazid ibn Thabit and bore him 'Umara. She became Muslim and gave allegiance to the Messenger of Allah.

Umm Salama

She is Su'ad bint Rafi'. Her mother was Rughayba bint Sahl. She married Aslam ibn Harish and bore him Salama who was present at Badr. She became Muslim and gave allegiance to the Prophet.

Umm Khalid bint Khalid al-Ansariyya

Her mother was Umm Thabit bint Thabit. She married Haritha ibn an-Nu'man and bore him 'Abdullah, 'Abdu'r-Rahman, Sawda, 'Amra, and Umm Hisham. She became Muslim and gave allegiance to the Messenger of Allah.

Umm Sulaym bint Khalid

She married Qays ibn Qahd and bore him Sulaym. She became Muslim and gave allegiance to the Messenger of Allah.

Ruqayya bint Thabit ibn Khalid

Muhammad ibn 'Umar mentioned that she became Muslim and gave allegiance to the Messenger of Allah.

Umm Zayd bint 'Amr

Muhammad ibn 'Umar mentioned that she became Muslim and gave allegiance to the Messenger of Allah.

Umm 'Atiyya al-Ansariyya

She became Muslim and gave allegiance to the Messenger of Allah and went on expeditions with him and related from him.

Umm 'Atiyya said, "I went on seven expeditions with the Messenger of Allah ﷺ. I prepared food for them and repaired their saddles, treated their wounded, and cared for the wounded.

Umm 'Atiyya said, "When Zaynab, the daughter of the Messenger of Allah, died, the Prophet said to us, 'Wash her an odd number of times - three or five - and put some camphor in the fifth. When you have washed her, inform me.' When we had washed her, we informed him and he gave us his wrapper and said, 'Wrap her in it.'"

Umm Sharahil, the client of Umm 'Atiyya, said, "'Ali ibn Abi Talib used to spend midday at Umm 'Atiyya's house."

Muhammad ibn 'Umar said that Umm 'Atiyya was present at Khaybar with the Messenger of Allah.

Khansa' bint Khudham al-Ansariyya

She became Muslim and gave allegiance to the Prophet.

Nafi' ibn Jubayr said, "Khansa' bint Khudham was widowed and her father gave her in marriage when she was unwilling. She went to the Prophet ﷺ and said, 'Messenger of Allah, my father has followed his own opinion and given me in marriage without consulting me.' He said, 'There is no marriage. Marry whom you wish.'" Her marriage was revoked and she married Abu Lubaba ibn 'Abu'l-Mundhir.

Sa'id ibn 'Abdu'r-Rahman al-Jahshi said, "There was a woman called Khansa' bint Khudham who was married to Unays ibn Qatada al-Ansari. He was killed on the Day of Uhud. Then her father gave her in marriage to a man. She went to the Prophet ﷺ and said, 'Messenger of Allah, my father has given me in marriage although I prefer my son's paternal uncle.' The Prophet gave her control over herself."

Umm Waraqa bint 'Abdullah ibn al-Harith

She became Muslim and gave allegiance to the Prophet. The Prophet used to visit Umm Waraqa bint 'Abdullah ibn al-Harith and he named her "the martyr". She collected the Qur'an. When the Messenger of Allah set out for Badr, she said to him, "Give me permission to go out with you to treat the wounded and nurse the sick. Perhaps Allah will give me martyrdom." He said, "Allah will grant you martyrdom." He named her "the martyr". The Prophet ﷺ commanded her to act as Imam for the people of her house. She had a *mu'adhdhin*. She used to act as Imam for the people of her house until a slave and slavegirl of hers attacked her, having plotted together to murder her, during the rule of 'Umar. He was told, "Umm Waraqa's slave and slavegirl have attacked and murdered her and fled." They were brought and he had them crucified. They were the first to be crucified in Madina. 'Umar said, "The Messenger of Allah spoke the truth when he said, 'Let us go and visit the martyr.'"

Tamima bint Wahb

It is related that Rifa'a ibn Samw'al divorced his wife, Tamima bint Wahb, three times in the time of the Messenger of Allah. Then 'Abdu'r-Rahman ibn az-Zubayr married her and then he felt averse to her and could not consummate the marriage. He divorced her and Rifa'a, who had been her first husband who had divorced her, wanted to remarry her. That was mentioned to the Messenger of Allah and he forbade him to marry her. He said, "She is not lawful to you until she has tasted the sweetness [of intercourse]."

Umm Mubashshir al-Ansariyya

Some variants call her Umm Bashir, but it is the same woman. She was the wife of Zayd ibn Haritha. She became Muslim and gave allegiance to the Messenger of Allah. She related from him and Jabir ibn 'Abdullah related from her.

Umm Bashir al-Ansariyya said, "The Messenger of Allah ﷺ visited me while I was among some palm trees of mine. He said,

'Who has cultivated them, Muslim or unbeliever?' I said, 'Muslim.' He said, 'There is not a Muslim who plants a plant or sows a crop and then a human being, bird or wild animal eats from it but that it is *sadaqa* for him.'"

It is related that Umm Mubashshir said that she heard the Messenger of Allah say when he was with Hafsa, "Allah willing, none of the people of the Tree who gave allegiance under it will enter the Fire." She said, "Yes, Messenger of Allah." He chided her and Hafsa said, "Some of them must come to it." The Prophet ﷺ said that Allah says, *"Then We will rescue those who were Godfearing but We will leave the wrongdoers there on their knees."* (19:72)

Umm al-'Ala' al-Ansariyya

She became Muslim and gave allegiance to the Messenger of Allah and related to him. She is the one who said, "The Ansar quarrelled about the Muhajirun so that they drew lots for them. We drew 'Uthman ibn Maz'un." Umm al-'Ala' was with the Messenger of Allah at Khaybar.

The aunt of Husayn ibn Mihsan

It is related that the aunt of Husayn ibn Mihsan went to the Messenger of Allah ﷺ about something she needed. When she had finished, he said, "Do you have a husband?" She said, "Yes." He said, "How are you with him?" She said, "I only fail in what I am incapable of doing." He said, "See where you are in relation to him. He is your garden or your fire."

Umm Bujayd

She was the grandmother of 'Abdu'r-Rahman ibn Bujayd. Umm Bujayd was one of those who gave allegiance to the Messenger of Allah. She said, "Messenger of Allah, a poor man comes to my door and I do not find anything to give him." The Messenger of Allah said to her, "If you do not find anything to give to him except a burnt hoof, then put it in his hand."

Umm Bujayd said, "The Messenger of Allah came to us among the Banu 'Amr ibn 'Awf and I made a mash for him in a wooden cup of mine. When he came, I gave it to him to drink. I said, 'Messenger of Allah, a beggar comes to me and I have little to give him.' He said, 'Place something in the beggar's hand, even if it is a burnt hoof.'"

Umm Hani' al-Ansariyya

It is related that Umm Hani' al-Ansariyya asked the Messenger of Allah, "Will we visit one another when we die, and see one another?" The Messenger of Allah ﷺ said, "The souls are birds which hang from the trees. On the Day of Rising, each soul will enter its body."

Hawwa', the grandmother of 'Amr ibn Mu'adh al-Ansari

Hawwa' said, "I heard the Messenger of Allah ﷺ say, 'Give something to the beggar, even if it is only a burned hoof.'"

Chapter Fourteen:
Women who did not relate from the Prophet, but related from his wives and others

Zaynab bint Abi Salama ibn 'Abdu'l-Asad

Of Makhzum. Her mother was Umm Salama, the wife of the Messenger of Allah. She married 'Abdullah ibn Zam'a and bore him 'Abdu'r-Rahman, Yazid, Wahb, Abu Salama, Kabir, Abu 'Ubayda, Qurayba, Umm Kulthum, and Umm Salama. Asma' bint Abi Bakr as-Siddiq was her wet-nurse. Zaynab's name had been Barra, and the Messenger of Allah ﷺ renamed her Zaynab. Zaynab related from her mother, and 'Urwa ibn az-Zubayr related from Zaynab. She was his brother by suckling.

Muhammad ibn 'Amr ibn 'Ata' said, "I named my daughter Barra and Zaynab bint Abi Salama said to me, 'The Messenger of Allah forbade this name. I was named Barra and the Messenger of Allah said, "Do not proclaim yourselves pure. Allah knows best who is the pious (*barr*) among you." They said, "What shall we name her?" He said, "Zaynab."'"

It is related that Zaynab bint Abi Salama died when Tariq was the amir of the people. Her bier was brought after the *Subh* prayer and placed at al-Baqi'. Tariq did *Subh* in the dark. Ibn Abi Harmala said, "I heard 'Abdullah ibn 'Umar say, to her family, 'Either you pray over your funeral now or you leave it until the sun has risen.'"

Umm Kulthum bint Abi Bakr as-Siddiq

Her mother was Habiba bint Kharija. She married Talha ibn 'Ubaydullah and bore him Zakariyya, Yusuf, who died as a child, and 'A'isha. Talha ibn 'Ubaydullah was killed in the Battle of the Camel.

'Ata' said that 'A'isha went on *hajj* with her sister Umm Kulthum during her waiting-period for her husband, Talha ibn 'Ubaydullah.

Muhammad ibn 'Umar tells us that after the death of Talha ibn 'Ubaydullah, Umm Kulthum married 'Abdu'r-Rahman ibn 'Abdullah of Makhzum and bore him Ibrahim al-Ahwal, Musa, Umm Humayd, and Umm 'Uthman. 'A'isha, *Umm al-Mu'minin*, sent Salim ibn 'Abdullah ibn 'Umar to Umm Kulthum so that she could give him milk so that he could visit her. She did this three times and then became ill.

Umm Kulthum bint 'Ali ibn Abi Talib

Her mother was Fatima, the daughter of the Prophet. She married 'Umar ibn al-Khattab when she was a young girl who had not yet reached puberty. She remained with him until he was killed and bore him Zayd and Ruqayya. Then she married 'Awn ibn Ja'far ibn Abi Talib, but he died. Then she married his brother, Muhammad ibn Ja'far, and he died. Then she married his brother, 'Abdullah ibn Ja'far, after her sister, Zaynab bint 'Ali. Umm Kulthum said, "I was not shy with Asma' bint 'Umays. Two of her sons died while married to me, but I did not fear this for the third." She died while married to him. She did not bear children to any of them.

It is related that 'Umar ibn al-Khattab asked 'Ali ibn Abi Talib for the hand of his daughter, Umm Kulthum. 'Ali said, "I am keeping my daughters for the sons of Ja'far." 'Umar said, "Marry her to me, 'Ali. By Allah, there is no man on the face of the earth who will treat her better than I will." 'Ali said, "I have done it." 'Umar went to the assembly of the Muhajirun sitting between the grave and the minbar. They were 'Ali, 'Uthman, az-Zubayr, Talha and 'Abdu'r-Rahman ibn 'Awf. When anything came to 'Umar from abroad, he would come to them and inform them about that and consult with them about it. 'Umar came and said, "Congratulate me" They congratulated him and said, "To whom, Amir al-Mu'minin?" He said, "To the daughter of 'Ali ibn Abi Talib." Then he told them that the Prophet ﷺ said, "Every lineage and means will be cut off on the Day of Rising except my lineage and means." Then he added, "I accompanied him, and I wanted to have this as well."

When 'Umar ibn al-Khattab asked to marry 'Ali's daughter, Umm Kulthum, he said, "Amir al-Mu'minin, she is still a child." He said, "By Allah, that is not your intention. We know what your intention is." 'Ali commanded that she be prepared and then commanded that a striped garment be wrapped up. He said, "Take this to the Amir al-Mu'minin and say, 'My father has sent me to greet you. He says, "If you are pleased with the garment, keep it. If it displeases you, return it.""" When she went to 'Umar, he said, "May Allah bless you and your father. We are pleased." She went back to her father and said, "He did not undo the garment nor look at anything except at me." So he married her to him and she bore him a son called Zayd.

'Amir said that Zayd ibn 'Umar and Umm Kulthum bint 'Ali died, and Ibn 'Umar prayed over them. Zayd was put closer to him, and Umm Kulthum next to the *qibla*. He gave four *takbirs* over them.

That is also related from ash-Sha'bi. He and others added that al-Hasan and al-Husayn, the sons of 'Ali, Muhammad ibn al-Hanafiyya, 'Abdullah ibn 'Abbas, and 'Abdullah ibn Ja'far, were behind him.

The client of the Banu Hashim said, "That day I saw them and Sa'id ibn al-'As prayed over the two of them. He was the amir of the people on that day. Eighty Companions of Muhammad ﷺ were behind him."

Zaynab bint 'Ali ibn Abi Talib

Her mother was Fatima, the daughter of the Messenger of Allah. She married 'Abdullah ibn Ja'far and bore him 'Ali, 'Awn the elder, 'Abbas, Muhammad, and Umm Kulthum.

It is related that 'Abdullah ibn Ja'far ibn Abi Talib married Zaynab bint 'Ali. He also married Layla bint Mas'ud, and they were both married to him at the same time.

Fatima bint 'Ali ibn Abi Talib

Her mother was an *umm walad*. She married Muhammad ibn Abi Sa'id ibn 'Aqil and bore him Hamida. Then she married Sa'id ibn al-Aswad and bore him Barza and Khalid. Then she married al-Mundhir ibn 'Ubayda and bore him 'Uthman and Kabra.

It is related that Fatima bint 'Ali ibn Abi Talib said, "My father said that the Messenger of Allah ﷺ said, 'Whoever frees a Muslim or a believing soul, Allah will protect every limb of his by his limb from the Fire.'"

It is related that 'Urwa ibn 'Abdullah said that he visited Fatima bint 'Ali. He said, "I saw a bracelet on her hand, a ring on her finger and a string of pearls on her neck. I asked her about that and she said, 'A woman should not resemble men.'"

It is related that 'Isa ibn 'Uthman said, "I was with Fatima bint 'Ali when a man came to praise her father in her presence. She picked up a handful of ashes and threw it in his face."

Umm Qutham bint al-'Abbas

It is related that Umm Qutham bint 'Abbas said, "'Ali ibn Abi Talib visited us while we were playing a game of fourteens. He said, 'What is this game?' She said, 'We were fasting and we wanted to play this.' He said, 'Shall I send someone to buy you a nut so that you can play with it and leave this?' She said, 'Yes.' He sent someone to buy them a nut, and they left it."

'A'isha bint Talha ibn 'Ubaydullah

Her mother was Umm Kulthum bint Abi Bakr. She married 'Abdullah ibn 'Abdu'r-Rahman ibn Abi Bakr. Then she married Mus'ab ibn az-Zubayr ibn al-'Awwam and he was killed. Then she married 'Umar ibn 'Ubaydullah at-Taymi. 'A'isha bint Talha related from 'A'isha, *Umm al-Mu'minin*.

'A'isha bint Sa'd ibn Abi Waqqas

Her mother was Zayn bint al-Harith. 'A'isha bint Sa'd related from her father Sa'd and from several of the wives of the Prophet. People related from 'A'isha bint Sa'd.

'A'isha bint Sa'd said, "I met six of the wives of the Prophet and was with them. I did not see any of them wearing a white garment. I used to visit them wearing jewellery, but they did not criticise me for that." She was asked, "What was it?" She said, "Gold and mixed gold necklaces."

'A'isha bint Sa'd said, "I saw six of the wives of the Prophet. They wore safflower red garments, and I did not ever seen them wearing white garments. I used to visit them and one of them would have me sit in her room and would pray for blessing for me. I was wearing gold jewellery." Ayyub said, "I asked what she was wearing and she said, 'Gold and mixed gold necklaces.'"

It is related that 'A'isha bint Sa'd had two silver rings which were on her ring fingers. When she did *wudu'*, she took them off.
Ibrahim ibn Sa'd said that he saw 'A'isha bint Sa'd several times at *'Isha'* among the women wearing safflower red.

Habib ibn Abi Mazruq said, "I met a woman at Madina outside the mosque with some other women with a candle. I asked about her and they said, 'This is the daughter of Sa'd ibn Abi Waqqas.'"

'A'isha bint Quddama ibn Maz'un

Her mother was Fatima bint Sufyan of Khuza'a. She married Ibrahim ibn Muhammad and bore him Quddama, 'Uthman al-Alim who was at Kufa and used slightly foul language, Muhammad, and Ibrahim. 'A'isha bint Quddama related from her father.

Hafsa bint 'Abdu'r-Rahman ibn Abi Bakr

Her mother was Qurayna the younger, daughter of Abi Umayya of Makhzum. 'A'isha *Umm al-Mu'minin* gave her in marriage to al-Mundhir ibn az-Zubayr ibn al-'Awwam while her father, 'Abdu'r-Rahman ibn Abi Bakr, was absent. When her father arrived, he did not allow that marriage. When he was given authority in the matter, he married her to him, and she bore him 'Abdu'r-Rahman, Ibrahim and Qurayna. Then she married Husayn ibn 'Ali ibn Abi Talib. Hafsa related from her father and her aunt, 'A'isha, and her maternal aunt, Umm Salama, the wife of the Prophet.

Asma' bint 'Abdu'r-Rahman ibn Abi Bakr

Her mother was an *umm walad*. She married al-Qasim ibn Muhammad ibn Abi Bakr and bore him 'Abdu'r-Rahman and Umm Farwa , Umm Hakim, and 'Abda. Asma' bint 'Abdu'r-Rahman related from 'A'isha *Umm al-Mu'minin*.

She related that 'A'isha said, "The Messenger of Allah returned from a journey and I had purchased a carpet for him which had pictures on it. I used it for a curtain over a shelf of my house. The Messenger of Allah entered and I could see in his face that he disliked the curtain. He said, 'Do you veil the wall?' I took the carpet and cut it up into two cushions. The Messenger of Allah ﷺ reclined on one of them."

Safiyya bint Shayba ibn 'Uthman

Safiyya was called Umm Hujayr. Her mother was Umm 'Uthman, Barra bint Sufyan. She married 'Abdullah ibn Khalid and bore him children. Safiyya related from the wives of the Messenger of Allah and others, and many people related from her.

Zaynab bint al-Muhajir al-Ahmasiyya

It is related that Zaynab bint al-Muhajir said, "I set out to make *hajj* accompanied by another woman. I set up a tent and vowed not to speak. A man came and stood at the door of the tent and said, 'Peace be upon you.' My companion returned the greeting. He said, 'What is wrong with your companion that she does not answer me?' She said. 'She has vowed not to speak.' He said, 'Speak. This is part of the practice of the Jahiliyya.' I said, 'Who are you, may Allah have mercy on you?' He said, 'One of the Muhajirun.' I said, 'Which of the Muhajirun?' He said, 'Quraysh.' I said, 'Which Quraysh?' He said, 'You ask a lot of questions. I am Abu Bakr.' I said, 'O khalif of the Messenger of Allah! We are close to the Jahiliyya and do not feel entirely safe from one another. Allah has brought what you see of the business. So how long will this last for us?' He said, 'As long as your Imams are righteous.' I said, 'Who are the Imams?' He said, 'Are

there not nobles among your people who are obeyed?' I said, 'Yes.'
He said, 'Those are the Imams.'"

Mayya bint Mihraz

She was a woman of the Balharith ibn Ka'b. She listened to
'Umar ibn al-Khattab and she was one of the people of Basra.

Musayka Umm Yusuf ibn Mahik

She related from 'Uthman ibn 'Affan.

It is related from Musayka, "A woman visited her people. She
was in a waiting-period, and she went into labour with them. They
sent me to 'Uthman after he had prayed *'Isha'* and gone to bed. By
Allah, I was not kept from him. I went in to him and said, 'So-and-so
visited her family while in her waiting-period, and she is now in
labour and about to be released. What is your opinion?' He said,
'Have her carried to her house.'"

Suhayya bint 'Umayr ash-Shaybaniyya

She related from 'Uthman and 'Ali. She was one of the people of
Basra.

It is related that Abu'l-Mulayh claimed that al-Hakam ibn Ayyub
sent him to Suhayya bint 'Umayr ash-Shaybaniyya. She said, "I was
told that my husband, Sayfi ibn Qusayl, had died at Qandabil. After
him I married al-'Abbas ibn Tarif, the brother of the Banu Qays.
Then my first husband appeared. So we went to 'Uthman and he
looked at us and said, 'How am I to judge between you, given my
present situation?' We said, 'We will be content with your judgement.' He let the first man choose between the dower and the
woman, and he chose the dower." She said that he took two thousand
dirhams, and two thousand dirhams from the other husband.

Umm Hakim bint Qarizh

She was the wife of 'Abdu'r-Rahman ibn 'Awf.

Umm Hakim bint Qarizh said to 'Abdu'r-Rahman ibn 'Awf, "More than one man has proposed to me. Marry me to whomever you think best." "He said, "Will you assign that to me?" She said, "Yes." He said, "I have married you." The marriage was allowed.

Safiyya bint Abi 'Ubayd ibn Mas'ud

Her mother was 'Atika bint Asyad. She married 'Abdullah ibn 'Umar ibn al-Khattab and bore him Abu Bakr, Abu 'Ubayda, Waqid, 'Abdullah, 'Umar, Hafsa, and Sawda. He married her during the khalifate of 'Umar ibn al-Khattab. She related from 'Umar ibn al-Khattab and Hafsa bint 'Umar, the wife of the Prophet. She was the sister of al-Mukhtar ibn Abi 'Ubayd.

Ibn 'Umar said, "'Umar ibn al-Khattab paid my dower to Safiyya bint Abi 'Ubayd which was 400 dirhams. I secretly added 200 to it."

Safiyya bint Abi 'Ubayd reported, "I heard 'Umar ibn al-Khattab recite *Surat al-Kahf* in the *Fajr* prayer."

It is related that Safiyya said, "Sometimes 'Umar hit me so that my belt came undone. Once he hit with a clothes hook."

Nafi' said, "When Safiyya was an old woman, she used to go between Safa and Marwa on a camel."

Umm Salama bint al-Mukhtar ibn Abi 'Ubayd

Her mother was Umm al-Walid bint 'Umayr. She married 'Abdullah ibn 'Abdullah ibn 'Umar ibn al-Khattab.

It is related that Nafi' said, "The daughter of al-Mukhtar ibn Abi 'Ubayd was married to 'Abdullah ibn 'Abdullah ibn 'Umar and bore him a child on the night of Muzdalifa. Safiyya bint Abi 'Ubayd, her aunt, looked after her until the sun set on the Day of Sacrifice. Then 'Abdullah ordered them to stone the Jamra and then go on."

Fatima bint Husayn ibn 'Ali

Her mother was Umm Ishaq bint Talha ibn 'Ubaydullah. She married her cousin, Hasan ibn Hasan ibn 'Ali and bore him 'Abdullah, Ibrahim, Hasan, and Zaynab. Then he died and she married 'Abdullah ibn 'Amr. Her son, 'Abdullah ibn Hasan, married her to him at her command and she bore him al-Qasim and Muhammad, who was called ad-Dibaj (silk brocade), because of his handsomeness, and Ruqayya. 'Abdullah ibn 'Amr was called al-Mutrif (admirable) because of his handsomeness. He died while married to her.

It is related that Yazid ibn 'Abdu'l-Malik appointed 'Abdu'r-Rahman ibn ad-Dahhak al-Fihri as governor of Madina. He proposed to Fatima bint Husayn. She said, "By Allah, I do not wish to marry." She began to keep away from him and she disliked to appear before him because of what she feared of him. He continued to importune her. He said, "By Allah, if you do not marry me, I will flog your eldest son for drinking." While the situation was like that, Yazid ibn 'Abdu'l-Malik wrote to Ibn Hurmuz, who was in charge of the *diwan* of Madina, to present the accounts. He went to Fatima to bid her farewell and said, "Do you need anything?" She said, "Tell the Amir al-Mu'minin what I have endured from Ibn ad-Dahhak and how he is treating me." She sent a messenger with a letter to Yazid to mention her lineage and the injury done to her by Ibn ad-Dahhak and his threat. Ibn Hurmuz went and informed Yazid and he read her letter. He arose from his seat and began to strike his cane on his hand, saying, "Ibn ad-Dahhak has been bold! A man whose voice I will hear while he is being punished!" He called for paper and wrote to 'Abdu'l-Wahid ibn 'Abdullah an-Nasri who was at Ta'if at that time, "I have appointed you over Madina. Fine Ibn ad-Dahhak 40,000 dinars and punish him so that I can hear his cries." The news reached Ibn ad-Dahhak and he fled to Syria and sought refuge with Maslama ibn 'Abdu'l-Malik who asked Yazid to spare him, but he refused. He said, "Should he be allowed to do what he did so that I let him go!" He returned him to an-Nasri in Madina. He fined him 40,000 dinars and punished him and paraded him around in a wool shirt.

Fatima bint Husayn used to glorify Allah using a knotted string.

Sukayna bint al-Husayn ibn 'Ali

Her mother was ar-Rabab bint Imru'l-Qays. She married Mus'ab ibn az-Zubayr ibn al-'Awwam and bore him Fatima. Then he was killed and she married 'Abdullah ibn 'Uthman and bore him 'Uthman, Hakim, and Rubayha. Then he died and she married Zayd ibn 'Amr. Then he died and she married Ibrahim ibn 'Abdu'r-Rahman az-Zuhri. She acted as her own guardian and he married her and she was with him for three months. Then Hisham ibn 'Abdu'l-Malik wrote to his governor in Madina to separate them. He separated them. One of the people of knowledge said, "Zayd ibn 'Amr died and she married al-Asbagh ibn 'Abdu'l-'Aziz."

It is related that Sukayna bint al-Husayn died while Khalid ibn 'Abdullah was in charge of Madina. He said, "Wait for me so that I can pray over her." He went out to al-Baqi' and did not enter until *Dhuhr.* They feared that he had changed his mind and so they bought her camphor for 30 dinars. When he entered, he ordered Shayba ibn Nassah to pray over her.

Umm 'Uthman bint 'Ubaydullah

Her mother was Zaynab bint 'Umar ibn al-Khattab. We find that she reported from Hafsa.

Umm Muhammad ibn Qays ibn Makhrama

Her mother was Durra bint 'Uqba. She related from Umm Salama, the wife of the Prophet.

Umm Muhammad ibn Yazid ibn al-Muhajir

Her mother was Umm Haram bint Sulayman. She related from Umm Salama, the wife of the Prophet. She said, "A woman prays in a loose outer garment and a head covering."

She said, "I asked Umm Salama about how many garments a woman should pray in. She said, 'In a head covering and an outer garment which covers the top of your feet.'"

Umm al-Hasan al-Basri

She related that she saw Umm Salama, the wife of the Prophet, pray in an outer garment and head covering.

Usama ibn Zayd reported that his mother said, "I saw Umm al-Hasan recounting to people."

Fatima bint al-Mundhir ibn az-Zubayr

Her mother was an *umm walad*. She married Hisham ibn 'Urwa ibn az-Zubayr and bore him 'Urwa and Muhammad. Fatima related from her grandmother, Asma' bint Abi Bakr.

Umm Salam bint Hudhayfa ibn al-Yaman

She related from her father that he forbade them to fast the day of doubt in Ramadan.

Umm Sa'd bint Sa'd ibn ar-Rabi'

Umm Sa'd's name was Jamila. Her mother was Khallada bint Anas. Sa'd ibn ar-Rabi' was killed at Uhud before Umm Sa'd was born and her mother gave birth to her some months after her father, Sa'd as-Sa'idi, had been killed. Umm Sa'd bint Sa'd married Zayd ibn Thabit and bore him Sa'd, Kharija, Sulayman, Yahya, Isma'il, 'Uthman and Umm Zayd.

Umm Sa'd bint Sa'd said, "I and Zayd ibn Thabit used to do *ghusl* from the same vessel." She was his wife.

Zayd ibn as-Sa'ib said, "I saw Umm Sa'd, the wife of Zayd ibn Thabit, the mother of Kharija ibn Zayd, and she had an ivory bracelet on her wrist and was wearing an ivory ring."

Kabsha bint Ka'b ibn Malik

Her mother was Safiyya, from Yemen. She married Thabit ibn Abi Qatada of the Banu Salam. Her daughter, Hamida bint 'Ubayd, related from her from Malik ibn Anas.

It is related that Kabsha bint Ka'b said, "Abu Qatada visited us and asked for *wudu'* water so he could do *wudu'*. It was brought to him. A cat came and went to the vessel and drank. Abu Qatada said, 'I heard the Messenger of Allah ﷺ say, "It is not impure. It is one of those who go round about you waiting on you."'"

Zaynab bint Nubayt ibn Jabir

Her mother was al-Fari'a or al-Furay'a bint Asa'd ibn Zurara. She married Anas ibn Malik.

It is related that Zaynab bint Nubayt, the wife of Anas ibn Malik, said, "Abu Umama, who is As'ad ibn Zurara, left a bequest for his mother and aunt to the Messenger of Allah. He sent him some gold and pearls and the Messenger of Allah adorned them from those pearls." She said, "I got that jewellery with my family."

Zaynab bint Ka'b

She related from al-Furay'a bint Malik, the sister of Abu Sa'id al-Khudri. Al-Furay'a listened to the Prophet.

Umm 'Amr bint Khawwat

It is related from Umm 'Amr bint Khawwat that a woman of the Ansar went to 'A'isha. While she was with her, she said, "My daughter is afflicted by a severe illness which has made her hair fall out. I cannot comb it. She is a bride about to be given to her husband. Can I add something to her hair so that I can comb it?" She said, "No, the Messenger of Allah ﷺ cursed the one who adds false hair and the one who has it added."

Umm Hafs bint 'Ubayd

She related from her uncle, al-Bara' ibn 'Azib. She reported from him that the Messenger of Allah said, "Whoever has my name should not have my *kunya*."

Hafsa bint Anas ibn Malik

Hafsa bint Anas is reported to have said, "My father used to adorn us with gold and clothe us in silk.

'Amra bint 'Abdu'r-Rahman ibn As'ad

Her mother was Salima bint Hakim. She married 'Abdu'r-Rahman ibn Haritha and bore him Muhammad, who is Abu'r-Rijal. Az-Zuhri related from 'Amra, as did 'Abdullah ibn Abi Bakr, Yahya ibn Sa'id al-Ansari and others. 'Amra related from 'A'isha and Umm Salama. She was a woman of knowledge.

'Umar ibn 'Abdu'l-'Aziz wrote to Abu Bakr ibn Muhammad ibn Hazm: "Seek out the existing *hadith* of the Messenger of Allah or a past *sunna* or the *hadith* of 'Amra, and write that down. I fear the erosion of knowledge and the departure of its people."

'Amra bint 'Abdu'r-Rahman and her sisters were in the room and presence of 'A'isha. She said, "We had jewellery, but we did not wear it all at the same time."

It is related that 'Amra bint 'Abdu'r-Rahman said to her nephews, "Give me a site for my grave in a garden." They had a garden next to al-Baqi'. "I heard 'A'isha say, 'The bones of the dead person are broken when he is dead as they are broken when he is alive.'"

Hind bint Ma'qil ibn Yasar

One of the people of Basra. She related from her father.

'Udaysa bint Ihban al-Ghifari

She related from her father, who was one of the Companions of the Messenger of Allah.

'Udaysa said, "'Ali went to my father and asked him to go out with him [to fight during the Fitna]. He said, 'My friend and the son of your uncle commanded me that when people were in conflict, I should take a wooden sword. I have taken it. If you wish I will go with you carrying it.' He left him."

Umayma bint an-Najjar

She met the wives of the Messenger of Allah ﷺ and reported from them.

Umayma bint an-Najjar said, "The wives of the Messenger of Allah ﷺ used to take bands which had *wars* and saffron on them and tie them round their heads under their hair on their brows before they went into *ihram*. Then they would go into *ihram* like that."

Sukhayra bint Jayfar

One of the people of Basra. She visited Safiyya bint Huyayy and related a *hadith* from her about the *nabidh* made in a jar.

Jumana bint al-Musayyab al-Fizari

Jumana bint al-Musayyab al-Fizari was married to Hudhayfa ibn Al-Yaman. He used to leave the *Fajr* prayer in Ramadan and go to her in her blanket which he wrapped around his back to warm himself by her presence, but he did not turn his face to her.

Hind bint al-Harith al-Firasiyya

She met the wives of the Prophet and related from Umm Salama, and she listened to Safiyya bint 'Abdu'l-Muttalib. Az-Zuhri related from Hind bint al-Harith.

Na'ila bint al-Farafisa al-Hanafiyya

She related from 'A'isha. She said, "'A'isha acted as Imam for us in the prayer and stood in the middle of us."

Rayta al-Hanafiyya

Rayta al-Hanafiyya said, "'A'isha acted as Imam for us in the prayer and stood in the middle of us."

Mu'adha al-'Adawiyya bint 'Abdullah

The wife of Sila ibn Uthaym, one of the people of Basra. She visited 'A'isha and related from her.

Ja'far ibn Kaysan said, "I saw Mu'adha with her legs drawn up and her garment wrapped about her with the women around her."

Ar-Rabab Umm ar-Ra'ih bint Sulay'

She related from Salman ibn 'Amr, and Hafsa bint Sirin related from her.

Hafsa bint Sirin

She is the sister of Muhammad ibn Sirin. She is also called Umm al-Hudhayl. She related from Salman ibn 'Amir, Umm 'Atiyya and Abu'l-'Aliyya.

It is related that Hafsa ibn Sirin was the oldest of the children of Sirin by Safiyya. Safiyya's children were Muhammad, Yahya, Hafsa, Karima, and Umm Sulaym.

Hafsa bint Sirin said, "Anas ibn Malik asked me how I would prefer to die. I said, 'By the plague.' He said, 'It is martyrdom for every Muslim.'"

Hurayth ibn as-Sa'ib said, "We were at the funeral of Hafsa bint Sirin. Al-Hasan said, 'Where is your companion?' meaning Muhammad ibn Sirin. They said, 'He is doing *wudu*'.' He said, 'Is he fetching the water then?'"

Hujayra

She related that Umm Salama acted as Imam for the women. 'Ammar adh-Dhahabi related from her. Hujayra said, "Umm Salama acted as Imam for us in the prayer and stood in the middle of us."

'A'isha bint 'Ajra, Umm al-Hajjaj al-Jadaliyya

It is related from Umm al-Hajjaj al-Jadaliyya that she was with 'A'isha in a red tent. Al-Ashtar came and said, "Umm al-Mu'minin, what do you say about the killing of this man?" meaning 'Uthman. She said, "We seek refuge with Allah from commanding the shedding of the blood of the Imam of the Muslims."

As-Sahba' bint Karim

As-Sahba' bint Karim said, "I said to 'A'isha, 'What can a man do with a woman when she is menstruating?' She said, 'Everything except intercourse.'"

Umm Musa

She related from 'Ali and al-Mughira ad-Dabbi related from her.

Umm Khidash

She related from 'Ali. Umm Khidash said, "I saw 'Ali using wine vinegar as a dye."

Umm Dharra

Umm Dharra related from 'A'isha about the money which Ibn az-Zubayr had sent to her and she distributed.

It is related that Umm Dharra covered 'A'isha's head with musk and amber when she was in *ihram*.

Umm Bakra al-Aslamiyya

It is said that Umm Bakra al-Aslamiyya, who was married to 'Abdullah ibn Asyad, asked for a *khul'* divorce. Then she regretted it as did he. He went to 'Uthman and told him. He said, "It is a divorce unless you did not stipulate the amount. If you named it, it is that." He took her back.

Umm Talq

Ibn ar-Rumi said, "I visited Umm Talq in her house and her ceiling was low. I said, 'How low your ceiling is, Umm Talq!' She said, ''Umar wrote to his governors not to make their buildings tall.' He said, 'The worst of your days will be the day when your buildings are tall.'"

Umm Shabib al-'Abdiyya

One of the people of Basra. She related from 'A'isha.

Umm Shabib said, "We asked 'A'isha about making hair black. She said, 'I wish that I had something to make my hair black.'"

Al-'Aliyya bint Ayfa'

The wife of Abu Ishaq as-Subay'i. She visited 'A'isha and questioned her and listened to her.

It is related that al-'Aliyya bint Ayfa' went on *hajj* with Umm Mahabba. She said, "We visited 'A'isha, *Umm al-Mu'minin,* and greeted her and questioned her and listened to her. I saw that 'A'isha was wearing a reddish outer garment and a head covering. When we wanted to leave, she said to them, 'It is unlawful for a woman among you to slander her husband.'"

The wife of Abu's-Safar

She said, "I asked 'A'isha about weaving hair on the head of a woman who had a scalp disease. She forbade it as strongly as possible."

Umm Mahabba

She questioned Ibn 'Abbas and listened to him, and Abu Ishaq transmitted from her.

'A'idha

A woman of the Banu Asad. She listened to 'Abdullah ibn Mas'ud and transmitted *hadith* from him.

'Amra bint at-Tubakh

'Amra bint at-Tubakh said, "I went to the market with a slavegirl of mine and we purchased an eel in a palm basket whose head and tail came out of the basket. 'Ali passed by and said, 'How much was this? This is abundant and good and will satisfy the family.'"

Maryam bint Tariq

It is related that Maryam bint Tariq said, "I visited 'A'isha during a *hajj* she made with some of the women of the Ansar. They began to ask her questions about the circumstances in which *nabidh* could be made. She said, 'Women of the believers! You ask me about various circumstances, but not many of them existed in the time of the Messenger of Allah ﷺ. Fear Allah. You should avoid whatever you make that becomes an intoxicant. If the water of grain becomes an intoxicant, you should avoid it. Every intoxicant is unlawful.'"

Jasra bint Dujjaja al-'Amiriyya

One of the people of Kufa. She transmitted directly from Abu Dharr from 'A'isha.

Layla bint Sa'd

She related from 'A'isha and people related from her.
Layla bint Sa'd said that she saw 'A'isha pray in an outer garment, head covering, and waist wrapper.

Baraka, Umm Muhammad ibn as-Sa'ib

She related from 'A'isha, and her son, Muhammad ibn as-Sa'ib, related from her.

'Amra bint Qays al-'Adawiyya

One of the people of Basra. She visited 'A'isha, listened to her and related from her.
'Amra bint Qays al-'Adawiyya said, "I visited 'A'isha and asked her about fleeing from the plague. She said that the Prophet ﷺ said, 'Fleeing from the plague is like fleeing from enemy.'"

Zhubayya bint al-Mu'allil

Zhubayya bint al-Mu'allil said, "I visited 'A'isha and a beggar came and she gave him a bunch of grapes. Then she looked at us and said, 'I see that you like this. This contains many atoms.'"

Diqra Umm 'Abdu'r-Rahman

She met 'A'isha *Umm al-Mu'minin* and listened to her and reported from her.

Umm 'Alqama, the client of 'A'isha

She related from 'A'isha and her son 'Alqama ibn Abi 'Alqama related sound *hadiths* from her.

Kabsha bint Abi Maryam

It is related from Kabsha bint Abi Maryam that they asked Umm Salama about drinks and she said, "I will tell you what the Messenger of Allah ﷺ forbade his family. He forbade them to mix dates with raisins, and to soak cooked date stones.

Safiyya

Safiyya said, "I saw Safiyya bint Huyayy pray four *rak'ats* before the Imam came out. She prayed the two *rak'ats* of *Jumu'a* with the Imam.

Umm Habib bint Dhu'ayb ibn Qays al-Muzniyya

She related from Safiyya's nephew from Safiyya bint Huyayy.

Tufayla, the client of al-Walid ibn 'Abdullah

She related from 'A'isha and al-Walid ibn 'Abdullah related from her.

Umm 'Isa ibn 'Abdu'r-Rahman as-Sulami

She related from 'A'isha and 'Isa ibn 'Abdu'r-Rahman as-Sulami related from her.

Umm 'Abdu Rabbihi ibn al-Hakam

The daughter of Ruqayqa, Umm 'Abdu Rabbihi ibn al-Hakam. She related from her mother from the Messenger of Allah.

It is related from the daughter of Ruqayqa that her mother told her that the Messenger of Allah ﷺ visited her when he came to Ta'if seeking help. She gave him some mash to drink. She said, "The Messenger of Allah said to me, 'Do not worship idols and do not pray to them.' She said, 'What if they kill me?' He said, 'If they say that to you, say, "My Lord is the Lord of this idol." When you pray, put it behind your back.' Then he left them." She said, "My brothers, Sufyan and Wahb, the sons of Qays, told me that when Thaqif became Muslim, they went to the Prophet, and the Prophet said, 'How is your mother?' They said, 'She died in the same condition as you left her.' He said, 'Then your mother was a Muslim.'"

Tamalluk

She was a woman of the people of Kufa. She related from Umm Salama and Abu Ishaq related from her.

It is related that Tamalluk questioned Umm Salama who said, "When you put the knife in the bread, mention the name of Allah and then eat."

Ghuzayla

She related from 'A'isha'.

It is related from Ghuzayla that she visited the *Umm al-Mu'minin*. She said, "A young slavegirl came in wearing a sash. I said, 'Umm al-Mu'minin, why didn't you order this one to veil herself?' She replied, 'She has not yet menstruated and she does not have to do so even after she starts to menstruate. She is a slavegirl.'" It is reported that the *Umm al-Mu'minin* referred to was 'A'isha.

Safiyya bint Ziyad

It is related that Safiyya bint Ziyad said, "Maymuna saw me

washing my garment after menstruation. She said, 'We used not to do this. We used to scrape it.'"

She said, "I heard Maymuna say, 'There is no harm in the sweat of the menstruating woman.'"

Qumayra

She was the wife of Masruq. She related from 'A'isha.

Kabsha bint al-Harith

She was the wife of Shurayh. It is reported that Shurayh divorced Kabsha bint al-Harith and he gave her a gift of 500 dirhams.

Umm Isma'il bint Abi Khalid

Her sister was Sukayna. They visited 'A'isha and listened to her.

Isma'il related from his mother and sister that they visited 'A'isha on the day of *tariyya* [after the *'Id al-Adha*] and a woman asked her, "Is it lawful for me to show my face while I am in *ihram*?" She lifted her head covering from her chest and put it above her head.

Zaynab, the wife of Qays ibn Abi Hazim

She related from 'A'isha, and her husband, Qays ibn Abi Hazim, related from her.

The grandmother of Salih ibn Hibban

It is related that she said, "There was no day harder on me than the day when the locusts descended on Madina. Safiyya bint Huyayy ordered a pan of hers containing some oil for her and she ate that."

Ar-Rabab, the grandmother of 'Uthman ibn Hakim

It is related from ar-Rabab that 'Uthman ibn Hunayf said, "Girl, hand me the shawl." She said, "I am not praying." He said, "Your menstruation is not in your hand." So she handed it to him. He prayed in a single garment and his cloak was hanging on a peg in the mosque and he did not get it.

Salma bint Ka'b al-Asadiyya

She related a *hadith* about the lost object from 'A'isha.

Umm Kulthum, the wife of Salim ibn 'Abdullah

It is related that Khalid ibn Abi Bakr said, "I saw Umm Kulthum, the wife of Salim, wearing a safflower red garment."

Umm Qays, the grandmother of 'Amr ibn Maymun

It is related that Umm Qays said, "I passed by Masruq at Salsala and I had sixty oxen with me which were carrying cheese and nuts. He said, 'Who are you?' I said, 'A woman with a *kitaba*.' He said, 'Let them go. There is no *zakat* on the property of someone with a *kitaba*.'"

Fatima bint Muhammad, the wife of 'Abdullah ibn Abi Bakr

It is reported that Fatima bint Muhammad was in the room of 'A'isha, *Umm al-Mu'minin*, and she said, "A woman of Quraysh sent 'Amra a box with a piece of cotton in it with yellow on it to ask her whether she thought that a woman who only saw this was pure of menstruation. She said, 'Not until she sees whiteness.'"

Nadba the client of Ibn 'Abbas

She related from 'Urwa. She said that when 'Urwa ibn az-Zubayr went out to the *hajj*, he went out with his family and commanded them not to make conditions.

Maymuna bint 'Abdullah ibn Ma'qil

She related a *hadith* from her father. He said that her father was asked about soaking raisins and he disliked it.

Umm Thawr

Jabir al-Ja'fi reported from her, and she reported from her husband, Bishr, that he asked Ibn 'Abbas about how many garments a woman should pray in.

Hunayda, the wife of Ibrahim an-Nakh'i

Shu'ayb ibn al-Habhab related from her.

Mulayka, the aunt of an-Nu'man ibn Qays

Muhammad ibn Fudayl related from her as did an-Nu'man ibn Qays.

Hajja bint Qurat and her daughter

Ruqayqa bint 'Abdu'r-Rahman

She reported that her mother, Hajja bint Qurat said, "The *Maqam* was cast down from heaven."

Glossary

Abu Qubays: a mountain outside Makka.

adhan: the call to prayer.

Ansar: the "Helpers", the people of Madina who welcomed and aided the Prophet.

'Aqaba: a pass where the Prophet met with the first Muslims from Madina and where two pledges of loyalty and support were given.

'aqiqa: an animal killed in celebration of the birth of a child.

ayat: a verse of the Qur'an.

Badr: the site of the first battle fought by the Muslims.

deen: the life-transaction, lit. the debt between two parties, in this usage between the Creator and created.

dhihar: an oath by a husband that his wife is like his mother's back, meaning sex with her is unlawful.

Dhuhr: the Midday Prayer.

diwan: accounts of the Bayt al-Mal (Muslim Treasury).

Fajr: dawn prayer

fitra: the first nature, the natural, primal condition of mankind in harmony with nature.

ghusl: the full ritual washing of the body.

hadith: reported speech of the Prophet.

hajj: pilgrimage to Makka.

hays: a mixture of dates, ghee and curd.

hijra: the emigration from Makka to Madina.

'id: a festival.

'idda: the waiting-period observed by a widow or divorced woman to ascertain whether or not she is pregnant.

ihram: a special condition adopted by someone making *hajj* or *'umra.*

'Isha': the Evening Prayer

Jahiliyya: the Time of Ignorance before the coming of Islam.

Jamra al-'Aqaba: one of the three *jamras* at Mina which are stoned during the *hajj.*

janaba: the state of impurity which requires a *ghusl.*

jihad: struggle, particularly fighting in the way of Allah to establish Islam.

jizya: a protection tax imposed on non-Muslims.

Jumu'a: the Friday Prayer.

khul': a form of divorce in which a woman seeking divorce returns her dowry in return for her freedom.

khums: the fifth of the booty set aside for the Amir to distribute in the cause of Islam.

khutba: a speech, especially the one given on *Jumu'a.*

kitaba: a contract by which a slave acquires his freedom against a future payment, or instalment payments, to his master.

kunya: a respectful but intimate way of addressing people as "the father of so-and-so" or "the mother of so-and-so."

Maghrib: the Sunset Prayer.

Maqam: the place where Ibrahim stood near the Ka'ba.

mawla: a person with whom a tie of *wala'* has been established, usually by having been a slave and then set free.

minbar: steps on which the Imam stands to give the Friday *khutba.*

mithqal: a weight which is a seventh of ten dirhams; also a certain coin.

Muhajirun: Companions of the Prophet who accepted Islam in Makka and then emigrated to Madina.

mudd: a measure of volume, approximately a double-handed scoop.

nabidh: a drink made by soaking grapes, or raisins, or dates, etc. in water without allowing them to ferment.

qasida: an ode.

qibla: the direction faced in the prayer, which is towards the Ka'ba in Makka.

rak'at: a unit of the prayer consisting of a series of standings, bowing, prostrations and sittings.

sa': a measure of volume equal to four *mudds*.

sadaqa: giving in the way of Allah in any form.

sahur: the early morning meal taken before first light when fasting.

Salaf: the early generations of the Muslims.

Subh: the Morning Prayer.

Suffa: the portico of the mosque where poor, homeless Muslims stayed.

Sunna: lit. a form, the customary practice of a person or group of people. The *Sunna* is the practice of the Prophet.

tafsir: commentary and explanation of the meaning of the Qur'an.

takbir: saying *"Allahu akbar"*- "Allah is Greater".

tashriq: the days of the 10th, 11th and 12th of Dhu'l-Hijja, when the pilgrims sacrifice their animals and stone the *jamras*.

tawaf: circling the Ka'ba.

Tawaf al-Ifada: the *tawaf* that pilgrims must perform after coming from Mina to Makka on the 10th of Dhu'l-Hijja.

umm walad: lit. the mother of a son, a slave-girl who has given birth to a child by her master and hence becomes free when he dies.

'umra: the lesser pilgrimage.

uqiyya: a measurement of silver equivalent to 40 dirhams or 123 grams.

wala': the tie of clientage, established between a freed person and the person who frees him.

wasq: a measure of volume equal to 60 *sa's*.

wars: a yellowish coloured type of scent.

witr: lit. odd, a single *rak'at* which makes uneven the number of *sunna* prayers, prayed between *'Isha'* and *Subh*.

wudu': ritual washing to be pure for the prayer.

zakat: wealth tax, one of the five fundamental practices of Islam.

Index